Need-Based Distributive Justice

Stefan Traub · Bernhard Kittel
Editors

Need-Based Distributive Justice

An Interdisciplinary Perspective

Springer

Editors
Stefan Traub
Department of Economics
and Social Sciences
Helmut Schmidt University Hamburg
Hamburg, Germany

Bernhard Kittel
Department of Economic Sociology
University of Vienna
Vienna, Austria

ISBN 978-3-030-44120-3 ISBN 978-3-030-44121-0 (eBook)
https://doi.org/10.1007/978-3-030-44121-0

This Springer imprint is published by the registered company Springer Nature Switzerland AG
The registered company address is: Gewerbestrasse 11, 6330 Cham, Switzerland

Preface

This edited volume is a product of the collective effort of an interdisciplinary group of researchers to better understand the role of need in the distribution of resources. The research group FOR 2104 “Need-based Justice and Distribution Procedures” has been funded by the Deutsche Forschungsgemeinschaft (DFG), the Austrian Science Fund (FWF, grant I3804-G27), and the Swiss National Fund (SNF, grant 10 0 019E_178317/1) in the framework of the DACH collaboration between these three funding institutions since 2015 for a 6-year period. The principal investigators of FOR 2104 and authors of the chapters of this book come from philosophy (Thomas Schramme, University of Liverpool; Mark Siebel, University of Oldenburg), psychology (Adele Diederich, Jacobs University Bremen), sociology (Bernhard Kittel, University of Vienna), political science (Frank Nullmeier, University of Bremen; Tanja Pritzlaff-Scheele, University of Bremen; Kai-Uwe Schnapp, University of Hamburg; Markus Tepe, University of Oldenburg), and economics (Andreas Nicklisch, HTW Chur; Fabian Paetzel, HSU Hamburg; Stefan Traub, HSU Hamburg). In eight subprojects, they all employ theoretical and laboratory experimental research designs in order to understand the various aspects of need as a principle of justice. The URL of FOR 2104’s website is `https://needs-based-justice.hsu-hh.de`.

The aim of this endeavor is to develop an empirically informed theory of distributive justice based on need. Its central distribution rule would be the *need principle*, demanding the distribution of resources to be guided by the satisfaction of socially or politically recognized needs. The research program is structured by two leading hypotheses on the relevance of transparency and expertise in the identification, recognition, dynamics, and economic sustainability of need and need-based (re)distribution. In the present volume, members of FOR 2104 take stock of the literature in the five disciplines from a disciplinary perspective, with an eye to the contribution of the discipline to the understanding of need-based justice. Moreover, it documents the variety of approaches, the complementarity and cumulative contribution of the disciplinary building blocks, and the substantial potential of convergence.

Apart from the principal investigators, who not only engaged in the discussion of the initial ideas and the writing of the proposals, but also made sure that this project stayed on tracks, the postdoc members and Ph.D. students employed in the project made it flourish as they developed fresh ideas out of the initial outline. Besides the members of FOR 2104, we are also indebted to many people who have contributed at different stages and in various ways to the success of the project, in alphabetic order: André Bächtiger, Wulf Gaertner, Peter Hammond, Guillermina Jasso, James Konow, Claudia Landwehr, Stefan Liebig, Christian List, Wolfgang J. Luhan, David Miller, Joe Oppenheimer, David Rueda, Christian Seidl, and Susumu Shikano. We are also indebted to the officials at the Deutsche Forschungsgemeinschaft, in particular Eckard Kämper and his team, who were available for all questions in the preparatory process, and to the team at Springer, in particular Martina Bihn, Niko Chtouris, and Yvonne Schwark-Reiber as well as to project manager Kokila Durairaj and her team of Scientific Publishing Services.

Hamburg, Germany
Vienna, Austria
January 2020

Stefan Traub
Bernhard Kittel

Contents

Chapter 1
Perspectives for a Theory of Need-Based Distributive Justice

Stefan Traub

Abstract This edited volume aims at exploring the foundations and prospects of a *theory of need-based distributive justice* by critically reviewing the literature on distributive justice from five different disciplines: philosophy, psychology, sociology, political science, and economics. This chapter has two main purposes. First, it provides a brief introduction to the subject of need-based distributive justice. Second, the chapter provides an outline of the book by summarizing the main arguments of each of the five disciplinary chapters and the concluding synthesis chapter.

1.1 Introduction

This edited volume aims at exploring the foundations and prospects of a *theory of need-based distributive justice* by critically reviewing the literature on distributive justice from five different disciplines: philosophy, psychology, sociology, political science, and economics. *Pluralistic* theories of justice that include need as a distribution criterion among others—usually equality and equity—were proposed, for example, by Lerner (1974), Deutsch (1975), Walzer (1983), Miller (1999), Konow and Schwettmann (2016), and Liebig and Sauer (2016). Wiggins (2005) and Brock (2012) belong to the few authors who claim to put need satisfaction center stage in a *monistic* theory of justice. However, in current normative debates on distributive justice in these disciplines, need has more often than not been ignored or treated as a second-tier principle of justice. Likewise, in empirical research in the social sciences and experimental research in psychology and economics, attitudes towards and behavior in-line with need-based justice have seldom been made an explicit research object. Notable exceptions are the early questionnaire experiments of psychologists Lamm and Schwinger (1980, 1983) and the social choice experiments of economists Yaari and Bar-Hillel (1984).

S. Traub (✉)
Department of Economics & FOR 2104, Helmut-Schmidt University, Holstenhofweg 85, 22043 Hamburg, Germany
e-mail: traubs@hsu-hh.de

S. Traub and B. Kittel (eds.), *Need-Based Distributive Justice*,
https://doi.org/10.1007/978-3-030-44121-0_1

The dominant justice principles and big competitors, equality and equity (the latter of which is also called the contribution principle), exhibit inherent legitimation problems by mutually excluding each other (apart from cases where everyone contributes the same input). Building a theory of justice on need, therefore, may have the advantage of giving rise to more legitimate distributive goals—geared to the satisfaction of needs—and more legitimate redistribution procedures that are also more in-line with people's *actual* distributive preferences. In a recent empirical study using the Basic Social Justice Orientations (BSJO) scale, Hülle et al. (2018) showed need to be the most preferred justice principle among the German population.[1] Using data from the 9th wave of the European Social Survey (ESS), Adriaans et al. (2019) assessed the perception of fairness of earned incomes for 33.972 households from 18 European countries. Respondents strongly approved need and equity as principles of fair distribution (approval rates of about 80%), approval was distinctly lower for equality (around 50%), and entitlement was rejected by about 90% of the people).[2]

Distributive justice and distributive decision-making are topics of philosophy, psychology, sociology, political science, economics, and other disciplines. A research agenda that is concerned with the normative and positive aspects of need-based justice inevitably affects questions that are relevant to more than one of these fields, for instance, regarding the identification and recognition of needs, and therefore, have to be studied from an interdisciplinary perspective. An interdisciplinary research agenda on need-based justice may contribute to solve the pressing questions of societal relevance. How can modern welfare states justly organize the distribution of scarce resources in consideration of more or less exogenous challenges such as globalization, technological change, demographic change, the sovereign debt crisis, migration, and climate change? In times of rising inequality and political polarization (see, e.g., Frank and Cook 1995; Frank 2007; Stiglitz 2012; Piketty 2014; Atkinson and Bourguignon 2015; OECD 2015), can social policies geared to the satisfaction of needs help to reduce societal conflict?

Since Rawls' (1971) fundamental contribution, the ongoing debate on social justice in the fields of social policy research, political philosophy, political theory, and distributive economics has been dominated by the dispute between egalitarians (such as Rawls himself and Dworkin 1977) and non-egalitarians (such as Nozick 1974). Approaches to distributive justice like (liberal) egalitarianism, on the one hand, and libertarianism, on the other hand, have provoked opposition related to the question of whether and how theories of social justice should try to incorporate *multiple* principles of justice (such as equality, equity, and need as showcased, e.g., by Miller 1999).

Walzer (1983), for example, denied the *universalistic* claim underlying egalitarianism and libertarianism. Instead, he argued in favor of a "complex" conception of equality that assigns to each delimited societal area ("sphere of justice") one specific

---

[1]Need received an average score of 4.58 on a scale from 1 (strong disagreement) to 5 (strong agreement) and excelled equity (4.02), equality (2.77), and entitlement (1.95).

[2]Interestingly, the approval for both need and equity was independent of the respondents' own gross incomes, whereas the approval for equality diminished with increasing gross income.

distributive criterion (such as need, desert, or free exchange) as the guiding principle of justice. Liberal egalitarians like Rawls only argued about *what* is to be distributed equally, whereas they agreed on declining equity and need as distribution principles (see Gosepath 2004). Rawls mentioned the term "need" when developing the list of basic needs that are required by citizens in order to exercise their basic liberties (compare Maffettone 2010). He then argued that in the original position from behind the veil of ignorance citizens would reject the "restricted" utilitarian model granting citizens only a societal minimum at the level of basic needs in favor of the difference principle that tolerates inequalities only if they are to the benefit of the worst off in society, because citizens that are granted only their basic needs would not feel like fully valid members of the society (Rawls 2001).

There have also been parallel debates on the equity-related concept of *desert* (see Sher 1987 and Nussbaum 2006 and the contributions in Pojman and McLeod 1999 and Olsaretti 2007) and the concept of need (see Braybrooke 1987; Doyal and Gough 1984, 1991; Wiggins 1998, 2005, and the contributions in Reader 2005), but rarely in connection with theories of distributive justice.

Much closer to what we would call a theory of need-based justice are the works of Sen and Nussbaum (e.g., Sen 2009; Nussbaum 2000, 2006, 2011, and the contributions in Nussbaum and Sen 1993) on their respective variants of the *capabilities approach*. Yet, the capabilities approach treats needs as goods requirements for certain human "capabilities" and "functionings" and therefore—in an *instrumental* sense—as a means to an end (see Sen 1992, 109). Our authors Frank Nullmeier, Tanja Pritzlaff-Scheele, Kai-Uwe Schnapp and Markus Tepe (see Sect. 5.6.2 in Chap. 5 of this volume) summarize Nussbaum and Sen's (1993) view of needs as follows: "Needs have no value; they are a transitory or intermediate stage in the discussion about what constitutes the quality of human life".

Sen's and Nussbaum's works shaped a new understanding of development policy and led to the construction of the Human Development Index (HDR 1990). In related contributions, several authors tried to determine lists of basic human rights (Shue 1996 [1980]; Brock 1998; Langan 1998; Dean 2013), and to derive yardsticks for global social policy and poverty prevention programs (Pogge 2008), as well as access to health goods (Daniels 2008). A further branch of the literature initiated by Elster (1992) is concerned with *local justice*, which bears some resemblance to Walzer's (1983) "spheres of justice". Elster argued that many allocation decisions about scarce goods are made at the local level. Decisions such as the allocation of organ transplants may be inconsiderable at the societal level but very important at the personal level. Here, he reasoned that due to the allocation methods involved (lotteries, waiting lines, points systems) aspects of *procedural justice* become of particular importance. Elster explicitly acknowledged need as one of the possible assessment criteria. None of the above mentioned theories, however, attempts to construct a theory of distributive justice primarily on the basis of acknowledged needs.

Why has need been treated with so much reservation and skepticism in the literature? Should need be made the basis of a theory of distributive justice at all? In the voluminous literature on social justice in general, and distributive justice in particular, need is in fact assigned a more fundamental and—simultaneously—more controversial role as compared to other prominent justice principles like equality, equity, desert, entitlement, and others (for a comprehensive overview, see the contributions in Sabbagh and Schmitt 2016). Need is more fundamental than the other principles because it refers to the basic conditions for human existence. Hence, what constitutes human existence and what constitutes the quality of human life needs to be clarified. Depending on the discipline, need may refer to motives that drive behavior (Lewin 1926), physiological basic needs (Galtung 1980), subjective feelings of deprivation (Runciman 1966), or—as noted above—a requirement for certain human capabilities and functionings in order to live a "decent life".

As outlined in the following chapters of this book, numerous classifications have been proposed in the literature with the objective of clarifying and sharpening the term need. Maslow's (1943) famous Theory of Human Motivation, for example, distinguishes between physiological needs, safety, love and belonging, esteem, and self-actualization. Maslow also postulated that lower level needs are stronger and would have to be satisfied first. Hence, one could be tempted to assume a lexicographic relationship between physiological, psychological, and social needs. The Basic Needs Approach, introduced by Rowntree (1901) to study the living circumstances of working-class families in the city of York at the end of the nineteenth century, followed exactly this approach by defining those families as living in poverty who had not enough financial means to purchase a certain food basket plus shelter and clothing. The necessary daily calorie intake of the family members was computed by experts like the agricultural chemist Wilbor Atwater. As an absolute concept of poverty directed at mere physical wellbeing, the Basic Needs Approach has for a long time dominated development policy, and the income associated with the basic needs threshold became the official poverty line of the International Labor Organization in 1976 (see Jolly 1976). Later, it was replaced by Sen's Human Development Approach, shifting the focus from consumption to "capabilities".

However, attempts to objectify needs by expert knowledge as in the Basic Needs Approach are questionable for several reasons. First, it has been emphasized that not only physiological needs but also psychological and social needs contribute to people's (mental) wellbeing (e.g. Deci and Ryan 2000; Ryan and Deci 2000). Though such hierarchies of needs follow from a logic of urgency, their strictly sequential application is missing the mark. Second, Wiggins (1998) and many other authors have pointed out that need claims have to be interpreted in relation to their respective cultural contexts. This was already noticed by Adam Smith who wrote: "By necessaries I understand not only the commodities which are indispensably necessary for the support of life, but whatever the custom of the country renders it indecent for creditable people, even the lowest order, to be without. [...] Custom [...] has rendered leather shoes a necessary of life in England. The poorest creditable person of either sex would be ashamed to appear in public without them." (Smith 1776 [1976], 869–870). Third, it has been argued that the objectification and "juridification" (Habermas 1987 [1981]) of needs in the welfare state leads to a depoliticization of the question of what needs are and to what extent they should be satisfied (Fraser 1989).

A purely subjective conception of need would lead to severe problems, too. The Theory of Relative Deprivation, introduced by Runciman (1966), holds that a person suffers a lack of resources if she does not have *X*, knows that other persons have *X*, *wants* to have *X*, and believes that obtaining *X* is realistic. It is quite obvious, however, that wanting or desiring something is different from needing something. It is questionable, therefore, whether society should care about the satisfaction of individual desires. In cases of doubt, societies would have to dedicate a potentially unlimited amount of resources for the satisfaction of unlimited wants (see, e.g., Vlastos 1962; Miller 2007; Brock 2012).

As Adele Diederich (see Chap. 3 of this book) and Bernhard Kittel (see Chap. 4 of this book) point out from their psychological and sociological disciplinary perspectives, the exceptional position of need in the distributive justice debate is also owing to the fact that the recognition and satisfaction of needs have been attributed in the literature to close interpersonal relationships with strong positive feelings towards the members of the group (see, e.g., Deutsch 1975). Such *affective relationships* are not required for equality and equity. Furthermore, it has been argued that the mutual recognition of needs is based on a certain level of societal equality: "If and when such patterns constitute actors as peers, capable of participating on a par with one another in social life, then we can speak of reciprocal recognition and status equality" (Fraser 2000, 113–115). If the satisfaction of recognized needs is mutual, then it gives rise to a *symmetric* and *reciprocal* relationship among equals (Gouldner 1960; Blau 1964). In contrast, if needs recognition is unidirectional, the satisfaction of needs becomes an act of humanitarian solidarity rather than a principle of social justice (Miller 1999).

Finally, because need has not been made the basis of a theory of distributive justice so far, it has—unlike equality—not been *formalized* as an allocation principle. The Pigou–Dalton Transfer Principle (Dalton 1920; Atkinson 1970), which holds that social welfare increases if, all other things being equal, income is transferred from a richer to a poorer person, still forms the normative-theoretical backbone of inequality measurement and welfare economics. The dominance of inequality measurement as an input for both scientific and public debates on (re)distribution, and the widespread understanding of distributive justice as a matter of (in)equality is certainly due to the availability of a wide range of ad-hoc and "ethical" (axiomatic) measures of inequality. Accordingly, several sections of this edited volume deal with measurement issues concerning need, previous attempts to formalize needs as an allocation principle, and with possible new departures for measuring need satisfaction and need-based justice.

In spite of all these challenges, we are optimistic that a theory of need-based justice is feasible if we carefully delineate between needs as *wants*, on the one hand, and needs as *legitimate claims*, on the other hand. To be legitimate, needs would have to be socially or politically recognized using *legitimate procedures*. Procedures for the recognition of needs would have to avoid the pitfalls of trying to objectify needs by means of detailed lists generated from expert knowledge. Apart from the established criteria of procedural justice (see, e.g., Rawls 1971), the *social objectification* of which individual need claims should count as legitimate must be made an integral part of such procedures. Assuming that social objectification is possible, the "need principle" becomes the central distribution rule of a theory of need-based justice. The need principle demands the distribution of resources to be guided by the satisfaction of socially or politically recognized needs. Consequently, a distribution of resources is called just in terms of need-based justice if all individuals' legitimate need claims have been satisfied.

In the opinion of the authors of this volume, a need-based theory of distributive justice would have to provide compelling answers to the following sets of questions: (1) How can needs be identified? How can specific distributions of resources be identified as sufficient for the satisfaction of individual needs? (2) How are needs socially and politically recognized? What is the relation of need to other justice principles, such as equity and equality? How do societies make decisions about procedures for the establishment of need-based justice? (3) What are the social dynamics of establishing the need principle as a central distribution principle? Will groups or societies develop a stable understanding of what counts as a need? What kinds of procedures should be applied in order to determine which need claims are legitimate? Does the application of the need principle give rise to (new) distributive conflicts? (4) What are the consequences of need-based redistribution for individual behavior, in particular? Are there trade-offs between need-based redistribution and efficiency?

The first set of questions is related to what we call the *identification* of needs. We distinguish between *positive* and *normative* aspects of the identification of needs. The positive, or descriptive, part deals with how people identify needs and render need-based justice judgments. Answering these questions requires theoretical models of behavior and data generated from experiments and surveys in order to test these models. The normative, or prescriptive part is concerned with how people *should* identify needs and render need-based justice judgments. An important requisite for the legitimacy of social policy and redistribution is its consistency. In order to make consistent justice judgments and redistribution decisions, a certain degree of *rationality* is required on the part of the decision maker. Countless studies both from psychology and economics have shown, however, that people regularly miss the ideal conception of the rational decision maker (see, e.g., the contributions in the *Handbook of Experimental Economics Results* edited by Plott and Smith 2008). Cognitive biases like *framing effects*—the phenomenon of people's judgments and decisions being affected by the description of the outcomes, for instance, as gains or losses (see Kahneman and Tversky 2000)—are likely to occur in the identification of needs, too. Hence, adequate behavioral models such as *dual process models* (see Kahneman and Frederick 2002 and Kahneman 2011) are required to describe people's need identification process correctly and to develop proper debiasing methods.

As noted above, a problem related to the identification of needs is the measurement of individual needs and need satisfaction, and the *aggregation* of individual degrees of need satisfaction to an index of need-based justice, comparable to approaches in inequality and poverty measurement (compare Atkinson 1970 and Sen 1976). Commitments have to be made with respect to scaling issues (ordinality vs. cardinality), problems of interpersonal comparability, and methods of aggregation. Furthermore, in order to enable an "ethical" interpretation of indices of need-based justice, one has to derive the index from a set of suitable axioms that also clarifies, for instance, whether and how the resources available to the non-needy should matter for judgments about the needy (comparable to Sen's Focus Axiom).

The second set of questions is related to what we call the *recognition* of needs. The recognition of needs refers to the establishment of a joint understanding of which needs count as a starting point for the application of the need principle. It can obviously take place in an informal way within small groups (*social recognition*) or it can take the form of a structured political process within a state (*political recognition*). Moreover, it involves two types of procedures: those for recognizing individual need claims within the scope of, for instance, a deliberation process, and those for allocating scarce resources among the needy.

From a normative point of view, the focus of the recognition step is on the *legitimacy* of these preference aggregation and resource allocation procedures. In this respect, it has been argued that *transparency* and *expertise* are suitable for improving political decision processes. It has been argued that transparency increases the legitimacy of the distributive decision making, by the provision of a better informational basis, and leads to greater public participation (see, e.g, Norris 1999, 2002, 2011; Smith 2009). Yet, there is also (experimental) counterevidence (de Fine Licht 2011). Deliberative processes may benefit from or even require some expert knowledge (see, e.g., Fischer 2003, 2009 and Landwehr 2009). Apart from the advantage of the objectification of debates, there is, however, the danger that political decision-making is shifted away from citizens and to expert committees (see, e.g., Collins and Evans 2007 and Bogner and Menz 2010).

The third set of questions deals with the *dynamics* of political need recognition and, from a normative perspective, with its *stability*. The implementation of the need principle crucially relies on adequate procedures. In order to be stable, just allocations in terms of the need principle should result from generally accepted fair procedures. It must not be possible to call the entire allocation procedure into question due to individual outcomes ("pure procedural fairness", Rawls 1971, 86). To this effect, the correct application of a purely procedural fair allocation procedure ensures the legitimacy and—in the long term—stability of the need principle.

Procedural fairness is a well researched subject in several disciplines. In political theory and philosophy, the focus is on the quality of deliberative democratic processes (see, e.g., Luhmann 1969; Goodin 2003; Forst 2007; Peter 2009, and Bächtiger et al. 2010). The research field of deliberative democratic processes has also sparked a number of experimental studies (see, e.g., Morrell 1999; Karpowitz and Mendelberg 2011; Dietz and Nullmeier 2011, and Neblo 2014). From the outset, justice research in social psychology has emphasized the significance of procedural aspects (e.g., Deutsch 1985, see also the works of Tyler and coauthors: Tyler 1990, 2011; Tyler and Blader 2000, and Tyler and van der Toorn 2013). An economic analysis of procedural fairness was provided, for example, by Frey et al. (2004).

The fourth set of questions focusses on the economic and fiscal *consequences* and, thus, the *sustainability* of need-based redistribution. A desired benefit of income redistribution is a more equal distribution of income and wealth. As income redistribution is achieved by distortionary taxation, that is, it provides negative work incentives, it unfortunately comes at a cost (see Sandmo 1998). Ballard et al. (1985)

estimated the welfare loss of income taxation ("marginal cost of public funds") for the US at about 33%. In other words, for each dollar the state took in, the private sector lost 1.33 dollars. However, estimations like Ballard's crucially depend on the elasticity of labor supply with respect to the wage rate. The higher the elasticity, the stronger the negative incentive effect of taxation, and the greater the welfare loss for society (for more estimates and literature overviews see Heckman 1993 and Saez 2002).

In the political economy literature, the Meltzer–Richard model (Meltzer and Richard 1981) utilizes the incentive-driven trade-off between equality and efficiency in order to explain in the framework of a median voter model the "size of government"—the level of taxation in democratic welfare states. The empirical evidence for the Meltzer–Richard model is mixed at best (see, e.g., Perotti 1996 and Milanovic 2000). The Meltzer–Richard model, or simplified versions of it, has also been tested experimentally in the laboratory. Agranov and Palfrey (2015) were the first to explicitly investigate the trade-off between efficiency and equality in their laboratory experiment. As predicted by the model, they found that ex-ante wage rate inequality led to higher tax rates. The implemented tax rates were close to the ideal tax rates of the median voter. Future research would have to address the question of whether need-based redistribution results in lower welfare losses as compared to the proportional or indirect progressive tax scales usually considered in these models.

The following section provides an outline of the book. It briefly summarizes the contents of each of the five disciplinary chapters and the concluding synthesis chapter. The authors of each chapter review the literature on distributive justice with a discipline-specific focus on the four sets of positive and normative questions concerning identification, recognition, dynamics, and the consequences of needs and need-based redistribution, respectively. We start with the philosophy of need-based justice in Chap. 2. While the emphasis of the chapter is on the normative aspects of distributive justice including measurement issues, it also examines positive approaches in terms of "what the people think" (Miller 1992). Chapter 3 investigates need from a psychological perspective. In particular, the chapter provides a thorough account of behavioral theories of need and need-based justice and their empirical applications. Chapter 4 reviews the sociological literature on need and need-based justice. Beyond that, it outlines a theoretical framework for the social recognition of needs. The political science chapter (Chap. 5) has five main sections dealing with need as a motive for political action, the political economy of need-based redistribution, needs as a matter of public policy, need-based social policy, and basic human needs. The economic view of need-based justice is outlined in Chap. 6. Here, the authors turn their attention to the cost of redistribution. Finally, Chap. 7 provides a synthesis and outlines a framework for a need-based theory of justice based on ten hypotheses derived from the previous disciplinary chapters.

1.2 Outline of the Book

Our quest for a theory of need-based distributive justice begins with the perspective of *philosophy*—or, to be precise, the perspective of ethics. From Chap. 2, written by Mark Siebel and Thomas Schramme, we expect three main contributions: First, the ethical significance of need as the core element of a theory of distributive justice has to be assessed using a suitable logical framework. It is self-evident that the outcome of this assessment is strongly related to whether it is possible to find consistent answers to our key questions regarding the identification of needs. Second, provided that need-based justice judgments have ethical significance, we would like to know how need satisfaction (or lack thereof) can be measured and aggregated to an index. That is, we expect a sketch of an axiomatic basis for need-based justice judgments. The third expectation is a methodological contribution. Since we are exploring the foundations and prospects of a theory of need-based distributive justice, it would be desirable to learn how such a theory can be generated and whether and to what extent the process of theory generation may involve empirical observations.

Right at the start of their chapter, Siebel and Schramme argue that a particular theory of justice can be regarded as a "template for political aims" (Sect. 2.2) that sets an ideal point for real social institutions. A theory of justice consists of three main ingredients (Page 2006): The *scope* defines the group of people who are included, the *shape* determines the distribution goal, and the *currency* identifies the "good" to be used to reach the distribution goal. According to Siebel and Schramme, the currency of need-based justice is the degree of need satisfaction rather than need itself, and its shape could, for instance, be equal need satisfaction.

Using this model as the starting point of their analysis, Siebel and Schramme discuss several fundamental questions regarding the concept of need-based justice. For instance, does need-based justice belong to the sphere of *non-comparative* or *comparative* theories of justice (the latter of which requires a societal reference point in terms of a *decent life*)? A further tricky question addressed by Chap. 2 is whether need satisfaction can be the currency of a theory of justice since needs are potentially limitless and resources are scarce. The authors suggest interpreting the term "scarcity" in a relational way and carefully distinguishing between (limitless) *desires* and *legitimate needs* in order to preserve need as a criterion of distributive justice.

In the third section of their chapter, Siebel and Schramme deal with our expectation regarding the measurement and axiomatic basis of need-based justice. They introduce *principles* of need-based justice, i.e., propositions about the conditions required for need-based justice to be fulfilled, and they distinguish between *qualitative* and *quantitative measures* of need-based justice. They also critically discuss Miller's (1999) Aristotelian approach to the measurement of need-based justice, and they extract Platonic measures of need-based justice from Jasso's (1999) theory of justice by replacing actual and just endowment with actual endowment and need in the so-called Justice Evaluation Function. The bottom line from this exercise is that there is still much needed for the development of axiomatic measures of need-based justice.

The fourth section of Chap. 2 is devoted to the *methodology* of need-based justice. Siebel and Schramme mainly focus on the issue of whether a *normative* theory of justice can be generated from *empirical* data. Siebel and Schramme argue with regard to Rawls' (1971, 1975) idea of a general reflective equilibrium that it is not sufficient to make assumptions about the moral beliefs of people and their convergence in order to justify a theory of justice. Such claims can, in principle, be tested empirically, as has been demonstrated by Frohlich and Oppenheimer (1990). Consequently, in Sect. 2.4.3, the authors turn towards the question of "how and by what measures [...] subjective opinions" can be converted "into relevant data for normative theory". Siebel and Schramme plead for an interdisciplinary research agenda capitalizing on experimental methods as used in psychology, economics, and the social sciences in order to overcome the potential weaknesses of empirical studies on "what the people think" (Miller 1992).

Chapter 3 explores need-based justice from the perspective of *psychology*. While the previous chapter reflected on needs as a currency for a theory of justice that provides behavioral guidelines for social institutions, this chapter, written by Adele Diederich, identifies needs and need-based justice as a *motive* for individual behavior. Hence, though the psychology chapter, too, mainly deals with the identification of needs, it has a positive focus. That is, we expect answers to the questions related to how people *actually* identify needs and render need-based justice judgments. While Sects. 3.2 and 3.3 deal with theoretical models of need identification and need as a principle of justice, Sect. 3.4 is concerned with the factors that may influence the preference for choosing one justice principle over another or that may determine the weights for different principles in a multiple-principles approach. The fifth section reviews empirical studies on (distributive) justice that explicitly take need into consideration.

Section 3.2 introduces several prominent psychological theories that involve specific notions or catalogs of needs. Diederich notes in the summary of this section that these theories are confined to *qualitative* accounts of needs, i.e., they identify and categorize needs. In order to establish a minimum requirement for each need and in order to compare the degree of need satisfaction among different needs, one would additionally need a *quantitative* account of needs. The latter would require that "[...] need can be converted into a common unit" (Sect. 3.2.6). Here, Diederich's assessment parallels Siebel and Schramme's distinction between qualitative and quantitative measures of need-based justice in Sect. 2.3. Section 3.3 then deals with need as a principle of justice. According to Diederich, "[...] psychological perspectives are interested in how people judge justice, think and feel about it, and how and why they act accordingly" (Sect. 3.2.6). According to Diederich, in psychology, need has rarely been treated as a self-contained principle of justice, but has rather been seen as one principle in a multidimensional approach (or it has been completely ignored).

In Sect. 3.4, Diederich distinguishes between situational and social determinants (Sect. 3.4.1) and individual determinants (Sect. 3.4.2) of justice preferences. In Sect. 3.4.2, she also presents a number of scales (tests) that have been proposed to measure social value orientations with respect to justice. For example, "beliefs in a just world" scales (introduced by Rubin and Peplau 1973, 1975). In most of these scales, need is not considered or not directly addressed. Section 3.5 reviews empirical studies on (distributive) justice that explicitly take need into consideration. Again Diederich distinguishes between situational and social determinants (Sect. 3.5.1) and individual determinants (Sect. 3.5.2). At the end of this section, Diederich calls for more *systematic* research on the situational, social, and individual factors that influence justice judgments.

After noting that a comprehensive normative theory of needs does not exist at present, the conclusion and outlook of the psychology chapter (Sect. 3.6) then discusses whether and how psychology could contribute to the development of such a theory. Diederich argues that the distinction between primary and secondary needs in many motivation theories "[...] might be reasonable, but only if the classification makes no demands that lower needs must be satisfied before higher needs". She emphasizes that measurement and scaling are underdeveloped issues in (empirical) social justice research, which usually relies on ordinal (e.g., Likert) scales that are not sufficient to compare or trade-off (differences in) needs. Diederich also issues a warning that individual justice judgments are "prone to all kinds of cognitive biases" and she suggests thoroughly studying the cognitive processes involved in the individual identification of needs and in justice judgments related to need.

Chapter 4, written by Bernhard Kittel, is concerned with the *sociology* of needs and need-based justice. As the author notes in the beginning of his chapter, the sociology of justice "places reciprocal relationships and structures center stage" (Sect. 4.1). The sociological perspective, therefore, is a key to understand the multiplicity of individual fairness motives that arise from different *structural* conditions. One could say that the sociological perspective complements the psychological perspective, which is concerned with the impact of different *cognitive* conditions. From Kittel's chapter, we, therefore, expect a theoretical framework for the *social recognition* of needs that provides answers to the following key questions: How are needs socially recognized? What is the relation of need to other justice principles, such as equity and equality? How do groups and societies make decisions about procedures for the establishment of need-based justice?

Section 4.2 explores the foundations of justice principles in sociological theory and develops the theoretical framework. Building on a classification of justice principles by Liebig and Sauer (2016) and Parsons' (1951) so-called $AGIL$ scheme of social functions, he develops a 2×2 matrix of four forms of sociality, where each form of sociality is characterized by four dimensions: social function, social relationship, justice principle, and relational model (see Table 4.1 on Sect. 4.2.1). In Sect. 4.3, Kittel turns to the "need principle" as a social norm. As in the philosophy chapter (see Chap. 2) and the psychology chapter (see Chap. 3), the discussion starts with a distinction between demands or wants, on the one hand, and "legitimate" needs, on the other hand. Next, Kittel analyzes how needs recognition works in a society (Sect. 4.3.2). In particular, he addresses the behavioral foundations of the need principle as a social norm: Is the mutual recognition of needs an expression of "weak reciprocity" (which is based on long-term relationships and low-cost strategies to avoid free-riding) or "strong reciprocity" (which assumes that cooperation can be established even in short-term relationships by means of costly punishment)?

Section 4.4 searches the sociological literature for empirical references to needs and need-based justice from three different perspectives: the individual perspective focusses on *attitudes*, the relational perspective focusses on *interactions* mostly in small groups, and the collective perspective focusses on the *operationalization* of justice principles by societies. The third—collective—perspective (see Sect. 4.4.3) also addresses procedural issues regarding the implementation of need-based justice in welfare states. A major problem associated with *means-testing* is the *stigmatization* of welfare recipients: At the individual and relational level, need recognition is borne out of trust and solidarity in small groups. At the collective level, such a direct mutual understanding of needs is not possible. Means-testing represents a potential solution to the problem of need recognition in large groups. It can, however, also be interpreted as an indication of mistrust towards potential free riders.

In the fifth section of his chapter, Kittel reflects on the potential contributions of sociology to a theory of need-based justice. He sees the adequate classification and description of different forms of sociality and their associated justice principle, as outlined in Sect. 4.2.1 and Table 4.1, as a core contribution to a theory of need-based justice. Moreover, he argues that a restriction of the *scope* of need-based justice (Miller 2013) is required: The scope restriction is a consequence of regarding needs as *instrumental* needs rather than *intrinsic* basic human needs with universal scope. Instrumental needs are always defined in relation to a societal reference point, a consensus about what counts as a "minimum decent life". In Kittel's words, need-based justice "[…] builds on the particularistic principle of entitlement to define the boundaries of the community, meaning the needs of 'others' may be recognized on humanitarian grounds but not as part of a reciprocal relationship" (Sect. 4.5).

Chapter 5, written by a quartet of authors (Frank Nullmeier, Tanja Pritzlaff-Scheele, Kai-Uwe Schnapp, and Markus Tepe), presents the main areas of theoretical thought and empirical research in political science related to need-based justice. In-line with our key questions regarding the feasibility of a theory of need-based distributive justice, the Chapter studies the normative and positive aspects of the *political recognition* of needs and the *dynamics* of establishing need as a central distribution principle. Sections 5.2–5.4 address the research topics of positive political theory: need as a motive for political action, the political economy of need-based (re)distribution, and needs in public policy. In this part of the chapter, we expect to gain information about models and procedures of political need recognition. Sections 5.5 and 5.6 deal with the normative aspects of political theory, respectively, justifications of the welfare state by justice principles such as equality, equity, and need, and the basic human needs approach.

At the beginning of Sect. 5.2, the authors remark that "recourses to needs as motives for [political] action are very rare". Inglehart's (1977, 1990) contributions to the post-materialism debate explicitly refer to Maslow's (1943) Theory of Human Motivation and his hierarchy of needs (also see Sect. 3.2.3 of the psychology chapter), attributing the two lower levels—the physiological and safety needs—to the area of materialist needs and the three upper levels to the area of post-materialist needs.

Section 5.3 reviews the literature on the political economy of (re)distribution. The authors point out that, in this literature, which merges ideas from political science and economics, self-interest rather than need or need satisfaction forms the motivational basis of individual behavior. Need satisfaction, therefore, could be seen as an *output* of collectively choosing a certain level of redistribution rather than an *input* in terms of a preference—which is an interesting twist of this perspective. The authors identify three branches of the literature that deals with collective decisions on inequality and redistribution: (1) studies on the choice of justice principles (this was pioneered by Frohlich and Oppenheimer 1990), (2) studies on redistributive choices in the framework of the Meltzer–Richard model (Meltzer and Richard 1981), and (3) studies focussing on the procedural aspects and legitimacy of income redistribution (e.g. Esaiasson et al. 2012). Interestingly, a number of studies revealed a stable predominance of the so-called "Boulding principle" (see Boulding 1962; Raphael 1980), that is, the maximization of the average income subject to a floor constraint.

Section 5.4 then reviews the literature that treats need as a matter of public policy. Dismissing conceptions of need that are associated with universal and unchanging lists of basic human needs, Nullmeier et al. plead for the recognition of needs through political processes: "Needs are contested political constructions that have to be developed and affirmed in political discourses and institutional procedures. Modern societies do agree on levels of need-based provisions of goods and on the extent of redistribution by way of political decisions". Like the authors of the previous chapters, Nullmeier and coauthors refer to a "minimum decent life". The "normal" participation standard could serve as a reference point in order to measure individual neediness, as well as for interpersonal comparisons of need (the measurement and scaling issues associated with this are also addressed in Diederich's psychology chapter).

Procedures used for the recognition of needs and the provision of recognized needs are addressed in Sect. 5.4.3. The subsection concentrates on *rationing* in the health sector, a procedure that becomes necessary if the resources required to satisfy all individually recognized needs exceed the resources made available by the society (see Landwehr 2006). Since *substantial* justice in terms of need satisfaction for everyone becomes unattainable, the focus has to shift from outcomes to procedures. Criteria of *procedural* justice are required, the development of which more often than not is delegated to experts and brain trusts.

The normative part of the political science chapter starts off in Sect. 5.5 with a review of the crisis of the welfare state in the 1980s. Nullmeier et al. remind their readers that Habermas (1987 [1981]) criticized the "juridification" of the definition of social situations in the welfare state and called for "[...] a recovery of needs not only within the legal system and in expert committees, but also within public discourse" (see Sect. 5.5 of the political science chapter). Section 5.6 is concerned with basic human needs in international politics. It has three subsections dealing with (i) basic human needs as a development strategy, (ii) the capabilities approach, and (iii) need-based global justice. In the first subsection, Nullmeier and coauthors illustrate how the basic needs strategy shaped a whole decade of development policy, beginning with an ILO world conference in 1976. Here, Maslow's (1943) hierarchy of needs served as the theoretical background. In the context of development policy, the Basic Needs Approach has mainly been criticized because it gives physiological needs absolute precedence over higher needs (see, e.g., Galtung 1980). The chapter then recounts how the focus of development policy shifted—at the beginning of the 1990s—from needs to capabilities (see Sect. 5.6.2) under the influence of Amartya Sen (see, e.g., Sen 1992).

Nullmeier and his coauthors conclude that "a certain degree of restraint, caution and reluctance dominates the debates in political science about the concept of need" (Sect. 5.7). Constant support for (basic) needs—often paired with other justice principles—shows in (re)distribution decisions in positive political theory. Whether or not basic needs, a list of capabilities, or something else should be made a yardstick for development policy is still a debated issue in normative political theory.

Chapter 6 outlines the *economic* view of need-based justice. While the previous chapters extensively address our key questions regarding the identification and recognition of needs and need-based justice, and the social dynamics of applying the need principle, Chap. 6 is concerned with the *consequences* of need-based redistribution for individual behavior. Are there trade-offs between need-based redistribution and efficiency? How *sustainable* is the application of the need principle?

The review starts with an apparent paradox: As most income (and wealth) distributions in rich democratic countries are right-skewed, the low-income majority of citizens seems to tolerate a considerable degree of income inequality "[...] despite having the voting power to eliminate that inequality by means of redistribution" (Sect. 6.1). The authors, Andreas Nicklisch and Fabian Paetzel, argue that—according to the "standard view" of economics—redistribution involves direct and indirect costs that diminish the size of the cake to be redistributed. The main focus of the chapter is on the indirect effects of redistributive taxation on welfare resulting from biased work incentives. The authors add new—and, perhaps, more realistic—perspectives on the efficiency-equity trade-off to the literature by allowing economic agents to exhibit fairness preferences, as well as by explicitly considering need-based redistribution (as compared to equity-based and equality-based redistribution).

Section 6.2 introduces the economic "standard view" of the cost of redistribution. The third section then introduces models of social preferences (Fehr and Schmidt 1999; Bolton and Ockenfels 2000), accounting for fairness considerations such as *equity* and *equality* as behavioral motives. Need as a fairness motive is addressed in Sect. 6.4. At the beginning of the section, the authors state that "[...] need-based justice acknowledges that people are heterogeneous with respect to their needs and adjust redistribution accordingly. Instead of focusing on the distribution of income within society (i.e., equality), or on the supply of resources within society (i.e., equity), need-based redistribution focuses on *socially accepted* needs" (emph. added). So, the main point here is that needs have to be socially or politically recognized before they can serve as a yardstick for redistribution. The recognition step invalidates the critique that the satisfaction of needs cannot be made a criterion of justice because of doubt about whether a group or society would—in the long-term—recognize needs that exceed the resources available for satisfying them (the issue of over and undersupply is taken up again by Frank Nullmeier in Sect. 7.7 of the synthesis chapter). However, the concrete procedures that could be used (or are already in use) to determine which needs are to be satisfied and to what extent are an understudied domain (see Sect. 6.4.2). In spite of these knowledge gaps, the authors conclude that need-based justice plays a prominent role in most modern welfare states because they pursue the objective of granting their citizens a "decent life" by means of means-tested social benefits.

How are the (indirect) costs of distribution affected by need-based redistribution? Section 6.5 extends the theoretical leisure consumption choice framework introduced in Sect. 6.2 by adding a minimum consumption threshold. The theoretical prediction is unambiguous: The stronger the worker's preference for leisure the greater is the likelihood that need-based redistribution impinges upon her willingness to work. Hence, if there is a large share of such workers, the cost of need-based redistribution might become excessive. This result, however, depends on the assumption that leisure is a normal good, i.e., decreasing the price of leisure consumption—the wage rate—by taxation leads to more leisure demand. Nicklisch and Paetzel mention a few empirical and experimental studies (e.g. Fehr and Goette 2007; Farber 2008) showing that, at least for some groups of workers with low incomes (e.g., cab drivers, bicycle messengers), this assumption might not reflect the reality.

The final chapter of this volume, written by Frank Nullmeier, attempts a synthesis of the five disciplinary chapters on need-based justice. In each of the ten sections of Chap. 7, a thesis on the further development of a theory of need-based justice is presented and discussed. Since the synthesis builds on the previous chapters, we will not repeat the arguments in detail here.

Nullmeier is cautiously optimistic that a meaningful theory of need-based distributive justice is feasible. In his opinion, the theory would consist of two main components. One component, in the form of a "normatively informed" positive theory, describes how needs are actually identified and recognized. The other component, in the form of a "positively informed" normative theory, prescribes how the need principle should be applied in reference to norms like consistency, legitimacy, stability, and sustainability. Such "[a]n integrated theory of need-based justice can be developed as part of a strong pluralistic theory of justice" (Sect. 7.10) if certain typologies of distributive and social situations are feasible. It would include needs as a "central and indispensable component". With respect to the normative dimension, the theory could even go a step further by giving need satisfaction *priority* over all other principles. Analogously to Rawls' "leximin" principle (the difference principle), the principle giving priority to needs could be called "lexineed". According to Nullmeier, "[t]he key argument in support of the priority of the criterion of need is that there is such a wealth of resources worldwide that the needs of all people could be met easily—and there would still be a huge surplus of resources" (Sect. 7.10).

Coming back to our starting point about exploring the foundations and prospects of a theory (or two separate positive and normative theories) of need-based distributive justice, we are convinced that the following six chapters make a good case for such a theory with a "lexineed" allocation principle at its core.

Acknowledgments This chapter has been written as part of DFG Research Group 2104 "Need-based Justice and Distributive Procedures", Project D2 "Need-based Justice as a Social Contract" (reference TR 458/6-1). This funding is gratefully acknowledged. I thank all members of FOR 2104 for making such a project possible.

References

Adriaans, J., Eisnecker, P., & Liebig, S. (2019). A comparison of earnings justice throughout Europe: Widespread approval in Germany for income distribution according to need and equity. *DIW Weekly Report*, *44*(45), 397–404.

Agranov, M., & Palfrey, T. R. (2015). Equilibrium tax rates and income redistribution: A laboratory study. *Journal of Public Economics*, *130*, 45–58.

Atkinson, A. B. (1970). On the measurement of inequality. *Journal of Economic Theory*, *2*(3), 244–263.

Atkinson, A. B., & Bourguignon, F. (2015). *Handbook of income distribution* (Vol. 2A). Amsterdam: North Holland.

Bächtiger, A., Niemeyer, S., Neblo, M., Steiner, J., & Steenbergen, M. R. (2010). Disentangling diversity in deliberative democracy: Competing theories, their blind-spots, and complementarities. *Journal of Political Philosophy*, *18*(1), 32–63.

Ballard, C. L., Shoven, J. B., & Whalley, J. (1985). General equilibrium computations of the marginal welfare costs of taxes in the United States. *American Economic Review*, *75*(1), 128–138.

Blau, P. M. (1964). *Exchange and power in social life*. New York: Wiley.

Bogner, A., & Menz, W. (2010). How politics deals with expert dissent: The case of ethics councils. *Science, Technology, and Human Values*, *35*, 888–914.

Bolton, G. E., & Ockenfels, A. (2000). ERC: A theory of equity, reciprocity, and competition. *American Economic Review*, *90*(1), 166–193.

Boulding, K. E. (1962). Social justice in social dynamics. In R. Brandt (Ed.), *Social justice* (pp. 73–92). Englewood Cliffs: Prentice Hall.

Braybrooke, D. (1987). *Meeting needs*. Princeton: Princeton University Press.

Brock, G. (Ed.). (1998). *Necessary goods. Our responsibilities to meet others' needs*. Oxford: Rowman and Littlefield.

Brock, G. (2012). Needs and distributive justice. In G. F. Gaus & F. D'Agostino (Eds.), *The Routledge companion to social and political philosophy* (pp. 444–455). New York: Routledge.

Collins, H., & Evans, R. (2007). *Rethinking expertise*. Chicago: University of Chicago Press.

Dalton, H. (1920). The measurement of the inequality of incomes. *Economic Journal*, *30*(119), 348–361.

Daniels, N. (2008). *Just health. Meeting health needs fairly*. Cambridge: Cambridge University Press.

Dean, H. (2013). The translation of needs into rights: Reconceptualising social citizenship as global phenomenon. *International Journal of Social Welfare*, *22*(S1), S32–S49.

Deci, E. R., & Ryan, R. M. (2000). The "what" and "why" of goal pursuits: Human needs and the self-determination of behavior. *Psychological Inquiry*, *11*(4), 227–268.

de Fine Licht, J. (2011). Do we really want to know? The potentially negative effect of transparency in decision making on perceived legitimacy. *Scandinavian Political Studies*, *34*(3), 183–204.

Deutsch, M. (1975). Equity, equality, and need: What determines which value will be used as the basis of distributive justice? *Journal of Social Issues*, *51*(3), 137–149.

Deutsch, M. (1985). *Distributive justice*. New Haven, CT: Yale University Press.

Dietz, M., & Nullmeier, F. (2011). Gesellschaftsberatung und deliberative Verfahren. *Zeitschrift für Politikberatung*, *3*(3/4), 307–329.

Doyal, L., & Gough, I. (1984). A theory of human need. *Critical Social Policy*, *4*(10), 6–38.

Doyal, L., & Gough, I. (1991). *A theory of human need*. Basingstoke: Macmillan.
Dworkin, R. (1977). *Taking rights seriously*. Cambridge, Mass.: Harvard University Press.
Elster, J. (1992). *Local justice: How institutions allocate scarce goods and necessary burdens*. New York: Sage.
Esaiasson, P., Gilljam, M., & Persson, M. (2012). Which decision-making arrangements generate the strongest legitimacy beliefs? Evidence from a randomised field experiment. *European Journal of Political Research, 51*(6), 785–808.
Farber, H. S. (2008). Reference-dependent preferences and labor supply: The case of New York city taxi drivers. *American Economic Review, 98*(3), 1069–1082.
Fehr, E., & Goette, L. (2007). Do workers work more if wages are high? Evidence from a randomized field experiment. *American Economic Review, 97*(1), 298–317.
Fehr, E., & Schmidt, K. M. (1999). A theory of fairness, competition, and cooperation. *Quarterly Journal of Economics, 114*(3), 817–868.
Fischer, F. (2003). *Reframing public policy. Discursive politics and deliberative practices*. Oxford: Oxford University Press.
Fischer, F. (2009). *Democracy and expertise. Reorienting policy inquiry*. Oxford: Oxford University Press.
Forst, R. (2007): *Das Recht auf Rechtfertigung. Elemente einer konstruktivistischen Theorie der Gerechtigkeit*, Frankfurt a.M.: Suhrkamp.
Frank, R. H. (2007). *How rising inequality harms the middle class*. Berkely: University of California Press.
Frank, R. H., & Cook, P. (1995). *The winner-take-all society*. New York: Free Press.
Fraser, N. (1989). Struggle over needs: Outline of a socialist-feminist critical theory of late capitalist political culture. In N. Fraser (Ed.), *Unruly practices. Power, discourse, and gender in contemporary social theory* (pp. 161–187). Minneapolis: University of Minnesota Press.
Fraser, N. (2000). Rethinking recognition. *New Left Review, 3*, 107–120.
Frey, B. S., Benz, M., & Stutzer, A. (2004). Introducing procedural utility: Not only what, but also how matters. *Journal of Institutional and Theoretical Economics, 160*(3), 377–401.
Frohlich, N., & Oppenheimer, J. A. (1990). Choosing justice in experimental democracies with production. *American Political Science Review, 84*(2), 461–477.
Galtung, J. (1980). The basic needs approach. In K. Lederer, J. Galtung, & D. Antal (Eds.), *Human needs. A contribution to the ongoing debate* (pp. 55–125). Cambridge: Oelschlager, Gunn and Hain.
Goodin, R. E. (2003). *Reflective democracy*. Oxford: Oxford University Press.
Gosepath, S. (2004): *Gleiche Gerechtigkeit. Grundlagen eines liberalen Egalitarismus*. Frankfurt a.M.: Suhrkamp.
Gouldner, A. W. (1960). The norm of reciprocity: A preliminary statement. *American Sociological Review, 25*, 161–178.
Habermas, J. (1987 [1981]): *The theory of communicative action, lifeworld and system. A critique of functionalist reason* (Vol. 2). Boston: Beacon Press.
HDR (1990). Human development report 1990. http://hdr.undp.org/en/global-reports.
Heckman, J. J. (1993). What has been learned about labor supply in the past twenty years? *American Economic Review, 83*(2), 116–121.
Hülle, S., Liebig, S., & May, M. J. (2018). Measuring attitudes toward distributive justice: The basic social justice orientations scale. *Social Indicators Research, 136*(2), 663–692.
Inglehart, R. (1977). *The silent revolution. Changing values and political styles among western publics*. Princeton: Princeton University Press.
Inglehart, R. (1990). *Culture shift in advanced industrial society*. Princeton: Princeton University Press.
Jasso, G. (1999). How much injustice is there in the world? Two new justice indexes. *American Sociological Review, 64*, 133–168.
Jolly, R. (1976). The world employment conference: The enthronement of basic needs. *Development Policy Review, 9*(2), 31–44.

Kahneman, D. (2011). *Thinking, fast and slow*. London: Penguin Books.
Kahneman, D., & Frederick, S. (2002). Representativeness revisited: Attribute substitution in intuitive judgment. In T. Gilovich, D. Griffin, & D. Kahneman (Eds.), *Heuristics and biases: The psychology of intuitive judgment*. Cambridge: Cambridge University Press.
Kahneman, D., & Tversky, A. (Eds.). (2000). *Choices, values, and frames*. Cambridge: Cambridge University Press.
Karpowitz, C. F., & Mendelberg, T. (2011). An experimental approach to citizen deliberation. In J. N. Druckman, D. P. Green, J. H. Kuklinski, & A. Lupia (Eds.), *Cambridge handbook of experimental political science* (pp. 258–272). Cambridge: Cambridge University Press.
Konow, J., & Schwettmann, L. (2016). The economics of justice. In C. Sabbagh & M. Schmitt (Eds.), *Handbook of social justice research* (pp. 83–106). Heidelberg: Springer.
Lamm, H., & Schwinger, T. (1980). Norms concerning distributive justice: Are needs taken into consideration in allocation decisions? *Social Psychology Quarterly*, *43*(4), 425–429.
Lamm, H., & Schwinger, T. (1983). Need consideration in allocation decisions: Is it just? *Journal of Social Psychology*, *119*, 205–209.
Landwehr, C. (2006). Kann über die Verteilung von Gesundheitsgütern demokratisch entschieden werden? *Forschungsjournal Neue Soziale Bewegungen*, *19*(4), 84–97.
Landwehr, C. (2009). *Political conflict and political preferences: Communicative interaction between facts. Norms and interests*. Colchester: ECPR Press.
Langan, M. (Ed.). (1998). *Welfare. Needs, rights, and risks*. London: Routledge.
Lerner, M. J. (1974). The justice motive: 'Equity' and 'parity' among children. *Journal of Personality and Social Sciences*, *29*(4), 539–550.
Lewin, K. (1926). Vorsatz, Wille und Bedürfnis. *Psychologische Forschung*, *7*, 330–385.
Liebig, S., & Sauer, C. (2016). Sociology of justice. In C. Sabbagh & M. Schmitt (Eds.), *Handbook of social justice theory and research* (pp. 37–59). Heidelberg: Springer.
Luhmann, N. (1969). *Legitimation durch Verfahren*. Neuwied: Luchterhand.
Maffettone, S. (2010). *Rawls: An introduction*. Cambridge: Polity Press.
Maslow, A. H. (1943). A theory of human motivation. *Psychological Review*, *50*, 370–396.
Meltzer, A. H., & Richard, S. F. (1981). A rational theory of the size of government. *Journal of Political Economy*, *89*(5), 914–927.
Milanovic, B. (2000). The median-voter hypothesis, income inequality, and income redistribution: An empirical test with the required data. *European Journal of Political Economy*, *16*, 367–410.
Miller, D. (1992). Distributive justice: What the people think. *Ethics*, *102*, 555–593.
Miller, D. (1999). *Principles of social justice*. Cambridge, Mass.: Harvard University Press.
Miller, D. (2007). *Human rights, basic needs, and scarcity*. Centre for the Study of Social Justice and Department of Politics and International Relations, Working Paper Series, SJ007.
Miller, D. (2013). *Justice for earthlings. Essays in political philosophy*. Cambridge: Cambridge University Press.
Morrell, M. E. (1999). Citizens' evaluations of participatory democratic procedures: Normative theory meets empirical science. *Political Research Quarterly*, *52*(2), 293–322.
Neblo, M. A. (2014). *Change for the better? Linking the mechanisms of deliberative opinion change to normative theory*. Working Paper, Ohio State University, Department of Political Sciences.
Norris, P. (Ed.). (1999). *Critical citizens. Global support for democratic governance*. Oxford: Oxford University Press.
Norris, P. (2002). *Democratic phoenix. Reinventing political activism*. Cambridge: Cambridge University Press.
Norris, P. (2011). *Democratic deficit: Critical citizens revisited*. Cambridge: Cambridge University Press.
Nozick, R. (1974). *Anarchy, state, and utopia*. New York: Basic Books.
Nussbaum, M. C. (2000). *Women and human development: The capabilities approach*. Cambridge and New York: Cambridge University Press.
Nussbaum, M. C. (2006). *Frontiers of justice. Disability, nationality, species membership*. Cambridge: Belknap Press, Harvard University Press.

Nussbaum, M. C. (2011). *Creating capabilities*. Cambridge, MA: Harvard University Press.
Nussbaum, M. C., & Sen, A. K. (Eds.). (1993). *The quality of life*. Oxford: Clarendon Press.
OECD (2015). *In it together: Why less inequality benefits all*. Paris: Organisation for Economic Cooperation and Development.
Olsaretti, S. (Ed.). (2007). *Desert and justice*. Oxford: Clarendon Press.
Page, E. A. (2006). *Climate change, justice and future generations*. Cheltenham: Edgar Elgar.
Parsons, T. (1951). *The social system*. London: Routledge.
Perotti, R. (1996). Growth, income distribution, and democracy: What the data say. *Journal of Economic Growth, 1*, 149–187.
Peter, F. (2009). *Democratic legitimacy*. New York: Routledge.
Piketty, T. (2014). *Capital in the twenty-first century*. Cambridge, MA: Harvard University Press.
Plott, C. R., & Smith, V. L. (Eds.). (2008). *Handbook of experimental economics results* (Vol. 1). Amsterdam: North-Holland.
Pogge, T. (2008). *World poverty and human rights*. Cambridge: Polity Press.
Pojman, L. P., & McLeod, O. (Eds.). (1999). *What do we deserve? A reader on justice and desert*. Oxford: Oxford University Press.
Raphael, D. D. (1980). *Justice and liberty*. London: Athlone Press.
Rawls, J. (1971). *A theory of justice*. Oxford: Oxford University Press.
Rawls, J. (1975). The independence of moral theory. *Proceedings and Addresses of the American Philosophical Association, 48*, 5–22.
Rawls, J. (2001). *Justice as fairness: A restatement*. Cambridge, MA: Harvard University Press.
Reader, S. (Ed.). (2005). *The philosophy of need*. Cambridge: Cambridge University Press.
Rowntree, B. S. (1901). *Poverty: A study of town life*. London: Macmillan.
Rubin, Z., & Peplau, A. (1973). Belief in a just world and reactions to another's lot: A study of participants in the national draft lottery. *Journal of Social Issues, 29*(4), 73–93.
Rubin, Z., & Peplau, A. (1975). Who beliefs in a just world? *Journal of Social Issues, 31*(3), 65–89.
Runciman, W. G. (1966). *Relative deprivation and social justice: Study attitudes social inequality in 20th century England*. London: Routledge.
Ryan, R. M., & Deci, E. L. (2000). Self-determination theory and the facilitation of intrinsic motivation, social development, and well-being. *American Psychologist, 55*(1), 68–78.
Sabbagh, C., & Schmitt, M. (Eds.). (2016). *Handbook of social justice theory and research*. Heidelberg: Springer.
Saez, E. (2002). Optimal income transfer programs: Intensive versus extensive labor supply responses. *Quarterly Journal of Economics, 117*, 1039–1073.
Sandmo, A. (1998). Redistribution and the marginal cost of public funds. *Journal of Public Economics, 70*(3), 365–382.
Sen, A. K. (1976). Poverty: An ordinal approach to measurement. *Econometrica, 44*(2), 219–231.
Sen, A. K. (1992). *Inequality reexamined*. Oxford: Oxford University Press.
Sen, A. K. (2009). *The idea of justice*. New York: Penguin.
Sher, G. (1987). *Desert*. Princeton: Princeton University Press.
Shue, H. (1996 [1980]): *Basic rights. Subsistence, affluence, and U.S. foreign policy* (2nd ed.). Princeton: Princeton University Press.
Smith, A. (1776 [1976]). An inquiry into the nature and causes of the wealth of nations. In R. H. Campbell & R. S. Skinner (Eds.), *The Glasgow edition of the works and correspondence of Adam Smith* (Vol. II). Oxford: Oxford University Press.
Smith, G. (2009). *Democratic innovations: Designing institutions for citizen participation*. Cambridge: Cambridge University Press.
Stiglitz, J. E. (2012). *The price of inequality: How today's divided society endangers our future*. New York: W. W. Norton & Company.
Tyler, T. R. (1990). *Why people obey the law*. New Haven/London: Yale University Press.
Tyler, T. R. (2011). *Why people cooperate. The role of social motivations*. Princeton: Princeton University Press.

Tyler, T. R., & Blader, S. (2000). *Cooperation in groups: Procedural justice, social identity, and behavioral engagement*. Philadelphia: Psychology Press.

Tyler, T. R., & van der Toorn, J. (2013). Social justice. In: L. Huddy, D. O. Sears, & J. S. Levy (Eds.), *The Oxford handbook of political psychology* (2nd ed., pp. 627–661). Oxford: Oxford University Press.

Vlastos, G. (1962). Justice and equality. In R. B. Brandt (Ed.), *Social justice* (pp. 31–72). Englewood Cliffs, New Jersey: Prentice Hall.

Walzer, M. (1983). *Spheres of justice: A defense of pluralism and equality*. New York: Basic Books.

Wiggins, D. (1998). *Needs, values, truth* (3rd ed.). Oxford: Clarendon Press.

Wiggins, D. (2005). An idea we cannot do without: What difference will it make (eg. to moral, political and environmental philosophy) to recognize and put to use a substantial conception of need?. In S. Reader (Ed.), *The philosophy of need* (pp. 25–50). Cambridge: Cambridge University Press.

Yaari, M. E., & Bar-Hillel, M. (1984). On dividing justly. *Social Choice and Welfare*, *1*(1), 1–24.

Chapter 2
Need-Based Justice from the Perspective of Philosophy

Mark Siebel and Thomas Schramme

Abstract The first part addresses the concept of needs and their moral significance. That includes the demarcation of needs from desires; subtypes of needs, such as categorical and basic needs; the role of a decent life in the specification of needs; and the claim that the satisfaction of needs takes priority over the satisfaction of desires. In the second part, qualitative principles, both comparative and non-comparative, and quantitative measures of need-based justice are discussed. The last part is concerned with methodological and justificatory questions. We analyse the reconstructive and the constructive method of developing a theory of justice and examine Rawls' model of reflective equilibrium. Special emphasis is placed on the ways in which theories of justice might draw on empirical findings.

2.1 Introduction

The philosophical perspective on justice is normative. Philosophers do not primarily want to describe existing beliefs about justice or to take stock of "what the people think", to use the catchy phrase of Miller (1992, 1999a). They rather intend to establish what the *right* beliefs about justice are, that is, what the people *should* think. This requires justification of a normative conception of justice. As we will see in Sect. 2.4, however, the very task of justifying normative claims might lead philosophers back to empirical studies.

In political philosophy, the term "justice" usually stands for what would more exactly be described as "social justice". The term "distributive justice", which is also commonly used, is somewhat insufficient because it is often restricted to tangible goods that, in the strict sense of the word, can be distributed. Social justice, on the other hand, may refer to other objects of justice than tangible goods. Briefly, the

M. Siebel (✉)
Carl von Ossiezky Universität Oldenburg & FOR 2104, 26111 Oldenburg, Germany
e-mail: mark.siebel@uni-oldenburg.de

T. Schramme
University of Liverpool & FOR 2104, Liverpool L69 7ZY, UK
e-mail: t.schramme@liverpool.ac.uk

S. Traub and B. Kittel (eds.), *Need-Based Distributive Justice*,
https://doi.org/10.1007/978-3-030-44121-0_2

concept of social justice refers to the way society organizes access to and allocation of specific resources, goods or benefits, and burdens (Miller 1976, 22).

In general usage, the concept of justice might also apply to the whole of right action and is then a concept of individual morality. In this sense, individual acts are deemed just or unjust. In political philosophy, however, it is usually institutions that are called just or unjust, so that the focus is not on individual persons and their behaviour. From such a perspective the following sentence, which is taken from the beginning of one of the most influential philosophical books on social justice, Rawls' (1971, 3) *A Theory of Justice*, clearly makes sense: "Justice is the first virtue of social institutions, as truth is of systems of thought".

Moral philosophers, who usually focus on individual conduct, would rather hold that justice is a virtue (perhaps the first virtue) of *persons*, i.e. a disposition to act in accordance with what is just. They might even claim that applying the concept of virtue to institutions is a category mistake since institutions do not have character traits. But if, from the perspective of political philosophy, we allow institutions to possess virtues, then we can see that Rawls is here actually making a normative claim, despite the apparently descriptive language ("justice *is* the first virtue of social institutions"). He does not interpret virtues as it is usually done in moral philosophy but means something like a normatively required aim, purpose or goal. A proper way to interpret Rawls' influential viewpoint would thus be to translate it as follows: social institutions' foremost aim should be to realize a just order. Obviously, we therefore need an account of just order, or in other words, a theory of justice.

The chapter proceeds as follows. Section 2.2 is concerned with the concept of needs and its moral significance. In Sect. 2.2.1, we introduce the role need satisfaction could play in a theory of justice as a currency of allocation. Section 2.2.2 presents the central characteristics of the concept of need and discusses its demarcation from the concept of desire. In Sect. 2.2.3, the reader will be acquainted with different specifications of basic needs. Since something like a decent life is often regarded as the central goal of need satisfaction, this notion is examined in Sect. 2.2.4. Section 2.2.5 discusses the moral significance of needs and especially the claim that the satisfaction of needs takes priority over the satisfaction of mere desires.

In Sect. 2.3, qualitative and quantitative accounts of need-based justice are discussed. Section 2.3.1 is concerned with principles of need-based justice, i.e. propositions laying down what conditions have to be fulfilled for need-based justice to obtain. We distinguish Aristotelian principles, which focus on equality of need satisfaction, from Platonic principles, which highlight that needs are satisfied in the first place. Section 2.3.2 examines Miller's tentative measure of need-based justice and the one resulting from Jasso's general theory of justice.

Section 2.4 assesses the methodology of need-based justice. In Sect. 2.4.1, we analyse two main methods of developing a theory of justice: a reconstructive and a constructive method. Section 2.4.2 focuses on issues of justification by scrutinizing Rawls' model of reflective equilibrium. As will be seen, on a plausible interpretation of this model, justification implies a reference to normative beliefs of real people. In Sect. 2.4.3, we therefore discuss different ways in which theories of justice, and political philosophy more generally, might draw on empirical findings. Altogether, we defend a perspective that demands a certain level of interdisciplinarity for any convincing theory of justice. Section 2.5 concludes the chapter.

2.2 The Concept of Need and Its Moral Significance

2.2.1 Need as a Criterion of Justice

A particular theory of justice can be seen as laying out a template for political aims. Such an ideal model is supposed to be used as a yardstick for real social institutions. When discussing such a model, it is useful to distinguish its *scope*, *shape* and *currency* (Page 2006, Chap. 3.1). The scope is the set of recipients whose endowments are to be taken into consideration. It may include, for example, the members of a particular society, all human beings or all living creatures. The shape determines the amount of a good that the relevant individuals should receive. One of the standard proposals here states that the good is to be distributed in such a way as to ensure equality; another one says that the distribution is to maximize well-being. Finally, the currency states the good that is to be distributed in the way given by the shape. Briefly, scope, shape and currency, in the prescribed order, answer the question "*who* should receive *how much* of *what*?".

To further illustrate the notion of currency, egalitarians have to make clear what has to be distributed equally for a distribution to be just (Sen 1980; Cohen 1989). A suggested currency might be specific resources, such as Rawls' social primary goods, including liberties, opportunities and income. Other theories focus on what people can do and achieve with resources. An influential account that has emerged from a critique of Rawls' theory is Sen's capabilities approach, which has been developed in collaboration with Nussbaum (1990). Here the currency is not tangible goods but what the authors call *capabilities* to achieve a number of *beings* and *doings*. The ability to participate in adequate health provision, or to engage with nature, could be capabilities in this sense (see Sect. 2.2.3). Obviously, different currencies might overlap. Especially the influential currency of opportunities implies tangible resources, e.g. money, as well as liberties.

Strictly speaking, proponents of need-based justice do not regard need itself as their currency but the degree to which it is satisfied. The shape of a corresponding theory might then consist in the claim that needs should be satisfied to the same degree for everyone. Analogously, advocates of effort-based justice maintain that the currency of justice is reward for effort, and they might add that a just distribution requires equal reward.[1] There is a variety of pluralistic theories that include need satisfaction as one important currency of justice, as well as monistic ones that are wholly based on the fulfilment of needs. For example, Wiggins (2005), Brock (2012)

[1] For lists of general principles of distributive justice, see Deutsch (1975), Konow (2001, 2003, 2009), Konow and Schwettmann (2016), Lerner (1974), Lamont and Favor (2017), Liebig and Sauer (2016), Miller (1999a), Sen (2009) and Walzer (1983).

and Reader (together with Brock 2004) hold that needs should take centre stage in moral theory. Miller (1999a) has introduced need as a criterion of just distribution within specific contexts of personal relationships. Frankfurt (1987, 1997, 2000) and many other so-called sufficientarians have developed theories focusing on what is *enough* to live a decent life. There are also theories of social justice that do not use the terminology of need but might be interpreted as sharing the concerns of need-based justice. The already mentioned capabilities approach is an example, as well as Margalit's account in his book *The Decent Society* (1996).

On the empirical side, it is well known that people make allowances for needs in their allocation decisions. For example, if there are two persons with equal productivity but different needs, subjects give the needier a greater amount of the corresponding good (Lamm and Schwinger 1980). This even holds if the needier person is less productive.[2] Similarly, participants in other experiments have kept a close eye on a minimum income for the worst off while trying to maximize the average income.[3] This behaviour is evocative of the so-called Boulding principle: "Society lays a modest table at which all can sup and a high table at which the deserving can feast" (Boulding 1962, 83; see also Raphael 1980, 54).

Conceptions of justice are sometimes divided into *comparative* and *non-comparative* conceptions (Feinberg 1974). Egalitarian justice is a clear case of comparative justice because the question of whether the allocation to an individual is just cannot be answered without taking into account what the other members of the group have. By contrast, need-based justice will usually be described as a variant of non-comparative justice because the needs of a person appear to depend on nothing but her intrinsic condition and are therefore to be determined independently of what other members need. But there are some complications to consider.

Many philosophers take the central goal of need satisfaction to be a decent life. Along these lines, welfare states usually base provision on necessary resources to live a decent life. Access to health care and educational institutions, or the provision for situations of threats to security, can all be seen as traditional goals of social-welfare institutions. In addition, many states also cater for so-called public goods, such as transport to secure mobility or parks to offer opportunities for recreation. These standards are an object of political concerns and social conflicts, and it is uncertain whether they can be determined in a purely objective way (see Sect. 2.2.4). What a decent life consists of might rather be influenced by comparative considerations, such as the relative wealth in a society. But then need-based justice would not be a non-comparative affair. The same follows from an Aristotelian principle of need-based justice to be discussed in Sect. 2.3.1: a distribution is just if and only if needs are met to the same degree. This principle is clearly comparative because it amounts to matching degrees of need satisfaction.

Philosophers sometimes tend to think that, despite the fact that important real-life examples of social justice in welfare states are based on provision for needs, need satisfaction cannot be a suitable currency of justice. One reason is that basing claims

[2]See Gaertner (1994), Gaertner et al. (2001) and Yaari and Bar-Hillel (1984).

[3]See Frohlich et al. (1987), Frohlich and Oppenheimer (1992) and Traub et al. (2005).

of justice on needs seems to require an enormous amount of resources (Vlastos 1962, 42; Miller 2007, 5). Needs, in this interpretation, are potentially limitless. Think, for instance, of the need for physical security: road traffic, work conditions or health care can always be improved. To fulfil needs thus seems to require ever-increasing provision. For this reason, focusing on needs might be considered unhelpful: there will always be scarcity because needs can never be fully met.

A second objection is also grounded on reflections on scarcity. Hume (1738–40/1978, 495; 1751/1975, 188) famously introduced scarcity as one feature of the circumstances in which rules of justice gain practical importance, the other features being individual motivation, mainly by self-interest, and rough equality of power (Barry 1978; Hope 2010; Hubin 1976). Rawls has a similar account of the circumstances of justice. To many philosophers, however, in a situation of scarcity it does not seem just to distribute goods on the basis of needs. Rather, equal distribution seems to be fair because everyone has the same moral status and therefore nobody can claim more goods than others initially. Only if someone has a special need, in terms of requiring more resources than others to achieve the same goal, can the currency of need satisfaction be added to the picture. An example would be a pupil who needs additional support to reach the same level of knowledge as others. Still, in this picture need would only be a *secondary* criterion. The goal of need satisfaction would not constitute straightforward normative claims because it becomes relevant only in an instrumental sense, namely as a means of achieving more equality. Altogether, scarcity as one of Hume's circumstances of justice appears to devalue need satisfaction as a currency of justice.

However, there are ways and means of dealing with these objections. First, the objection that needs are potentially limitless apparently equates needs with desires. The background idea might be that some desires have no limits and thus give rise to needs that can never be met (Hubin 1989, 185). However, it will be shown in the next subsection that this understanding of needs is inadequate. Even if there are boundless desires, there may very well be limitations to needs.

Furthermore, one can take issue with the definition of scarcity implicit in Hume's and Rawls' accounts. The most significant problem is that it does not take into account justified objections to claims of need. Many resources, for instance crude oil or coal, are available only in a limited amount. But in what sense are they scarce? If we interpret "scarcity" as an *absolute* concept, that is, if we refer to limitation, then these resources are indeed scarce because there is only a finite amount of them. However, "scarcity" can also be interpreted in a *relational* way: goods are scarce for someone in order to do something. If we see scarcity in that way, then it transpires that whether a specific resource is scarce or not depends on *demand* no less than on *supply* because the goals we need resources for can be contested. If we only focus on the supply side, like many theorists of justice do, then we end up with the assertion that all instrumentally valuable resources are scarce. However, we should also focus our normative concerns on the demand side, that is, examine whether the goals for which resources are needed are legitimate or not. Then it may turn out that there is enough for satisfying all human needs even if resources are not provided in abundance.

The demand for a certain resource is influenced by at least two aspects. First, the amount of resources people need when aiming at certain goals depends on the instrumentally required level of consumption. If a certain technology, say, a petrol engine, becomes more efficient, then people may need fewer resources. This aspect concerns only the means people require in the pursuit of certain goals, which are themselves taken for granted. In this respect, the level of scarcity is mainly driven by empirical issues, especially technological developments. Second, however, the amount of resources people consume also depends on their goals, in terms of their preferences, and whether these goals are permissible is a crucial normative question. It is possible, for example, to question the legitimacy of a specific practice because it is not environmentally friendly or based on addiction.

Many theorists of justice systematically avoid raising this question of legitimate claims and therefore ignore an important aspect of scarcity. They only deal with the problem of how to justly distribute a certain amount of goods among people who want to have as much as possible. Claims are then justified on the basis of a maximal demand. Given the mentioned circumstances of justice, especially scarcity of goods, the demand for as many resources as possible seems reasonable. Indeed, on such an account all finite goods are scarce by definition because not all demands can be fulfilled.

However, whether we should actually recognize the claim for a maximal share, i.e. whether we should accept the desire for as much as possible, is a normative issue that needs to be raised prior to the questions that Rawls and other theorists deal with. Among other things, it is to be decided independently of the amount of goods available for distribution. If theorists of justice would not accept the claim for the biggest possible amount of certain goods as justifying a default entitlement, then goods might actually not be scarce—now seen from a normative perspective—because the actual supply can fulfil all the justified demand. Using the common metaphor of a cake that ought to be distributed justly, it may be possible to save a piece even where several slices of the cake are shared out. Although the cake is of a limited size, it might nevertheless not be scarce for the fulfilment of all legitimate demands. In Rawls' contract apparatus, however, all available social primary goods are to be distributed because the initial maximal demand is not normatively challenged.

The reason why Rawls and other theorists avoid a discussion of the legitimacy of initial claims is that they believe that theorists would need a substantive theory of the good in order to query legitimacy. Since Rawls does not want to endorse a view he regards as perfectionist and accordingly not value-neutral, his theory of the good for persons centres around the idea of a life-plan, which supposedly amounts to a purely formal definition of the good (Rawls 1971, 424). A request addressed at persons to moderate their desires cannot be put forward on Rawls' account. Neither can their initial maximizing demand be disregarded on the basis of a theory of human needs.

In contrast, there might be enough goods for the fulfilment of all legitimate demands if and when the rationale of maximizing the individual share of social primary goods is put into doubt. We should therefore conceive of scarcity in a normative perspective. Accordingly, a theory of legitimate demands has to be based on a more ambitious theory of the good for human beings than Rawls' idea of a rational life-plan. It requires something along the lines of a substantive conception of a decent life that provides framework conditions for what is a need (see Sect. 2.4). As has been pointed out, this is the very reason why many liberal thinkers reject such an approach. However, it clearly seems possible to develop such a theory without sacrificing basic liberal ideals. Along these lines, Keynes (1930/1963, 326) sets *absolute* needs apart from *relative* needs. The latter may be insatiable because "their satisfaction lifts us above, makes us feel superior to, our fellows". But in the case of the former "a point may soon be reached, much sooner perhaps than we are all of us aware of, when these needs are satisfied in the sense that we prefer to devote our further energies to non-economic purposes" (see also Xenos 1987).

2.2.2 *The Concept of Need*

Needs may be attributed by the locution "S needs x in order to ϕ". In the context of justice, S typically refers to persons, but we may equally think of households, companies, etc. The term x designates the object of a need, i.e. the thing needed. This can be a material resource, but also other goods, such as personal relationships. The expression ϕ stands for the goal to be achieved with x, which may be an action, a status, an opportunity, etc. In any case, by claiming that S needs x in order to ϕ, it is stated that x is necessary for S to achieve ϕ.

The claimed necessity is not a strong metaphysical one. The assertion is not that there can be no world whatsoever in which S achieves ϕ without x. After all, in a possible world with favourable conditions, shelter is not necessary for people to survive, so there would be no need for shelter. We are rather invited to imagine a realistic setting in which S is not endowed with x. If, in such a setting, there is no chance for S to achieve ϕ, S needs x in order to ϕ (Wiggins 1987, 64f.; 1998, 14f.). Furthermore, the necessity might be grounded not only in universal human conditions, such as physical make-up, but also in quite specific circumstances. Human beings need food to survive. If there are different kinds of food available, such that eating cake is not necessary for survival, it is wrong to say that a person in these circumstances needs cake. However, if the only food available is in fact cake, it is correct to claim that, given this constraint, the person needs cake. Thomson (1987, 21) calls the latter needs "circumstantial" and the former "constitutional".

The word "need" contains two independent ambiguities. The first one is a state/object-ambiguity. When we talk about an individual's need for something, we may mean either the state of need she is in or the object she needs (White 1975, 104). For the second ambiguity, consider a family of two adults and four children that should have at least $120\,m^2$ of housing space available but lives in a $90\,m^2$ flat. Then both the threshold of $120\,m^2$ and the missing space of $30\,m^2$ may be called the household's need. For the sake of disambiguation, we will use "need" for the threshold and dub the missing amount "need gap". Note that there is a need in the sense of a threshold even if the need is satisfied.[4] Our family needs $120\,m^2$ regardless of whether it has this living space at its disposal or not. According to Thomson (1987, 12), the gap-sense is secondary because it can be defined by recourse to the threshold-sense: to need something in the former sense is to lack a part of what one needs in the latter sense.

The concept of need is not very popular in ethics and political philosophy. Specifically, many deem it too flexible to work as a criterion of social justice because it seems that every fancy wish may become a need. However, needs are clearly different from wishes, desires, wants, preferences and the like. Wiggins (1987, 62) describes the essential difference as follows: "What I need depends not on thought or the working of my mind (or not only on these), as wanting or desiring do, but depends on the way things really are". That is, while a desire is a paradigm of a mental state and thus a subjective affair, a need is objective in some sense.[5] Let us set out what this means.

First, while lower animals, plants and even artefacts need many things, only beings with certain cognitive abilities are able to have a desire (White 1975, 111). Second, a *desire* requires possession of the concepts included in its content. Consider Anne who has a terrible headache. To desire ibuprofen, and not acetylsalicyclic acid, she must know what ibuprofen is. Otherwise, her thoughts cannot be directed at ibuprofen. On the other hand, Anne does not have to possess the concept of ibuprofen in order to need ibuprofen. Even if she believes that ibuprofen is by definition poisonous, she might need it in order to get rid of her headache. Third, statements about desires are referentially opaque and thus intensional whereas statements about needs are referentially transparent and thus extensional. Since the way in which a person conceptualizes the wanted thing is essential, someone may want something under one description but not under a different description. Even if Anne desires to take the headache pill Bill offers her, and this pill is an ibuprofen pill, Anne need not desire to take the ibuprofen pill because, again, it might be the case that she regards ibuprofen as poisonous. More generally, "S wants x" and "$x = y$" do not imply "S wants y". By contrast, if S needs x and $x = y$, then S needs y because what satisfies a need is independent of the mental attitudes of the needy person.

Some scholars hold that the shorter locution "S needs x" is in general elliptical for "S needs x in order to ϕ" because there is always a goal ϕ which has to be specified to fully spell out the need.[6] Thus, a need claim boils down to a claim of necessity, which in itself is neutral: "x is necessary for S to achieve ϕ" may be true even if both the good x and the goal ϕ are unacceptable. Whether a need is morally relevant, and therefore puts pressure on society to satisfy it, would then depend, among other

[4]See Braybrooke (1987, 29), White (1975, 107f.) and Thomson (1987, 11f.). Contrast Gustavsson (2014, 26) and Wollheim (1974, 174).

[5]See Braybrooke (1987, 91), Doyal and Gough (1991, 39, 42f.), Frankfurt (1984, 2), Mac Carthaigh (2014, 461), Lowe (2005, 170), Miller (1976, 128–130), Thomson (1987, 10f., Chap. VII; 2005, 175), White (1975, 108–116) and Wiggins (1998, 5f.). See Hamilton (2009, 48) for some causal connections between needs and desires.

[6]See Flew (1977), Frankfurt (1984, 2), Mac Carthaigh (2014, 460) and White (1975, 105, 121).

things, on the moral significance of the goal ϕ.[7] Some claims of need are clearly non-normative, for example, "An element needs a free electron in order to conduct electricity" (Thomson 1987, 3; see also White 1975, 103f.). Or consider a person saying "I need £100 to buy a coat". She merely claims that the money is necessary for the goal—to get the coat—whereas it is not said that the goal itself is in any way important, let alone necessary, for the person. It is thus possible to challenge the need for that coat. The person in the example would have to explain why she needs the coat; and to work as a claim of justice, it appears that the need would have to be recognized by others insofar as they accept the corresponding aim as something that ought to be accomplished.

Other scholars distinguish such an *instrumental* sense of "*S* needs *x*" from a *categorical* (*absolute* or *intrinsic*) one. While in the latter sense this locution also refers to a goal, it is assumed to be fixed by the meaning of "need". This analytically given goal is often taken to be negatively defined, focusing on the avoidance of something (significantly) bad for the person, such as (serious) harm or living a life that is (vitally) impaired.[8] However, the goal might also be some positively valued good, such as living a (minimally) decent life; living in accordance with our nature; performing the tasks assigned to a combination of basic social roles, such as parent or citizen; agency or flourishing.[9] Since these goals are regarded as something that ought to be realized, it is assumed that the categorical sense of "*S* needs *x*" has normative force.[10] For example, if Ben needs a coat to stop feeling cold, he has a categorical need and thus a right to be helped. But if he needs the coat to swagger about, then it does not seem that he has a right to be helped because to keep someone from swaggering hardly means to do him wrong.

The aim most commonly used to characterize categorical needs is *avoidance of harm*. It is seldom seen that, given the standard understanding of "harm", this characterisation is problematic. Let us assume that Anne stopped consuming food because she has a terminal disease she does not want to live with anymore. Since she practises meditation, her food refusal does not result in pain or any other misery. If a need requires that harm results when not being met, then Anne does not have a need for food because no harm is generated by her refusal to subsist. However, "food" is one of the first entries on every list of basic needs and is thus regarded as being universal. Hence, either the link to harm is not necessary for a need, or there are basic needs that are not universal.

One could react to this objection by pointing out that lists of basic needs are not discredited by rare exceptions (Braybrooke 1987, 45). The need for food is real, as it were, even if a minority of people has a strong desire for not consuming food. In the

[7] Cf. Connolly (1983, 62), Goodin (1985, 624), Mac Carthaigh (2014, 462), Plant et al. (1980, 28) and White (1975, 106f.).

[8] See Doyal and Gough (1991, 39–45), Feinberg (1973, 111), Frankfurt (1984, 7), Hamilton (2009, 47), Miller (1976, 126–128, 130f.; 1999a, 206f.), Thomson (1987, 8f., 14–16; 2005, 175) and Wiggins (1987, 63f.; 1998, 7–10; 2005, 29–31).

[9] See Braybrooke (1987, 48), Brock (2005, 56), Miller (1999a, 207f., 210, 212), S. Miller (2005, 142), Reader and Brock (2004, 252, 254) and Thomson (2005, 185).

[10] See Frankfurt (1984, 6), Hamilton (2009, 47), Thomson (1987, 4–9) and Wiggins (1998, 11).

following, we will therefore exclude exceptions such as suicidal Anne from further considerations.

A more serious problem is that it is also uncertain whether the link to harm is *sufficient* for a need because it may occur in cases of what appear to be mere desires. Someone who strongly strives after an aircraft fleet but does not get it may severely suffer because his greatest wish does not come true. But suffering appears to be an obvious case of harm. A scholar who takes needs to be grounded in the avoidance of harm should therefore concede that such a person has a need for an aircraft fleet. To use a more mundane example, if a football fan's desire for her team winning the championship is so pervasive that she will be heavy-hearted if the desire remains unsatisfied, then we have to assign her a need (Schuppert 2013, 35). Or even more strikingly, consider a mother whose desire for killing her children is so deeply entrenched that she will suffer torment if she is prevented from realizing it. Assume, furthermore, that there is no way of curing her from this desire. Again, since the mother's suffering seems to fall under the rubric "harm", she would have a need for killing her children. The given characterisation of needs would thus force us to accept that people might not only have needs for colossal things like aircraft fleets, or quite individual needs such as the one for a team's championship win, but also needs for horrible crimes.

For such reasons, Doyal and Gough (1991, 50), Miller (1999a, 222f., 321) and Thomson (1987, Chap. III) demarcate *harm* in an objective sense from subjective feelings such as *suffering*, *anxiety* or *sadness*. They would argue that, whereas the homicidal mother, the football fan and the aircraft-fleet enthusiast suffer when not getting what they want, this does not cause harm to them in an objective sense of the word. However, what does this sense amount to?

As we saw above, a couple of philosophers characterize categorical needs by the positive aim of living a decent life instead of referring to the negative aim of avoiding harm. Miller (1999a, 207f., 210) even argues that these aims are identical because harm is what results if human beings are not allowed to live a minimally decent life. Miller would thus say that the mother who wants to kill her children, the football fan and the aircraft-fleet enthusiast, although they suffer when their desires are not fulfilled, do not come to harm because the desired activities do not belong to a decent life. Not all proponents of need-based justice make use of the term "decent life". Nevertheless, it seems that all of them have in mind some kind of *adequate* life that categorical needs are directed at. This becomes even more apparent in the case of *basic* needs.

2.2.3 Basic Needs

There are quite a few distinctions between categorical needs to be found in the literature. A common thread in many of them is that some needs are marked as *basic* or *fundamental*, accompanied by the claim that satisfaction of these needs is the highest priority. If someone faces a situation that involves a threat to such basic needs, e.g. food shortage or deprivation of personal freedoms, people will immediately understand her claim of need (and they usually believe it to require an explanation when someone in this situation does not claim to be in need). Basic needs are supposed to be grounded in the universal vulnerabilities of people and could therefore allow for criticism of other societies. However, a closer look reveals that the given terms are defined in a variety of ways. Sometimes, they are even defined in the same way as categorical needs, so that they do not form a strict subset of them. Future debate could therefore profit from bringing more systematicity in the use of these terms.

Thomson (1987, 18–22) takes basic needs, which he also calls non-derivative needs, to be categorical needs *directly* serving the purpose of such needs, namely avoidance of harm. Given that the need for food is categorical, if the only way for a person to obtain food is buying it, then she has a categorical need for money. This need is derivative, however, insofar as it exists just because the person needs something else, namely food. The need for food, on the other hand, is non-derivative because it directly serves the prevention of harm and is thus not had in virtue of needing something else which is necessary to accomplish this goal. More generally, let there be a need claim "S needs x". This claim can be questioned by asking for the purpose that cannot be accomplished without x. If the need is (partly) justified by providing its purpose, one may further ask why S has a need for accomplishing this purpose. In this manner, the justification of a need may be reiterated until it reaches a point where one can merely assert that the person will be harmed without the thing in question. Then all needs in this justificational chain are categorical, but only the need we end up with is basic.[11]

Thomson picks out basic needs by their *proximity* to the aim of categorical needs. Wiggins takes a different route by defining basic needs through the further *causes* of the harm that results when these needs are not met. He argues that needs are basic if "laws of nature, unalterable and invariable environmental facts, or facts about human constitution" ensure that the person will be harmed when not getting what she needs (Wiggins 1987, 65; 1998, 15). Insofar as the use of money to get food is not an unalterable and invariable environmental fact, Wiggins will not call the need for money a basic need. However, the need for food is an obvious example of a basic need in his sense because biological laws are responsible for the lack of food resulting in harm.

Wiggins' reference to "laws of nature" and "facts about human constitution" suggests the assumption that he confines the category of basic needs to what may be called *physical* (*biological* or *vital*) needs, i.e. needs directed at bare survival. His conception would then be redolent of the lowest level in Maslow (1943) hierarchy of needs, including food, shelter, sleep, etc. or the Basic Needs Approach, whose main target is physical integrity (Jolly 1976; Ghai 1978). However, since Wiggins (1987,

[11] See also Thomson (2005, 175, 177) where he seems to identify a subclass of non-derivative needs: a *fundamental* need is a "non-derivative, non-circumstantially specific and inescapable necessary condition in order for the person not to undergo serious harm".

65; our emphasis) also mentions needs that are "basic at least partly in virtue of [...] *psychological* facts", it is evident that his category of basic needs is broader.

Physical needs promise the highest objectivity and, due to their vital importance, the greatest moral significance. Nonetheless, only a minority does not go beyond them (e.g. Daniels 1985, Chap. 2). It is much more common to hold that there are basic needs beyond the biological minimum qualifying for satisfaction no less than physical needs. Such needs are often derived by asking what is necessary for conditions such as "human agency", "good human functioning", "a recognizably human life", "our ability to function as human agents" (Brock 2005, 62; 2012, 448), "functioning normally" (Braybrooke 1987, 31), "a normal range of opportunities" (Daniels 1981, 154), "minimal agency", viz. the ability "to form intentions, identify and process reasons, and act on the basis of his/her intentions and reasons" (Schuppert 2013, 30), "characteristics a being must possess if it can intelligibly be said to be a person rather than, say, an animal or a plant" or "goals which must be achieved if any individual is to achieve any other goal" (Doyal and Gough 1984, 9f., 14; cf. 1991, 54).

The idea behind these objectives is that any life deserving the title "human" does not only call for physical but also for mental and action-oriented integrity.[12] Along these lines, Miller (2007, 3) argues that "[h]uman beings are social as well as biological creatures" and takes "basic needs" to be the "conditions for a decent human life in any society" while "societal needs" are the additional "requirements for a decent life in the particular society to which the person belongs". Basic needs are further separated into "biological or quasi-biological needs" and "socially defined needs that are replicated across societies" (Miller 1999a, 319). While the satisfaction of basic needs is an obligation on the whole of humankind, needs obtaining in a particular society put a pressure only on fellow members (Miller 1999b).

Note that Reader and Brock (2004, 255) advocate a completely different notion of basic needs because their focus is on what they call "public morality". A need is basic, on their account, if the whole "constituency" in question has it. The constituency here may be all human beings but also just a small community. A basic need in this sense may thus be a merely societal need in Miller's sense.

After having promoted a primary goal of basic needs, some scholars continue by identifying specific resources and conditions that are necessary for reaching this goal. In this way, lists of basic needs are generated. For example, Doyal and Gough (1991, Chap. 4; 1984, Sect. 4) argue that being a person in a Kantian sense who acts responsibly and successfully is possible only if the *individual needs* "survival/health" and "autonomy/learning" are met. That is, such a person does not only have to be alive but also physically and mentally healthy. Moreover, her actions must not be imposed on her but initiated by her, and since autonomous action does not emerge by itself, the person has to learn from other people how to do it. For Doyal and Gough (1991, Chap. 5; 1984, Sect. 5), the social process of teaching is a starting point to maintain

[12]Hamilton (2003, Chap. 1; 2009, 46f.) distinguishes between vital needs (e.g. food, shelter and social entertainment), agency needs (e.g. autonomy, recognition and creative expression) and particular social needs (e.g. a car or public transport). By combining the first two categories, we obtain a set of needs that is similar to basic needs in the above-mentioned sense.

societal preconditions for meeting the given individual needs, namely "production", "reproduction", "cultural transmission" and "authority".[13] Along these lines, it is necessary for the maintenance of any society, and thus for teaching Kantian action, to produce food and shelter and to reproduce.

In a highly similar fashion, Brock (2005, 63) derives a comparable list of basic needs. Her point of departure is *human agency*. Since human agency requires the ability to deliberate and choose, and since this ability requires "physical and mental health", "sufficient security to be able to act", "understanding of what one is choosing between" and "a certain amount of autonomy", they are all considered basic needs. While Brock takes these four needs to already flow from the definition of human agency, she adds a fifth need on empirical grounds. According to Brock, research from different areas, such as psychology, has shown that human beings are social animals insofar as satisfying the former needs requires "decent social relations with at least some others".

Braybrooke's (1987, 31, 48) criterion for putting something on the Minimum Standard of Provision List is broader. He seeks what is necessary for the normal functioning of human beings, which means that it is "indispensable to mind or body in performing the tasks assigned a given person under a combination of basic social roles, namely, the roles of parent, householder, worker, and citizen". According to Braybrooke (1987, 36), "physical functioning" necessitates things such as food, excretion, exercise and rest, while "functioning as a social being" requires companionship, education, social acceptance, etc.

Braybrooke's account is strongly reminiscent of an approach to which Miller (1999a, b, 210) explicitly refers when explaining what he means by a decent life: the capability approach of Sen and Nussbaum.[14] Proponents of the capability approach argue that all human beings should have the *capabilities* to achieve a number of *functionings*, which are split into *beings* and *doings*. This means that they should be provided with the opportunity to be in certain states and undertake certain activities. Since people want to be in quite different states and undertake quite different activities, and since these include even morally reprehensible ones, the relevant functionings are restricted to what is constitutive of a valuable human life. Nussbaum (2000) even offers a list of ten capabilities she takes to be necessary for a life to be worthy of the dignity of a human being: survival; bodily health; bodily integrity; senses, imagination and thought; emotions; practical reason; affiliation; other species; play; and control over one's environment. These capabilities may be interpreted as basic needs that have to be met within a society in order to guarantee all members a decent life.

Whatever such lists of basic needs include in detail, all of them arise from a certain conception of what a "normal", "good", "valuable" or "decent" human life consists of.

---

[13]Doyal and Gough (1991, 81) identify these four preconditions with the four social roles that, according to Braybrooke (1987, 48–50), are included in normal human functioning. In an earlier paper, the preconditions were called "needs" (cf. Doyal and Gough 1984, 18).

[14]See, inter alia, Sen (2009) and Nussbaum (2000, 2011). We do not dwell on the particular differences between their accounts. See Reader (2006) for a reply to the criticisms proponents of the capability approach put against the basic needs approach.

The reason for such an approach is obvious. The associated needs would be intrinsic to all human beings and thus tailor-made for global theories of justice because they provide a universal currency applicable in different historical and cultural contexts. On the downside, however, such approaches are liable to paternalism. Let us therefore have a closer look at the expanse philosophers ascribe to their conception of an adequate life. We will adhere to the term "decent life" because it is the expression most frequently used to refer to the way of life basic needs, or all categorical needs, are directed at.

2.2.4 Decent Life

The crucial question is whether a conception of a decent life is meant to be *universal* or *culture-bound*; and the most pressing challenge accompanying this distinction is to sidestep both the Scylla of *paternalism* and the Charybdis of *relativism*. Many of the scholars mentioned in the last subsection defend universalism by arguing that their conception applies to all human beings. However, given the plurality of societies on earth and the further plurality within many of them, one has to go out on a limb to argue for a way of life all humans should subscribe to. The danger here is to inch one's way towards something like the distinction between "true" (or "genuine") and "false" needs discussed especially in the Marxian tradition.[15] In the words of Fehér et al. (1983), need-based justice might end up in an illiberal "Dictatorship over Needs" (Goodin 1988, 31). What is wanted is thus a notion of a decent life that is not biased by the particular beliefs and preferences of the person who promotes it. That is, it must neither be based on an idiosyncratic anthropological view nor on an all too specific view of society.

By way of illustration, Thomson (1987, Chaps. III and IV) makes use of a distinction between desires and *interests*. He starts by regarding harm as a type of deprivation. On its own, this idea does not help because, say, the football fan is deprived of the overwhelming feelings she would have had if her favourite team had won the championship, but she does not have a need for the championship win. However, Thomson continues by explaining deprivation in terms of interests. According to him, interests are the roots of desires insofar as they cause them. In contrast to a desire, however, an interest is not directed at specific objects. As an example, Thomson describes a man who works hard because he wants to impress his friends. Unbeknown to him, his desire is caused by his interest in affection, an interest that can be satisfied not only by the impression hard work makes on his friends but also by other kinds of behaviour. To lead a decent life thus means not to be deprived of something that is in one's interest. Applied to the football fan, for example, Thomson

[15] See Sadurski (1983) for a critique of this distinction. Nussbaum (2000, 51–59) provides arguments to the effect that a modest form of paternalism is desirable. Frankfurt (1984, 12) suggests that false needs are those needs that result in merely only because the person has a *desire* for the corresponding object.

would argue that her desire for the championship does not constitute a categorical need because the championship is not in her interest. The interest behind is rather of a more general type and can be satisfied by other things.

In the case of Thomson's theory, the danger of paternalism lies in the fact that one may ascribe interests to people that they deny, arguing that they *should* have these interests because they are linked to a decent life. Conversely, one may deny that people have particular interests, despite their insistence on them, because one thinks that a decent life does not include them. As Thomson (1987, 14; our emphasis) himself writes, "A person's needs have a bearing on how he *ought* to live". The challenge is thus not to end up in an extensive assignment of Freudian delusion.

To have a reasonable chance of success, a universal conception of a decent life has to fix as little as possible. This holds most likely for conceptions such as Brock's (2005, 63), Doyal and Gough's (1984, 9f., 14; cf. 1991, 54) or Schuppert's (2013, 30), which focus on *agency*, i.e. the ability to deliberate, choose and act on one's reasons. After all, an organism without this ability can hardly be called a person, let alone a human being.

On the other hand, there are many proponents of need-based justice who do not try to develop a universal notion of a decent life but agree that such notions are *culturally relative* (Wiggins 1987, 63; 1998, 11; Hamilton 2009, 49).[16] Along these lines, Miller (1999a, 212) says that "needs above the biological minimum have to be defined in terms of social norms about what constitutes a minimally decent life".[17] An example of such a context-specific need could be access to the internet. In an affluent society where media play an important role in public life, to have no access to the internet is a serious harm. However, this will not be the case in every society. The background idea here is that the significance of the goal has to be established in a social context. In other words, need claims have to be recognized in order to gain normative impact, and this recognition takes place within particular societies.

However, specifying categorical needs in this way circuits the Scylla of paternalism at the expense of heading for the Charybdis of relativism. If categorical needs are defined as what is necessary for living a decent life, and if there are only culture-bound notions of a decent life, then the concept of categorical needs inherits a further relatum (Miller 1999a, 212). To fully spell out such a need, we have to use locutions of the form "*S* needs *x* in order to live the sort of life conceived as decent in society *O*". But this hampers cross-cultural criticism of apparent undersupply. For example, if the duties a society assigns to females do not require schooling, then the question is how this society's keeping girls away from school could be criticized (Doyal and Gough 1991, Chaps. 2f.; Mac Carthaigh 2014, 462). After all, the given society's social norms about what constitutes a decent life for females do not require schooling. We may of course claim that girls need schooling to lead the sort of life

[16] As a matter of fact, Doyal and Gough (1984, 16), who at first glance belong to the "universalists", emphasize that even the concept of physical health includes a reference to a culture-bound notion of abnormality.

[17] Similarly, in his early work *Social Justice*, Miller (1976, 13f.) adds to his explication of harm as interference with a person's plan of life that "the plan must be intelligible to us".

conceived as decent in *our* society. However, this amounts to a serious objection only if it can be shown in addition that our way of life is somehow better than the one regarded as decent in the society we are criticizing.

Miller (1999a, 213) quite rightly adds that we do not have to appreciate a society's way of life in order to recognize that its members are harmed if they cannot participate in this way of life. However, this merely means that we can criticize the society for excluding people from the elements that are part of a local interpretation of "a decent life". It does not permit us to raise a complaint if the needs recognized by a society are satisfied but we think that there are further needs to be met, such as schooling for girls. Here, we have to refer either to a universalizable notion of a decent life or to some other reason why what we take to be a need should also be regarded as a need in the given society.

2.2.5 The Moral Significance of Needs

Proponents of need-based justice do not only assume that needs are different from desires but also that their satisfaction is morally more relevant than satisfaction of desires. However, since people do not only suffer when their needs are unmet but may suffer even more when strong desires remain unfulfilled, it appears at first glance that even categorical needs could be outranked by desires.

To argue for a Principle of Precedence of categorical needs over desires, Frankfurt distinguishes *volitional* from *non-volitional* needs. A need is volitional if the needed thing is necessary for achieving something the person wants; and it is non-volitional if, independently from the person's desires, the thing is necessary for avoiding harm (Frankfurt 1984, 4, 6). A volitional need, in turn, is *free* or *constrained*, depending on whether the underlying want is voluntary or not. Free volitional needs, Frankfurt (Frankfurt 1984, 5–8) argues, are not morally superior to mere desires. For since the desire from which the need derives is voluntary, harm can be avoided not only by meeting the need but also by relinquishing the desire. Constrained volitional needs, on the other hand, are just as categorical as non-volitional needs because there is no other way to avoid harm than meeting them (Frankfurt 1984, 9f.).

Non-volitional and constrained volitional needs are regarded by Frankfurt as being morally prior to mere desires for two reasons. First, meeting needs results in the avoidance of something bad while satisfying desires generates a benefit. The latter is less significant from a moral point of view because making the world better is less important than preventing it from getting worse (Frankfurt 1984, 6f.). Second, "whether or not the harm ensues is outside the person's voluntary control" if she has a non-volitional or a constrained volitional need (Frankfurt 1984, 7). She has thus a stronger right to be helped because prevention of harm is not in her hands.

Goodin (1985, 617–619; 1988, 33f., 40–42) objects to both arguments. First, compare a person whose non-volitional or constrained volitional need for something is met with a person whose mere desire for the same kind of thing is satisfied. If the desire is strong enough, not satisfying it anymore results in the same harm as not meeting the need anymore. Such a desire is thus on a par with a non-volitional or constrained volitional need for the same object because the satisfaction of both avoids harm. Second, the lack of voluntary control is not confined to non-volitional and constrained volitional needs but may also occur in the case of desires. Frankfurt (1984, 4) himself says that there are desires that are not under voluntary control. Hence, this feature also cannot make for a general distinction between the moral force of needs and desires. There could even be a desire possessing both of the given features, i.e. an involuntary desire whose fulfilment prevents harm. Contrary to Frankfurt's Principle of Precedence, a need for the same thing would not have a stronger right to be satisfied.

A problem that is analogous to Goodin's first objection was already mentioned in Sect. 2.2.2. The prevention of harm seems not to be sufficient for a need because, if we understand "harm" in the standard way, not satisfying even murderous desires might result in harm as much as not meeting a need. Remember that advocates of need-based justice therefore deploy a special understanding of "harm" under which this condition results only if a person is kept from leading a decent life. Goodin's objection could be handled in the same way. Needs, whether volitional or non-volitional, are superior to mere desires because they are, by definition, directed at a decent life. That is, if a need remains unmet, the corresponding individual is not able to lead a decent life and is thus in this strong sense affected by harm. However, if a desire is unsatisfied, the resulting harm need not be of this type because the desire might be directed at something unnecessary for a decent life. On the other hand, if it is directed at such a thing, then it is not a mere desire anymore but a categorical need. For example, although the mother who wants to kill her children suffers if her wish remains unsatisfied, this type of harm is negligible because killing one's children is not necessary for living a decent life.

To be sure, this solution presupposes that there is either a universally valid conception of a decent life not ending up in paternalism or culture-bound conceptions not ending up in relativism (see the previous subsection). A further challenge is posed by self-inflicted need gaps. If a farmer does not have enough wood for heating his cottage to a tolerable temperature because he was lazy, some people would say that there is no obligation to help him despite the fact that he would thus be prevented from living a decent life. From this point of view, even an unmet categorical need is morally relevant only if the gap is grounded in third-party responsibility. In other words, self-inflicted need gaps are unworthy of being filled.

A related topic deserving closer attention are addictions. According to Frankfurt (1984, 10f.), an addict has both a constrained volitional and a non-volitional need for the drug. There is a constrained volitional need because the addict has a desire for the drug she cannot free herself from even if she strongly wants to. There is also a non-volitional need because, even if she suddenly lost the desire for the drug, not getting it would still cause harm to her owing to the resulting withdrawal symptoms. Since the drug addict would thus have a need that is twice entrenched, one may speculate that it has a stronger right to be satisfied than the need of an ill person who needs the same drug for pain therapy and thus has no motive to get rid of her desire for the drug. Nevertheless, it is far from certain that an addict's need for a drug puts pressure on society to meet it at all. If the addict in fact has a morally relevant need, it rather appears to be her need for therapy (Braybrooke 1987, 265–267). Moreover, while withdrawal surely results in an impaired life for a time, the life of most drug addicts hardly deserves the title "decent" (Doyal and Gough 1991, 36). Along these lines, Thomson (2005, 176) argues that fundamental needs outrank addictions because, while one might be better off not having the addiction, there is no question of whether one ought to have one's needs met.

To conclude this subsection with a further topic for future debate, note that previous work on the moral significance of needs concentrated on the *goal* side of needs. The question was which goals, such as a decent life, are sufficient for putting pressure on society to meet the need in question. However, we should take into account the *object* side of needs as well, i.e. the moral status of *what is needed* to satisfy the goal. Sometimes, something bad might be necessary for achieving something good, and then it is far from obvious that there is an obligation to satisfy the need.[18]

2.3 Qualitative and Quantitative Accounts of Need-Based Justice

2.3.1 Principles of Need-Based Justice

By a *principle* of need-based justice, we mean a proposition stating what conditions have to be fulfilled for need-based justice to hold. Such a principle is *qualitative* in distinguishing just from unjust distributions without saying anything about how just or unjust a distribution is. For judgements of the latter type we need a *quantitative* account, i.e. a *measure* of need-based justice. Such measures will be discussed in the next subsection. To be as precise as possible right from the start, we introduce some notation. Let there be a set I of n individuals. These individuals could be persons, households, companies, etc. Each individual $i \in I$ is endowed with a particular amount ω_i of a good and exhibits a certain need ν_i of that good. An individual i is thus undersupplied if $\omega_i < \nu_i$, exactly supplied if $\omega_i = \nu_i$ and oversupplied if $\omega_i > \nu_i$.

Aristotle's famous proportionality conception of justice from book V of the *Nicomachean Ethics* can be used as a starting point for a principle of need-based justice (Aristotle 2009, 84f.):

> The just, then, is a species of the proportionate [...]. For proportion is equality of ratios, and involves four terms at least [...]; and the just, too, involves at least four terms, and the ratio between one pair is the same as that between the other pair; for there is a similar distinction between the persons and between the things. As the term A, then, is to B, so will C be to D, and therefore, *alternando*, as A is to C, B will be to D.

The "things" are the actual endowments of the persons. Aristotle is thus saying that a distribution is just if the ratio between these endowments is identical to the

[18]See Miller (2007, 6–9) for some cases in which needs may not entail a right to be satisfied.

ratio between the "persons". But what does the latter mean? In order not to commit ourselves to a specific reading, let us assume that Aristotle is talking here about what the persons, for whatever reasons, *should* receive. Then a distribution is just if the ratio between what the persons receives and what they should receive is the same for all of them. The Aristotelian approach may also be formulated by saying that we are to ensure equal ratios between actual and legitimate endowments.

' So far, there is only a formal characterization. To obtain a substantial principle, the legitimate endowments have to be defined. Since we are after *need*-based justice, it immediately suggests itself to equate them with the *needs* of the recipients. By recourse to our notation, the Aristotelian principle thus reads as follows (see Miller 2007, 8):

AP 1 *A distribution among the individuals in a set I is just with respect to needs if and only if the ratio ω_i / ν_i is the same for all $i \in I$.*

The ratio of endowment to need provides information on how much the given need is satisfied. For example, a ratio of 1/2 means that the need is only half-satisfied while 2/1 means that the individual has twice as much as it needs. From this perspective, principle (AP 1) states that all needs should be fulfilled to the same degree. In the terminology introduced in Sect. 2.2.1, we may also say that (AP 1) suggests need satisfaction as the *currency* of justice and equality as its *shape*.

(AP 1) rules goods to be distributed in proportion to needs not only under but also above the threshold. One could argue that proportionality beyond the threshold is universally valid for *effort*-based justice: if all participants have got what they deserve on the basis of their effort, then a surplus is also to be distributed so as to attain equal ratios of endowments to efforts. However, it is not obvious that the same holds for *need*-based justice. A second way to address situations of abundance is thus to impose no restrictions at all. If all needs are met, then other currencies, such as reward of effort, might become relevant, but from the perspective of need-based justice there is nothing to complain about. The corresponding variant of the Aristotelian principle states:

AP 2 *A distribution among the individuals in a set I is just with respect to needs if and only if either the ratio ω_i / ν_i is the same for all $i \in I$ or $\omega_i \geq \omega_i$ for all $i \in I$.*

The currency here is still need satisfaction, but (AP 2) promotes a different shape, namely equality up to the point at which all needs are met.

However, both (AP 1) and (AP 2) are debatable because they are purely *comparative*. They take into account only how much the individual ratios of endowments to needs resemble each other, and thereby ignore the non-comparative issue of whether the recipients' needs are satisfied in the first place. For example, even if households have to live in flats that are too small, a distribution is just according to both principles if all of them have, say, only half of what they require.[19] Of course, if there is no more housing space available, such a distribution may be called "as fair as possible

[19]See Feinberg (1974, 300), Jasso (1978, 1402), Miller (2007, 9) and the levelling-down objection to egalitarianism discussed in Nozick (1974, 229) and Temkin (1993, 247f.).

given the circumstances". But this could be understood as merely saying that the distribution is the least unjust.

From Plato's *Republic* (Plato 1998, 332b–c, 433e), we may extract a principle that is not subject to this objection because it is non-comparative:

> Simonides, then, after the manner of poets, would seem to have spoken darkly of the nature of justice; for he really meant to say that justice is the giving to each man what is proper to him, and this he termed a debt. [...] Then on this view also justice will be admitted to be the having and doing what is a man's own and belongs to him.

Although Plato is more interested in the mentioned aspect of doing, we will concentrate on the element of having because it is a better match for distributive justice. The fundamental idea was later summarized in the phrase "To each his own" ("Suum cuique")—which was popularized by Cicero and horribly abused when it was put at the gate of a Nazi concentration camp at Buchenwald. An application of this idea to distributions could be that we have to ensure that everyone receives what they should receive. In the case of *need*-based justice, what one should receive is nothing but the *need* of the given individual. The corresponding phrase is thus "To each what he needs".

Just as in the case of the Aristotelian account, the question is how to treat oversupply. On the one hand, "To each what he needs" could mean that neither more nor less is allowed such that all deviations from exact satisfaction of needs are unjust. Then the Platonic principle states that endowments ω_i have to be identical with needs ν_i. Or to put it equivalently:

PP 1 *A distribution among the individuals in a set I is just with respect to needs if and only if* $\omega_i/\nu_i = 1$ *for all* $i \in I$.

On the other hand, the land of milk and honey does not appear to be unjust just because everyone lives in abundance. A principle considering this argument would state that endowments ω_i could also be higher than needs ν_i:

PP 2 *A distribution among the individuals in a set I is just with respect to needs if and only if* $\omega_i/\nu_i \geq 1$ *for all* $i \in I$.

The latter approach is evocative of Sen's (1981, 186) Focus Axiom for the measurement of poverty. Just as the Focus Axiom states that poverty is not influenced by income changes among the non-poor (as long as they do not become poor), so (PP 2) implies that justice is not influenced by endowment changes among the oversupplied (as long as they do not become undersupplied). (PP 2) should also be acceptable for strong sufficientarians. They do not only hold the positive thesis that people must have enough to live a decent life but also the negative thesis that "if everyone had enough, it would be of no moral consequence whether some had more than others" (Frankfurt 1987, 21; see Casal 2007 for a critique).

Just as the Aristotelian principles, the Platonic ones assume need satisfaction as the *currency* of justice. However, there is a crucial difference in *shape*. The Aristotelian principles promote equality: at least up to the point at which all needs are fulfilled, they prescribe identical degrees of need satisfaction independently of their size. In contrast, the Platonic principles require particular degrees of need satisfaction: 100% in the case of (PP 1) and 100% or more in the case of (PP 2).

More generally, the Platonic approaches differ from the Aristotelian ones in being non-comparative in an essential sense. To be sure, both of them focus on the individuals' degrees of need satisfaction and therefore compare for each individual its endowment with its need. However, only Aristotle proceeds by also comparing the *results*, that is, by examining whether there is equal *need satisfaction*. Consequently, a distribution is just on the Aristotelian principles (AP 1) and (AP 2), but not on the Platonic principles (PP 1) and (PP 2), if all participants are undersupplied in the same proportion. Conversely, the definiens of (PP 1) implies both the one of (AP 1) and the one of (AP 2): if all needs are exactly satisfied, they are satisfied to the same extent. The same holds for (PP 2) and (AP 2): if all needs are fulfilled or overfulfilled, the first disjunct of (AP 2)'s definiens is made true. Nevertheless, there is no inference from (PP 2) to (AP 1) because needs can be overfulfilled to a variable extent.

(PP 2) is not sensitive to whether needs are satisfied to the same degree or not. For this reason (and in contrast to the Aristotelian principles), it regards all cases of undersupply unjust, whether or not the size of undersupply is the same. For the same reason, however, (PP 2) fails when faced with undersupply accompanied by different degrees of oversupply. Consider two households, both needing 90 m^2 of housing space, and compare two distributions. In both distributions, one of the households receives only 45 m^2. In distribution A, the other household receives 95 m^2 and therefore only a little bit more than it needs; in distribution B, it receives 270 m^2 and is thus massively oversupplied. Distribution B is clearly more unjust than distribution A because the oversupplied household would suffer no serious harm if it passed 45 m^2 to the other household, in order that it is not undersupplied anymore. The difficulty with the Platonic principle (PP 2) is that it is not able to reproduce this line of reasoning. For insignificant oversupply is attributed the same influence on justice as extreme oversupply, and this even holds if there are undersupplied individuals. With (PP 2) glasses on, we merely see two distributions in which the endowment of one household is higher than its need while the endowment of the other household meets only half of its need. There is thus no discernible reason for discriminating between these cases.

One could try to solve these problems by merging the Platonic with the Aristotelian approach. For example, one may combine the principles (PP2) and (AP1):

A distribution among the individuals in a set I is just with respect to needs if and only if (P) $\omega_i / \nu_i \geq 1$ *for all* $i \in I$, *and (A)* ω_i / ν_i *is the same for all* $i \in I$.

The underlying idea is that need-based *justice* consists in need *satisfaction* complying with the ideals prescribed by the clauses (P) and (A). The Platonic part (P) simply states that needs are to be met. However, need-based justice does not exhaust itself in need satisfaction because it also includes equality, with "equality" not meaning sameness of endowments in the sense of naive egalitarianism but equal degrees of need satisfaction. That is, we are not interested in whether all parties receive the same amount of a good but whether what they receive is able to fulfil their needs to the same extent. This is the Aristotelian part (A). Future research will show whether this combination of Platonic and Aristotelian principles, or another one, is tenable.

2.3.2 Measures of Need-Based Justice

The principles discussed in the previous subsection merely rule under which conditions a distribution is just or unjust but remain silent on *how* just or unjust it is. To answer the latter question, we need a *measure* (or as social scientists say: an *index*) of need-based justice. Again, let there be a set I of n individuals who are endowed with a particular amount ω_i of a good and exhibit a certain need ν_i of that good. A measure of need-based justice can then be characterized as a function whose arguments are the individual endowments ω_1 to ω_n and the individual needs ν_1 to ν_n and whose values are numbers representing a degree of need-based justice.

Advocates of the equality principle can draw on a wide range of measures of inequality, such as the Gini coefficient, the Atkinson index or the Theil index (Gini 1921; Atkinson 1970; Theil 1967). On the other hand, there exist hardly any considerations on how to measure need-based justice.[20] This is unfortunate because, among other things, situations of scarcity call for quantitative considerations. If the total amount of a good does not suffice to satisfy all needs, the question arises what distribution would be the least unjust. This question cannot be answered without doing some mathematics. For even if the answer is simply that we should see to it that as many needs as possible are satisfied, the arithmetic operation of addition is in play. Or consider the answer that the amount of unmet need should be minimized. This answer remains vague until it is clarified in which way unmet need is to be calculated. Moreover, the pressure to use mathematics is quite a helpful impetus for stating more precisely what need-based justice is, or to contrast different kinds of need-based justice hitherto conflated, and thus to achieve a deeper understanding of this topic.

The simplest way to measure need-based justice is to add the number of individuals whose needs are satisfied; a more sophisticated way is to calculate the ratio of individuals with satisfied needs to all individuals. The latter measure bears analogy to the so-called Head-Count Ratio, measuring poverty by the fraction of people below the poverty line (Seidl 1988, 90). It tells us what percentage is exactly supplied or oversupplied and thus, by implication, what percentage is undersupplied. For example, if four out of ten households receive the housing space they need and two receive more than they need, then this measure gives 60%, entailing that 40% are undersupplied. However, even the more sophisticated measure specifies only the *incidence* of need satisfaction while ignoring the *degree* to which individuals are over- or undersupplied. A distribution in which 40% lack half of what they need will be deemed just as unfair as a distribution in which 40% lack only a tiny amount. To avoid this oversimplification, we need an account of the degree to which people are undersupplied or oversupplied.

Such an account is provided by Miller who is the only scholar up to now having introduced a measure of need-based justice. This measure is based on the Aristotelian approach that a distribution is the more unjust the more inequality there is in unmet

[20]For some considerations on indirect measures of need satisfaction see Doyal and Gough (1991, Chap. 8).

need (Miller 1999a, 217f.). Conversely, "injustice is reduced to zero when people end up at the same relative point on the scale of need" (Miller 1999a, 219). In contrast to Aristotle, however, Miller (1999a, 320, fn. 27) measures unmet need by the *difference* between an individual's endowment and her need. Likewise, the divergence between two unsatisfied needs is given by the absolute value of the difference between these need gaps.

The overall injustice of a distribution is then calculated by adding all of the latter quantities, namely the difference between individual 1's need gap and individual 2's need gap, the difference between individual 1's and individual 3's need gaps, the difference between 2's and 3's gaps, and so on. Strictly speaking, there is a need gap only if a need is not satisfied, implying that there is no need gap if a need is exactly satisfied. However, Miller's examples show that he includes such cases of exact supply by assigning a need gap of 0. In other words, oversupplied participants do not enter into the calculation while all those whose endowments ω_i are smaller than or equal to their needs v_i are counted:

$$JM1 = \sum_{i=1}^{n-1} \sum_{j=i+1}^{n} \left|(\omega_i - v_i) - (\omega_j - v_j)\right|,$$

where $\omega_i \leq v_i$ and $\omega_j \leq v_j$.

Miller (1999a, 219f.) is well aware that his measure is not without shortcomings. Among other things, it allows for reaching perfect justice by decreasing the endowment of a recipient because such a decrease may equalize unmet need.[21] As Miller himself diagnoses, the problem here is that, although such a result complies with the principle that need gaps should not differ, it violates a second principle that is essential for need-based justice, namely that there ought to be no unmet need. Miller's diagnosis could be reformulated by saying that his index captures the Aristotelian comparative approach to the exclusion of the Platonic non-comparative approach. Note, however, that Hassoun ascribes recognition of the Platonic ideal to Miller. In her view, Miller does not simply equate need-based injustice with inequality in need gaps but "adds the total amount of remaining need to this inequality to give a score for need improvement" (Hassoun 2009, 262). Miller's index would accordingly read as follows:

$$JM2 = JM1 + \sum_{i=1}^{n} |(\omega_i - v_i)|,$$

where $\omega_i \leq v_i$.

Hassoun's interpretation is in conflict with most of what Miller writes about his measure. Among other things, it does not dovetail with the already cited remark that, on his account, "injustice is reduced to zero when people end up at the same relative point on the scale of need" (Miller 1999a, 219). The only advantage of Hassoun's interpretation is that it is able to explain the injustice values assigned by Miller when

[21] See Footnote 19 for the levelling-down objection.

he discusses a concrete example (Miller 1999a, 218). However, more important than the hermeneutic question is that Hassoun's Miller-like index $JM2$ does not solve the above-mentioned problem (Hassoun 2009, 263f.). Let there be three households needing 90 m^2 each. If one of them has 90 m^2, the second one 60 m^2 and the third 30 m^2, $JM2$ offers an injustice value of 210 m^2. But if we downgrade households 2 and 3 to 30 m^2, there is no inequality in need gaps anymore, with the result that the remaining injustice is due to nothing but unmet need and thus amounts to only 180 m^2.

There are further difficulties not mentioned by Miller. Remember that, to measure unmet need, he makes use of the *difference* between what the person has and what she needs. His index thus provides values in the unit by which the corresponding good is measured. If the good is, say, housing space measured in square metres, then justice will also be measured in square metres. This is odd in itself because square metres do not seem to be meaningful justice units (Jasso 1978, 1403). In addition, it has the unwelcome consequence that Miller's measure is neither unit-invariant nor scale-invariant. Concretely, the values for the previous examples do not stay the same if housing space is measured in square inches instead of square metres, and they change if both endowments and needs are doubled or multiplied by another number.

A second measure may be extracted from Guillermina Jasso's general theory of justice.[22] This theory includes the so-called Justice Evaluation Function (JEF) on which an index is based. JEF gives the degree of justice pertaining to the endowment of a single individual. This degree results from comparing the *actual* endowment ω_i with the *just* endowment, i.e. with what the individual should receive if the distribution were fair. In close proximity to Aristotle, Jasso argues that the degree of justice is to be identified with the natural logarithm of the ratio between actual and just endowment.

JEF leaves open how the just endowment is to be determined. To obtain a measure of *need*-based justice, we may again identify it with the *need* ν_i of a given individual:

$$JEF1_i = \ln(\omega_i/\nu_i).$$

This measure leads to the value 0, standing for perfect justice, if endowment and need are identical; it provides negative numbers in case of undersupply and positive numbers in case of oversupply. Second, it is monotonic both in ω_i and ν_i: the higher the endowment, the greater the justice value; and the higher the need, the lower this value. Third, it is invariant relative to unit and scale. Fourth, a consequence of the logarithm is that undersupply is treated as more unjust than oversupply of equal absolute value. If a person needs 100 units, then giving 80 units will be considered more unfair than giving 120 units.

But how can the values given by JEF be aggregated in order to arrive at a justice value for a whole distribution? Jasso (1999, 143f.) discusses two candidates, the arithmetic mean of the individual degrees of justice and the arithmetic mean of their

[22] See, inter alia, Jasso (1978, 1980, 1990, 1999, 2007) and Jasso and Wegener (1997).

absolute values:

$$JJ1 = \sum_{i \in I} \ln(\omega_i/\nu_i)/n.$$

$$JJ2 = \sum_{i \in I} \ln|(\omega_i/\nu_i)|/n.$$

Jasso herself points out a serious difficulty with $JJ1$: it merges positive values for oversupply and negative values for undersupply and thereby allows for unfortunate compensation. A distribution exactly satisfying the needs of two persons will be as just as a distribution in which one of them gets half of what she needs and the other one twice as much. $JJ2$ is superior in this respect because the arithmetic mean of the absolute justice values is 0 only if there is neither undersupply nor oversupply. On the other hand, $JJ2$'s values may be identical regardless of whether there is only undersupply or only oversupply. The injustice emerging from two individuals endowed with half of what they need is identical with the injustice given by two individuals possessing twice as much.

Furthermore, just as Miller's index $JM1$ is purely Aristotelian in not factoring in whether needs are satisfied in the first place, Jasso's indexes are purely Platonic in just aggregating, but not comparing, the individual amounts of need satisfaction. To make things worse, Jasso's indexes are geared to the inferior Platonic principle (PP 1). For not only undersupply but also oversupply entails a deviation from the value representing perfect justice. Admittedly, this problem can be evaded by fixing the value for oversupply to 0:

$$JEF2_i = \min(\ln(\omega_i/\nu_i), 0).$$

This would be in line with the Platonic principle (PP 2) because all degrees of oversupply are treated in the same way. However, it then becomes impossible to distinguish a distribution in which one household is undersupplied and the other one slightly oversupplied from a distribution in which the other household is massively oversupplied. Hence, although Jasso's theory has some advantages over Miller's because it does not start with the difference but the ratio of endowment and need, it is insufficient as well because it does not give due attention to the comparative dimension attached to the Aristotelian approach. These difficulties may be evaded by developing a measure that is based on a combination of Platonic and Aristotelian principles. In the former subsection, we mentioned the combination of (PP 2) and (AP 1), stating that a distribution is just if needs are not only satisfied but also satisfied to the same degree. To convert such a qualitative conception into a measure, one could draw on the simple idea that a distribution is more unjust the more the actual degrees of need satisfaction diverge from the ideal degrees prescribed by the given account. Applied to the given combination, this means that a distribution is more unjust the more divergence there is from satisfied needs (i.e. the Platonic ideal) and identical degrees of need satisfaction (i.e. the Aristotelian ideal).

2.4 The Methodology of Need-Based Justice

2.4.1 Generating Theories of Justice

At the outset, it was pointed out that the philosophical perspective on justice is normative. Philosophers do not focus on what people actually think about justice but what they *should* think. This raises a methodological question. What people actually think has to be examined by empirical research, and corresponding theories will thus be supported or undermined by empirical data. But how can a *normative* theory of justice be generated and justified? Do empirical data play a role here, too?

A theory of justice can be developed by different methods. It may be *reconstructed* from actual social institutions, or from normative beliefs identified in a society. Alternatively, it can be *constructed* on the basis of normative assumptions in combination with mechanisms of theory design, such as hypothetical choices of persons. These are the most influential versions of theory generation in political philosophy.

Different methods lead to different kinds of theories, but they also have significant impact on the substantive content of conceptions of justice. Whether a theory of justice puts needs at the centre or at the periphery is strongly related to its methodology. As we will see, a theory that aims to be in line with real institutions will normally have a strong link to needs whereas a theory that develops an ideal usually does not see needs as an important consideration. There might not be a necessary connection between methodologies and substantive aspects, but any theory of need-based justice should not merely be assessed in terms of its content but also its methodology.

Probably the most important social institutions within states to be linked to criteria of social justice are the legal constitution and welfare state elements. A theory of justice built by the method of reconstruction accordingly studies these political institutions and attempts to distill a particular account of a normative social order. This might be done in a mainly descriptive manner, for instance, by analysing real welfare states. Along these lines, the typology developed by Esping-Andersen (1990) and others, describing types of welfare state capitalism, might be read as a classification of theories of justice. A philosophical variant of the method of reconstructing a theory of justice can be found in Walzer's book *Spheres of Justice* (1983). Walzer develops a theory by way of interpreting a real society, the United States, especially in terms of the way citizens themselves see the significance of particular goods and how they want to organize access to these goods. In contrast to the sociological perspective of Esping-Andersen, who focuses on the *institutional* mechanisms of organizing access to resources within societies, Walzer is interested in "what the *people* think". Walzer focuses on specific social goods, for instance, welfare, leisure, work, etc. and reconstructs a multi-spherical theory of justice by way of interpreting these goods and their nature in combination with people's beliefs about these goods. A variant of such a method can be found in Honneth's (2014) recent work on social freedom. He is more historically minded than Walzer and refers to actual social struggles over the right way to organize institutions, most importantly the market, the family and the law.

The reconstructive method usually allows for a plurality of viewpoints on justice. Surely, theorists using this method have additional criteria to favour a particular theory. For example, they might hold that it fits better with the normative beliefs of actual people. Some possible theories might even be ruled out as justifiable or feasible on such an account. However, according to the reconstructive method there is not only one right theory of justice but several.

An important alternative to the reconstructive method in political philosophy is the constructive method. Here, a theory of justice is generated by certain basic assumptions and mechanisms of theory generation. Basic assumptions can be both descriptive and normative. Among other things, every (convincing) theory of justice is based on an assumption of the moral equality of all human beings. There might be more contested empirical assumptions, concerning, say, the role of incentives in the motivational structure of persons or the actual scarcity of certain goods.

Rawls (1971, Chap. III) used a constructive method. In order to generate principles of justice, he assumed a fair choice situation in which parties were supposed to choose principles for themselves. Hence, this method does not simply describe or interpret what citizens actually prefer or institutionalize in their societies, but models a hypothetical choice situation. Obviously, this initial situation needs to be adequate for the task of generating principles of justice. In Rawls' theory, the choice situation, which he dubs "original position", restricts the parties' knowledge about their social status, their gender, their economic income, etc. This is because Rawls plausibly assumes that, on the basis of selfish motivations, we will not be able to generate just principles. He claims that from the description of the just choice situation in combination with theoretical assumptions about the parties' motives specific principles will follow.

Dworkin (2000, 65ff.) offers a similar constructive account. He assumes a situation of no prior rights attached to resources, illustrated by shipwrecked people landing on an island. Since individuals have different preferences and conceptions of their own good, allocation of resources should be based on individual choices. This is modelled by setting an initially fair situation in which everyone gets an equal share of convertible goods, which are then traded on a market into preferred goods and services. Prices for these goods are established via an auction, and certain insurances are established for disadvantages due to bad luck. Eventually, such a hypothetical society will allocate resources to individuals until nobody envies any other person's bundle. The result is a just allocation, according to Dworkin. Again, as in Rawls' theory, he uses a method we can call constructive because it includes certain assumptions about an initially fair situation and mechanisms to let people determine for themselves what they deem just.

A constructive theorist of justice might be content with devising a theory of an initially fair choice situation and then leave it to actual people to identify substantive principles of justice in a fair procedure. This procedure may consist in collective deliberation about the preferred principles (see, e.g., Habermas 1996 and Forst 2002). Such versions of constructivism thus focus on the preconditions of determining just institutions in the real world. It should also be noted that such versions allow for a plurality of justified substantive principles of justice—at least theoretically, depending on the criteria of justification.

Utilitarianism can also be seen as following a constructive method. For it builds on an axiom, the principle of utility, and adds certain mechanisms of calculation, including standards of assessment and aggregation. This method is supposed to determine just institutions. An important difference to Rawls' and Dworkin's models is that utilitarianism does not require individuals themselves to choose certain principles or outcomes as just, but involves individual preferences merely as data in an objective calculation that might be performed by an impartial spectator. The latter is a counterfactual, if imaginable, device of theory construction. Utilitarianism is a philosophical theory well established in ethics, but it is also applied to issues of social justice. Many accounts in economic theory have been heavily influenced by it, especially in social choice theory.

There are, of course, more methods than the ones mentioned so far. For example, similar to theories in the natural sciences, political philosophers might assume a normative reality or a theory of essences or ideas, as in Plato's *Republic*. According to such a method, a theory of justice mirrors the real world of justice, albeit in an imperfect way. We may call this subject-external account a method of discovery. It has become unfashionable in political philosophy, most importantly because the epistemic access to such a normative world remains unclear.

Reconstructive theories seem more prone to need-based justice because they have a strong connection to the real world and the justice beliefs of people, as well as to real institutions. Most people do indeed believe that needs play an important role in questions of justice. It should be said, however, that constructive theories might also include need satisfaction as a currency of justice. For instance, Rawls' theory of primary social goods could be interpreted in this way, though probably in violation of his own inclinations.

In summary, both the reconstructive and the constructive method see justice in close connection to the choices of people. The main difference consists in how they model the involved parties and institutions. Whereas the reconstructive method relies on reality to a significant degree—although the corresponding theories involve a certain amount of abstraction and generalization—constructive models build in idealisations and normative assumptions right from the start. This brings us to the important issue of justification.

2.4.2 Justifying Theories of Justice

A possible rationale for regarding a theory of justice as justified would be directly analogous to what is done in the empirical sciences. We can test the latter type of theories against reality, and although we might never end up in a justification "once and for all", we still have valid reasons for preferring one theory over another on the basis of how well it fits reality. However, as mentioned before, in the normative domain there does not seem to be such a reality, or at least the epistemic access to any normative reality is doubtful. Given this situation, the best basis for justification consists in the convergence of the normative beliefs of all people. If everybody were to agree with a particular theory of justice in a free and informed choice, theorists would seem to have all they can reasonably hope for when aiming at justification.

Perhaps the strength of such a method of justification has led to the privileged position of contract theory in political philosophy. However, the price of such a method is its requirement of abstracting from reality. After all, in reality, people—even if sufficiently reasonable and informed—do not agree on particular principles of justice, or on any version of the welfare state as being most just. The way to deal with this lack of consensus is to introduce an idealized account of justification. This might be based, again, on an ideal situation of collective choice or common deliberation. Alternatively, it might be based on the convergence of the individual normative beliefs of people who have reached an ideal stage of deliberation about issues of justice. The latter idea has been called *(general) reflective equilibrium* by Rawls, and it has received considerable support in normative philosophical theory as a method of justification Floyd (2017).

Reflective equilibrium is a subject-internal state that is accomplished by a method of reflection guided by the criterion of coherence. The elements brought into coherence in reflective equilibrium are, however, not merely subjective, or perhaps even purely intuitive, beliefs. The relevant judgements are supposed to be *considered* judgements; they are critically scrutinized in light of moral principles and background theories. Considered judgements are thus judgements made in specific circumstances, without distorting influences on deliberative abilities and untainted by egoistic interests. "[C]onsidered judgements are simply those rendered under conditions favourable to the exercise of the sense of justice, and therefore in circumstances where the more common excuses and explanations for making a mistake do not obtain" (Rawls 1971, 47f.).

For Rawls, considered moral judgements are not the final authority of justification. The reflective method does not merely aim at a coherent internal viewpoint. Other considerations, which are independent of an individual person's point of view, are also to be included, namely theoretical insights. Every single considered judgement can come under scrutiny in reflective equilibrium and has to stand the test. Hence, "there are no judgements on any level of generality that are in principle immune to revision" (Rawls 1975 [1999], 289; see also Daniels 1979, 26ff.).

To make the inclusion of background theories more visible, Rawls (1975 [1999], 289) later distinguished *narrow* and *wide* reflective equilibrium. Narrow reflective equilibrium achieves internal order and coherence between a person's beliefs. Some individual judgements may conflict with a person's principled beliefs, but such conflicts merely set the task to sort out conflicts with ourselves. In wide reflective equilibrium, there are a couple of further considerations added to the search for a balance. These can be philosophical considerations, for example about human agency, the nature of persons, the role of morality, but also scientific facts and theories, such as findings concerning the mechanisms of economic markets (Daniels 1979, 260; Timmons 1990, 104; 1999, 236f.). In Daniels's (1979, 22) summary, "[t]he method of wide reflective equilibrium is an attempt to produce coherence in an ordered triple of sets of beliefs held by a particular person, namely, (a) a set of considered moral judgments, (b) a set of moral principles, and (c) a set of relevant background theories".

One might wonder whether the convergence of individual reflective equilibria is likely at all. Rawls' own viewpoint is not entirely clear. On the one hand, he explicitly states that several reasonable conceptions of justice might be possible: "[O]ne seeks the conception, or plurality of conceptions, that would survive the rational consideration of all feasible conceptions and all reasonable arguments for them" (Rawls 1975 [1999], 289). On the other hand, he promotes two routes to achieving a *general* reflective equilibrium, i.e. convergence in people's beliefs. The first route employs specific idealisations, especially an assumption regarding a well-ordered society. This route settles the issue by stipulation. The second route is more realistic but apparently ends in wishful thinking. To understand some of the tensions between ideal normative political philosophy and more realistically minded approaches, it is instructive to look more closely at the two routes available to Rawls.

The idealist argument for general reflective equilibrium consists in the claim that in a well-ordered society all parties agree on the same conception of justice: "Recall that a well-ordered society is a society effectively regulated by a public conception of justice. Think of each citizen in such a society as having achieved wide (versus narrow) reflective equilibrium. But since citizens recognize that they affirm the same public conception of political justice, reflective equilibrium is also general: the same conception is affirmed in everyone's considered judgements" (Rawls 2001, 31; see also 1971, 4f.). This, of course, simply begs the question. Rawls' conception of justice is allegedly justified in general reflective equilibrium, but general reflective equilibrium can only be secured by reference to the idea of a well-ordered society, which is nothing more than a stipulation. Therefore, this argument for general reflective equilibrium is a non-starter.

By taking the other route, Rawls claims that he merely describes a possible convergence in the reflective equilibria of persons. He adopts the role of an "observing moral theorist" (Rawls 1975 [1999], 289) and does not prescribe particular judgements, nor does he refer to them as the only correct ones. In contrast, Rawls states that persons actually converge in their beliefs when they are in wide reflective equilibrium. Allegedly, all people would then endorse his conception of justice. Thus, Rawls' theory of justice, according to this reading, is justified because of the fact that people do really accept it in an idealized deliberative situation. In this reading, his method of reflective equilibrium is a test of "psychological fit" between the normative theoretical claims and the normative beliefs of people (Sayre-McCord 1985, 171).

As long as some persons have not reached wide reflective equilibrium, however, it is an unfounded claim that Rawls' theory of justice would be preferred to other conceptions. Generally speaking, the method of justification via general reflective equilibrium is based on a claim about the possible convergence of individual reflective equilibria. This is an *empirical* claim that should in principle be able to be tested. An early attempt at such empirical testing are Frohlich and Oppenheimer's experiments on what principles subjects choose in a situation that emulates Rawls' original position. Since then, a number of experimental approaches have been developed in political science and economic theory (Frohlich and Oppenheimer (1992), Sabbagh and Schmitt 2016). In conclusion, if the moral beliefs of real people are to be used in a method of normative justification, then it seems that these beliefs need to be taken seriously. It is then not sufficient to make assumptions about their possible substance and convergence in the abstract.

2.4.3 Empirically Minded Political Philosophy

Rawls' method of reflective equilibrium is an example of how empirical findings might have an impact on developing a normative theory of justice. Background theories are at least partly empirical in that they include data such as psychological findings about the structure of human motivation. More importantly, Rawls' account, at least in one interpretation, also includes reference to facts about the normative beliefs of people. In this subsection, we want to address the question of the significance of such data more closely.

Beliefs about normative issues have an important role to play in the construction of theories because they determine what is *regarded* as right or wrong, for instance as just or unjust, in a particular society. In other words, it is unlikely that there is a method that is able to establish *convincing* normative claims without any reference to those beliefs. However, it is also obvious that we cannot simply use "bare beliefs" as material for constructing a political theory. They have to be somehow filtered in order to avoid a naive conventionalism (Bell and Schokkaert 1992). We therefore face another methodological problem, namely how and by what measures to convert subjective opinions into relevant data for normative theory.

There is a general philosophical problem in trying to tackle normative questions by using empirical data. After all, it is a *normative* issue one is trying to solve, and empirical findings are merely *descriptions*. Many philosophers have pointed out that we cannot reduce normative concerns to empirical ones. For normative theories it seems to be important what people *ought* to think, not what they do *in fact* think (Swift 1999, 341). Yet this antireductionist stance does not imply that normative issues can be addressed by taking a point of view completely unrelated to what people think. As long as we do not have a method of deriving normative claims from a normative reality, the only starting point seems to be the normative beliefs of people. It is true, of course, that descriptions of normative beliefs are *empirical* data, but they are descriptions of *normative* perspectives after all. The main challenge is how to integrate those empirical data in a meaningful way into normative considerations.

Another argument against bringing normative beliefs into play is that they are not useful for theoretical purposes because they might be biased and impaired by distorting influences. For instance, if we ask people what kind of institutions or distributions they regard as just, they might simply prefer the ones that best fit their personal desires. However, this objection need not result in a general rejection of the approach. It rather raises the methodological question how empirical studies could be designed such that genuine, or pure, normative beliefs are filtered out. Simple multiple-choice questionnaires conducted without any additional measures will certainly not do. For instance, test subjects might need information about the nature of normative issues and perhaps about relevant reasons underlying different normative viewpoints, which they might then endorse or reject. More theoretical measures include, for instance, impartial spectator models (Harsanyi 1982) or models appealing to empathetic preferences (Binmore 2005).

Another weakness of empirical studies about normative beliefs consists in the fact that people tend to be impressed by the unalterability of a situation. If people are of the opinion that a certain state of affairs cannot be changed anyway, or only with enormous costs, they might not assess it as unjust. This common psychological aspect could result in judgements that simply confirm reality. Again, this is not a knockdown argument against empirical studies but merely shows that we have to work on an adequate methodology. One way to get around this problem is not to ask what people think ought to be changed, but rather what they disapprove of, independent of the probability of change.

As long as empirical studies of normative beliefs cater for the mentioned and perhaps further methodological provisos, the results are relevant in constructing and assessing political theories. If common normative beliefs, filtered by proper methodological constraints, disagree fundamentally with a theory of justice, then this theory is not acceptable, at least not under the current social circumstances. To be sure, such a theory might still claim significance as a utopian account of a perfect society. However, a normative theory of justice can only reach wide acceptance if it is in line with the reflective normative beliefs of people to whom it claims to be plausible.

Since Miller (1992, 1999a) uses the criterion of "what the people think" to establish principles of justice, his theory seems to be a suitable candidate for improving Rawls' account of reflective equilibrium. Indeed, Stears (2005, 339; our emphasis) refers to Miller's approach as aiming at "*genuine* reflective equilibrium". Miller claims that different principles of justice guide people in different contexts. These contexts vary according to different relationships people have. There is some ambiguity as to how those principles follow from reality. Do relationships themselves ground principles, or are they derived from the normative beliefs of people in these relationships? This ambiguity need not pose a problem, however, as it might well be both influences—lived relationships and beliefs—that determine normative principles. Indeed, it seems that the ambiguity is Miller's way of providing external checks of normative beliefs. This is not a shortcoming of his methodology; it is rather an important ingredient because the check against corresponding relationships allows normative beliefs to be incorrect and be changed. Miller's methodology is therefore not conventionalist. "What the people think" is not fixed once and for all; neither is it sacrosanct. Miller's theory rather implies a non-vicious circularity between individual evaluations and theoretical considerations.

In conclusion, it has been argued that political philosophy can be genuinely normative, i.e. aim at an account of justice that does not simply describe real social institutions or beliefs on justice, and, at the same time, be connected to "what the people think". To flesh out theories of justice according to the methodology outlined here, we need not only philosophical expertise but have to involve other disciplines. Hence, a genuinely interdisciplinary approach is called for. Experimental methodologies are of specific importance from such a perspective. They allow to filter normative beliefs on justice and to model collective political processes of deliberation and decision-making about issues of justice on a small scale. Need-based justice can accordingly be developed in philosophical theories of justice and, at the same time, be an object of experimental studies.

2.5 Conclusion

In this chapter, we introduced need-based justice from a philosophical point of view. This means that, besides conceptual considerations, the focus was on normative issues. For need satisfaction to become a currency of justice, it is not necessary that need-based justice be the only legitimate notion of justice. It might as well be an integral part of a pluralistic conception including further currencies, for instance effort. This idea was defended against objections regarding the viability and significance of claims of need for issues of justice, especially the objection that there will always be scarcity because needs are limitless and can therefore never be fully met. We replied to this objection that demands may be challenged on normative grounds, namely by a substantive conception of a decent life providing framework conditions for what could be called a need. Then an ever-increasing desire does not automatically constitute an ever-increasing need.

The decent life was a recurring theme. We also referred to it when assessing the concept of need and its demarcation from the concept of desire. An essential distinction within the class of needs is the one between instrumental and categorical needs. While the former are morally significant only if the condition they aim at is also morally significant, the latter are meant to possess an inherent significance because they are defined by being necessary for the avoidance of harm. However, since harm in the standard sense of the word may also occur when a mere desire remains unsatisfied, it must be interpreted in quite a specific way. At this point, it is common to revert to some notion of a decent life or the like. Harm is then taken to be what results if people are kept from leading a decent life, and needs are the conditions that have to be satisfied in order to live in the given way. Philosophers differ, however, in the scope they ascribe to their notion of a decent life. While one camp tries to develop a universally valid conception from fundamental characteristics of humanity, the other camp thinks that our world is too pluralistic to allow for more than culture-bound conceptions. The former camp has to circuit the Scylla of paternalism and the latter camp the Charybdis of relativism.

Philosophers from both camps highlight some needs as basic and point out that satisfaction of these needs has the highest priority because they arise from the universal vulnerabilities of human beings. These approaches frequently include lists of basic needs derived by considering what is necessary for reaching the particular goal of basic needs. To argue for the priority of meeting needs in general, whether basic or not, over the satisfaction of mere desires, the conception of a decent life was required again. The argument here was that, if a categorical need remains unmet, the person is by definition exposed to harm in a significant way because she is kept from leading a decent life. Not satisfying a desire, on the other hand, need not have this consequence because the desire can be directed at something unnecessary for leading such a life.

Afterwards, we discussed principles of need-based justice, i.e. qualitative accounts, and measures of need-based justice, i.e. quantitative accounts. The central opposition here was the one between Aristotelian and Platonic principles. Aristotelian principles of need-based justice are purely comparative in focusing on equal degrees of need satisfaction without paying attention to whether needs are satisfied in the first place. Platonic principles are purely non-comparative in aiming at the satisfaction of needs without comparing degrees of need satisfaction. We tentatively proposed combining Aristotelian and Platonic principles in order to reach an adequate account of need-based justice. A measure might then indicate how much the actual degrees of need satisfaction deviate from the ideal degrees prescribed by the Aristotelian and the Platonic components.

Finally, the methodologies of generating and justifying theories of justice were addressed. We introduced two main methods for generating a theory, a reconstructive and a constructive method. We then evaluated the model of reflective equilibrium as a justificational procedure for theories of justice. Since this model includes a reference to the normative beliefs of real people, we discussed different ways in which empirical research may become relevant to theories of justice, or political philosophy as a whole. The proposed methodology calls for an interdisciplinary approach, which is further developed in this volume.

Acknowledgments This chapter has been written as part of DFG Research Group 2104 "Needs-based Justice and Distribution Procedures", Projects A2 "Measures of Need-Based Justice, Expertise and Coherence" (Siebel, reference SI 1731/2 – 1) and C1 "Limits of Proceduralism? Experimental Studies on the Stability of Procedures of Needs Determination" (Schramme, reference SCHR 1161/3 – 1). This funding is gratefully acknowledged. The chapter occasionally draws on earlier publications and a working paper (Schramme 2006, 2008, 2017; Siebel 2018). We would like to thank David Miller and an anonymous reviewer for helpful comments, and Andrew Fassett for editorial assistance.

References

Aristotle (2009). *Nicomachean ethics*, transl. by W.D. Ross. New York: Oxford University Press.

Atkinson, A. B. (1970). On the measurement of inequality. *Journal of Economic Theory*, *2*, 244–263.

Barry, B. (1978). Circumstances of justice and future generations. In R. I. Sikora & B. M. Barry (Eds.), *Obligations to future generations* (pp. 204–248). Philadelphia: White Horse Press.

Bell, J., & Schokkaert, E. (1992). Interdisciplinary theory and research on justice. In K. R. Scherer (Ed.), *Justice: Interdisciplinary perspectives* (pp. 237–253). Cambridge: Cambridge University Press.

Binmore, K. (2005). *Natural justice*. Oxford: Oxford University Press.
Boulding, K. E. (1962). Social justice in social dynamics. In R. Brandt (Ed.), *Social justice* (pp. 73–92). Englewood Cliffs: Prentice Hall.
Brandt, R. B. (1979). *A theory of the good and the right*. New York: Oxford University Press.
Braybrooke, D. (1987). *Meeting needs*. Princeton, NJ: Princeton University Press.
Braybrooke, D. (2005). Where does the moral force of the concept of need reside and when? In S. Reader (Ed.), *The philosophy of need* (pp. 209–228). Cambridge: Cambridge University Press.
Brock, G. (2005). Needs and global justice. In S. Reader (Ed.), *The philosophy of need* (pp. 52–72). Cambridge: Cambridge University Press.
Brock, G. (2009). *Global justice. A cosmopolitan approach*. New York: Oxford University Press.
Brock, G. (2012). Needs and distributive justice. In G. F. Gaus & F. D'Agostino (Eds.), *The Routledge companion to social and political philosophy* (pp. 444–455). New York: Routledge.
Casal, P. (2007). Why sufficiency is not enough. *Ethics, 117*, 296–326.
Cohen, G. A. (1989). On the currency of egalitarian justice. *Ethics, 99*, 906–944.
Cohen, G. A. (2011). How to do political philosophy. In *On the currency of egalitarian justice, and other essays in political philosophy* (pp. 225–235). Princeton: Princeton University Press.
Connolly, W. E. (1983). *The terms of political discourse*. Oxford: Martin Robertson.
Daniels, N. (1979). Wide reflective equilibrium and theory acceptance in ethics. *Journal of Philosophy, 76*(5), 256–282.
Daniels, N. (1981). Health care needs and distributive justice. *Philosophy and Public Affairs, 10*(2), 146–179.
Daniels, N. (1985). *Just health care*. Cambridge: Cambridge University Press.
Deutsch, M. (1975). Equity, equality, and need: What determines which value will be used as the basis of distributive justice? *Journal of Social Issues, 51*, 137–149.
Doyal, L., & Gough, I. (1984). A theory of human needs. *Critical Social Policy, 4*(10), 6–38.
Doyal, L., & Gough, I. (1991). *A theory of human need*. Hampshire: Macmillan Press.
Dworkin, R. (2000). *Sovereign virtue: The theory and practice of equality*. Cambridge, Mass.: Harvard University Press.
Esping-Andersen, G. (1990). *The three worlds of welfare capitalism*. Princeton: Princeton University Press.
Fehér, F., Heller, A., & Márkus, G. (1983). *The dictatorship over needs. An analysis of soviet societies*. Oxford: Basil Blackwell.
Feinberg, J. (1973). *Social philosophy*. Englewood Cliffs, N.J.: Prentice-Hall.
Feinberg, J. (1974). Non-comparative justice. *Philosophical Review, 83*, 197–338.
Flew, A. (1977). Wants or needs, choices or commands? In R. Fitzgerald (Ed.), *Human needs and politics* (pp. 213–228). Headington: Pergamon.
Floyd, J. (2017). Rawls' methodological blueprint. *European Journal of Political Theory, 16*(3), 367–381.
Forst, R. (2002). *Contexts of justice: Political philosophy beyond liberalism and communitarianism*. Berkeley: University of California Press.
Frankfurt, H. G. (1984). Necessity and desire. *Philosophy and Phenomenological Research, 45*, 1–13.
Frankfurt, H. G. (1987). Equality as a moral ideal. *Ethics, 98*(1), 21–43.
Frankfurt, H. G. (1997). Equality and respect. *Social Research, 64*, 3–15.
Frankfurt, H. G. (2000). The moral irrelevance of equality. *Public Affairs Quarterly, 14*(2), 87–103.
Frohlich, N., Oppenheimer, J. A., & Eavey, C. L. (1987). Choices of principles of distributive justice in experimental groups. *American Journal of Political Science, 31*, 606–636.
Frohlich, N., & Oppenheimer, J. A. (1992). *Choosing justice. An experimental approach to ethical theory*. Berkeley: University of California Press.
Gaertner, W. (1994). Distributive justice: Theoretical foundations and empirical findings. *European Economic Review, 38*, 711–720.
Gaertner, W., Jungeilges, J., & Neck, R. (2001). Cross-cultural equity evaluations: A questionnaire-experimental approach. *European Economic Review, 45*, 953–963.

Ghai, D. (1978). Basic needs and its critics. *Institute of Development Studies*, *9*, 16–18.
Gini, C. (1921). Measurement of inequality of incomes. *Economic Journal*, *31*, 124–126.
Goodin, R. E. (1985). The priority of need. *Philosophy and Phenomenological Research*, *45*, 615–625.
Goodin, R. E. (1988). *Reasons for welfare: The political theory of the welfare state*. Princeton: Princeton University Press.
Gustavsson, E. (2014). From needs to health care needs. *Health Care Analysis*, *22*, 22–35.
Habermas, J. (1996). *Between facts and norms: Contributions to a discourse theory of law and democracy*. Cambridge: Polity Press.
Hamilton, L. A. (2003). *The political philosophy of needs*. Cambridge: Cambridge University Press.
Hamilton, L. A. (2009). Human needs and political judgment. In B. de Bruin & C. F. Zurn (Eds.), *New waves in political philosophy* (pp. 40–62). Basingstoke: Palgrave Macmillan.
Harsanyi, J. C. (1982). Morality and the theory of rational behaviour. In A. Sen & B. Williams (Eds.), *Utilitarianism and beyond* (pp. 39–62). Cambridge: Cambridge University Press.
Hassoun, N. (2009). Meeting need. *Utilitas*, *21*, 250–275.
Honneth, A. (2014). *Freedom's right: The social foundations of democratic life*. Cambridge: Polity Press.
Hope, S. (2010). The circumstances of justice. *Hume Studies*, *36*, 125–148.
Hubin, D. C. (1976). Justice and future generations. *Philosophy and Public Affairs*, *6*(1), 70–83.
Hubin, D. C. (1989). Scarcity and the demands of justice. *Capital University Law Review*, *18*, 185–199.
Hume, D. (1738–40/1978). *A treatise of human nature*, ed. L. A. Selby-Bigge, rev. by P. H. Nidditch (2nd ed.). Oxford: Clarendon Press.
Hume, D. (1751/1975). *An enquiry concerning the principles of morals*, ed. L. A. Selby-Bigge, rev. by P. H. Nidditch (3rd ed.). Oxford: Clarendon Press.
Jasso, G. (1978). On the justice of earnings: A new specification of the justice evaluation function. *American Journal of Sociology*, *83*, 1398–1419.
Jasso, G. (1980). A new theory of distributive justice. *American Sociological Review*, *45*, 3–32.
Jasso, G. (1990). Methods for the theoretical and empirical analysis of comparison processes. *Sociological Methodology*, *20*, 369–419.
Jasso, G. (1999). How much injustice is there in the world? Two new justice indexes. *American Sociological Review*, *64*, 133–168.
Jasso, G. (2007). Studying justice: Measurement, estimation, and analysis of the actual reward and the just reward. In K. Törnblom, & R. Vermunt (Eds.), *Distributive and procedural justice* (pp. 225–254). London: Routledge.
Jasso, G., & Wegener, B. (1997). Methods for empirical justice analysis: Part I-framework, models, and quantities. *Social Justice Research*, *10*, 393–430.
Jolly, R. (1976). The world employment conference: The enthronement of basic needs. *Development Policy Review*, *A9*, 31–44.
Keynes, J. M. (1930/1963). Economic possibilities for our grandchildren. In *Essays in persuasion* (pp. 321–332). New York and London: W. W. Norton 1963; originally publ. in: *The Nation and Athenaeum*, part I: October 11, 1930, 36–37, part II: October 18, 1930, 96–98.
Konow, J. (2001). Fair and square: The four sides of distributive justice. *Journal of Economic Behavior and Organization*, *46*, 137–164.
Konow, J. (2003). Which is the fairest one of all? A positive analysis of justice theories. *Journal of Economic Literature*, *41*, 1186–1237.
Konow, J. (2009). Is fairness in the eye of the beholder? An impartial spectator analysis of justice. *Social Choice and Welfare*, *33*, 101–127.
Konow, J., & Schwettmann, L. (2016). The economics of justice. In C. Sabbagh & M. Schmitt (Eds.), *Handbook of social justice theory and research* (pp. 83–106). Heidelberg: Springer.
Lamm, H., & Schwinger, T. (1980). Norms concerning distributive justice: Are needs taken into consideration in allocation decisions? *Social Psychology Quarterly*, *43*, 425–429.

Lamont, J., & Favor, C. (2017). Distributive justice. In E. N. Zalta (Ed.), *The stanford encyclopedia of philosophy*. https://plato.stanford.edu/entries/justice-distributive/
Lerner, M. J. (1974). The justice motive: 'Equity' and 'parity' among children. *Journal of Personality and Social Sciences*, *29*, 539–550.
Liebig, S., & Sauer, C. (2016). Sociology of justice. In C. Sabbagh & M. Schmitt (Eds.), *Handbook of social justice theory and research* (pp. 837–859). Heidelberg: Springer.
Lowe, J. (2005). Needs, facts, goodness, and truth. In S. Reader (Ed.), *The philosophy of need* (pp. 161–173). Cambridge: Cambridge University Press.
Mac Carthaigh, S. (2014). Need and poverty. *Policy and Politics*, *42*, 459–473.
Margalit, A. (1996). *The decent society*. Cambridge, Mass.: Harvard University Press.
Maslow, A. (1943). A theory of human motivation. *Psychological Review*, *50*, 370–396.
McLeod, S. (2014). Absolute biological needs. *Bioethics*, *28*(6), 293–301.
Mill, J. S. (1861 [1991]). Utilitarianism. In J. Gray (Ed.), *On liberty and other essays* (pp. 131–205). Oxford: Oxford University Press.
Miller, D. (1976). *Social justice*. Oxford: Clarendon Press.
Miller, D. (1992). Distributive justice: What the people think. *Ethics*, *102*, 555–593.
Miller, D. (1999a). *Principles of social justice*. Cambridge, Mass.: Harvard University Press.
Miller, D. (1999b). Justice and global inequality. In A. Hurrell & N. Woods (Eds.), *Inequality, globalization, and world politics* (pp. 187–210). Oxford: Oxford University Press.
Miller, D. (2007). *Human rights, basic needs, and scarcity*. Centre for the Study of Social Justice and Department of Politics and International Relations, Working Paper Series, SJ007.
Miller, S. C. (2005). Need, care and obligation. In S. Reader (Ed.), *The philosophy of need* (pp. 137–160). Cambridge: Cambridge University Press.
Nozick, R. (1974). *Anarchy, state, and utopia*. New York: Basic Books.
Nussbaum, M. (1990). Aristotelian social democracy. In R. B. Douglass, G. M. Mora, & H. S. Richardson (Eds.), *Liberalism and the good* (pp. 203–252). New York and London: Routledge.
Nussbaum, M. (2000). *Women and human development: The capabilities approach*. Cambridge and New York: Cambridge University Press.
Nussbaum, M. (2011). *Creating capabilities*. Cambridge, MA: Harvard University Press.
Page, E. A. (2006). *Climate change, justice and future generations*. Cheltenham: Edgar Elgar.
Plant, R., Lesser, H., & Taylor-Gooby, P. (1980). *Political philosophy and social welfare*. London: Routledge and Kegan Paul.
Plato. (1998). *The republic*. In R. Waterfield (Ed.), *Oxford world's classic*. Oxford: Oxford University Press.
Raphael, D. D. (1980). *Justice and liberty*. London: Athlone Press.
Rawls, J. (1971). *A theory of justice*. Oxford: Oxford University Press.
Rawls, J. (1975 [1999]). The independence of moral theory. *Proceedings and Addresses of the American Philosophical Association*, 48, 5–22 (reprinted in: S. Freeman (Ed.), *Collected papers* (pp. 286–302). Cambridge, Mass.: Harvard University Press).
Rawls, J. (2001). *Justice as fairness: A restatement*. Cambridge, Mass.: Harvard University Press.
Reader, S. (2006). Does a basic needs approach need capabilities? *Journal of Political Philosophy*, *14*, 337–350.
Reader, S., & Brock, G. (2004). Needs, moral demands and moral theory. *Utilitas*, *16*, 251–266.
Sabbagh, C., & Schmitt, M. (Eds.). (2016). *Handbook of social justice theory and research*. New York: Springer.
Sadurski, W. (1983). To each according to his (genuine?) needs. *Political Theory*, *11*(3), 419–431.
Sayre-McCord, G. (1985). Coherence and models for moral theorizing. *Pacific Philosophical Quarterly*, *6*, 170–190.
Schramme, T. (2006). *Gerechtigkeit und soziale Praxis*. Frankfurt/New York: Campus.
Schramme, T. (2008). On the relationship(s) between empirical research and political theory. *Analyse und Kritik*, *30*(2), 613–626.
Schramme, T. (2017). Mill and Miller: Some thoughts on the methodology of political theory. Forthcoming in *Contemporary Political Theory*.

Seidl, C. (1988). Poverty measurement: A survey. In D. Bös, M. Rose, & C. Seidl (Eds.), *Welfare and efficiency in public economics* (pp. 71–147). Heidelberg: Springer.
Sen, A. (1980). Equality of what? In *The Tanner lecture on human values* (Vol. I, pp. 197–220). Cambridge: Cambridge University Press.
Sen, A. (1981). *Poverty and famines. An essay on entitlement and deprivation*. Oxford: Clarendon Press.
Sen, A. (2009). *The idea of justice*. New York: Penguin.
Schuppert, F. (2013). Distinguishing basic needs and fundamental interests. *Critical Review of International Social and Political Philosophy, 16*(1), 24–44.
Siebel, M. (2018). *A plaristonic measure of need-based justice*, Working Paper, Research Group Need-based Justice and Distribution Procedures, Hamburg.
Stears, M. (2005). The vocation of political theory: Principles, empirical inquiry and the politics of opportunity. *European Journal of Political Theory, 4*(4), 325–350.
Swift, A. (1999). Public opinion and political philosophy: The relation between social-scientific and philosophical analyses of distributive justice. *Ethical Theory and Moral Practice, 2*, 337–363.
Temkin, L. (1993). *Inequality*. Oxford: Oxford University Press.
Theil, H. (1967). *Economics and information theory*. Chicago: Rand McNally and Company.
Thomson, G. (1987). *Needs*. London: Routledge.
Thomson, G. (2005). Fundamental needs. In S. Reader (Ed.), *The philosophy of need* (pp. 175–186). Cambridge: Cambridge University Press.
Timmons, M. (1990). On the epistemic status of considered moral judgements. *Southern Journal of Philosophy, XXIX*(Supplement), 97–129.
Timmons, M. (1999). *Morality without foundations: A defense of ethical contextualism*. Oxford: Oxford University Press.
Traub, S., Seidl, C., Schmidt, U., & Levati, M. V. (2005). Friedman, Harsanyi, Rawls, Boulding–or somebody else? An experimental investigation of distributive justice. *Social Choice and Welfare, 24*, 283–309.
Vlastos, G. (1962). Justice and equality. In R. B. Brandt (Ed.), *Social justice* (pp. 31–72). Englewood Cliffs, New Jersey: Prentice Hall.
Walzer, M. (1983). *Spheres of justice: A defence of pluralism and equality*. New York: Basic Books.
White, A. R. (1975). *Modal thinking*. Oxford: Basil Blackwell.
Wiggins, D. (1987). Needs, need, needing. *Journal of Medical Ethics, 13*, 62–68.
Wiggins, D. (1998). Claims of need. In T. Honderich (Ed.), *Morality and objectivity: A tribute to John L. Mackie* (3rd ed., pp. 1–57). London: Routledge.
Wiggins, D. (2005). An idea we cannot do without: What difference will it make (eg. to moral, political and environmental philosophy) to recognize and put to use a substantial conception of need? In: S. Reader (Ed.), *The philosophy of need* (pp. 25–50). Cambridge: Cambridge University Press.
Wollheim, R. (1974). Needs, desires and moral turpitude. *Royal Institute of Philosophy Lectures, 8*, 162–179.
Xenos, N. (1987). Liberalism and the postulate of scarcity. *Political Theory, 15*(2), 225–243.
Yaari, M. E., & Bar-Hillel, M. (1984). On dividing justly. *Social Choice and Welfare, 1*, 1–24.

Chapter 3
Identifying Needs: The Psychological Perspective

Adele Diederich

Abstract This chapter discusses five topics related to the role and types of needs in justice-related judgments: (1) Need as a motive, particularly as conceptualized in theories that may contribute to the overarching goal of identifying needs relevant to justice judgments from the psychological perspective. (2) Need as one justice principle in the triad with equity and equality. The focus is on formal models of justice principles, which allow for the identification of needs. (3) The influence of the situational and social circumstances of the receiving person and framings of decision problems on the decision maker's justice judgments, as well as the personal traits of the decision maker on his or her justice judgments. (4) Empirical studies that investigate the need principle related to the aforementioned determinants. Each section includes a short evaluation. (5) Perspectives on how to bring the different concepts together to contribute to an informed normative theory of need.

3.1 Introduction

In psychology, the concept of *need* or *needs* is used differently in different contexts and sub-disciplines with different meanings. Needs may refer to an actual state of deprivation or merely a feeling of deficiency that drives the individual to engage in action to satisfy them. In this sense needs are motivational forces that activate behavior for the attainment of goals. They range from physiological or basic survival needs such as breathing, food, sex, and sleep, which are common to all animals, to psychological needs such as cultural, intellectual, and social needs. Sometimes physiological needs are called drives; sometimes need and drive are used as synonyms (e.g., Maslow 1943). In recent motivation theories, needs are related to, or replaced by, the notion of motives (e.g., Metz-Göckel 2014; Gollwitzer and Moskowitz 1996;

A. Diederich (✉)
Jacobs University Bremen & FOR 2104, Campus Ring 1, 28759 Bremen, Germany
e-mail: a.diederich@jacobs-university.de

S. Traub and B. Kittel (eds.), *Need-Based Distributive Justice*,
https://doi.org/10.1007/978-3-030-44121-0_3

Heckhausen and Heckhausen 2010). Sometimes, biological needs are called needs while psychological needs are called motives. Needs/motives also play a role in (psychological) learning theories and theories of personality. In the context of need-based justice, need is a (subjectively) felt deficiency, i.e., a want or desire. Identifying needs means providing a list of needs essential for goal directed behavior.

Research on justice is a multidisciplinary approach rooted in philosophy and absorbed into the social sciences. Here, the term *need* describes one principle for the fair allocation of resources and has a meaning slightly different from that in motivation theories. Needs as actual or felt deficiencies are satisfied by necessities or necessaries, entities that the individual requires to survive or to live satisfactorily. These entities are often called needs as well. Unlike economics, psychology takes little interest in necessities and necessaries as objects of study. In the current context, need is defined as (monetarily) evaluated individual demand to satisfy a need, i.e., a want. Needs in the sense of motives and needs as necessities and goods may be inferred from the context. Identifying needs here is then related to a demand a person has and its accomplishment.

Another strand of research combines justice and motives by assuming that human behavior is based on a justice motive, that is, the extent to which a person is motivated to promote fairness for others (e.g., Lerner 1975, 2003) rather than for themselves. In this strand of research, the need principle itself is a motive and identified as such. According to Lerner (1974) the more general justice motive takes various forms: the Marxian justice of need, the justice of equity, the justice of parity, and the justice of laws (Lerner 1974, 539). These ideas that fairness motives affect the behavior of people have more recently also been adopted by economists (see Konow 2003 for a review), unfortunately without referencing the original sources. This topic is not covered here in depth. For further details, including a comprehensive history of research on the justice motive, see Sabbagh and Schmitt (2016).

Most theoretical approaches on need as motive go back to the first half of the 20th century. We will focus on those that may contribute to our main objective of identifying needs in the context of justice. Theoretical psychological research on justice started in the 1970s and may have peaked in the 1980s. What has followed is mainly applications to various domains, in particular to the working environment. Theoretical approaches have been adopted and developed further by other disciplines, including sociology and behavioral economics. Again, we will focus on those theories that may lead to a general approach of identifying needs from the psychological perspective. Identifying needs implies that we can measure need, preferably in terms of measurement-theoretical principles and psychological scaling. Therefore, we concentrate on models that allow for a certain formalism. The identification of needs may be influenced by situational and individual factors. Most work on individual differences in justice evaluation deals with justice in a very broad sense. In particular, in psychology the focus has shifted to the emotions of specific types of people (e.g., victim, perpetrator) in specific situations (e.g., illness, assault). Again, we will limit analyses to studies that explicitly include need in their consideration.

The chapter is organized as follows. Section 3.2 discusses need as motive, limited to those theories that may contribute to the overarching goal of identifying needs from the psychological perspective. Section 3.3 focuses on need as a justice principle. It often appears in a trio with equity and equality. Because research on equity is most advanced with respect to formal development, it is discussed in more depth as a candidate for enhancing research on need. Section 3.4 discusses the determinants of justice principles, i.e., how the situational and social circumstances and individual traits of individuals determine which of the three principles is chosen. Section 3.5 summarizes empirical studies that investigate the need principle related to those determinants. Each section includes a short evaluation. The final section integrates the findings as an initial step towards building an informed normative theory of need.

3.2 Need as Motive

Research on needs, motives, and motivation is a very active field in psychology with a long history and overwhelmingly diverse approaches and studies. We will concentrate on those theories that focus on needs rather than on motives and that may contribute to identifying needs in justice research.

3.2.1 Lewin's Quasi-needs and Field Theory

Early research divided needs into categories. Lewin (1926), for instance, distinguishes true needs (echte Bedürfnisse, Triebbedürfnisse[1]), which are biological needs, from quasi-needs (Quasibedürfnisse), which are short-lived and deduced from true needs. The latter are mainly created by intention. Lewin's Field Theory postulates a functional relation between behavior (B), person variables (P) and environmental variables (E), $B = f(P, E)$. Field Theory is a very complex system describing motivational processes, conflict, group dynamic, and more. Lewin (1943, 294) describes it as a method of analyzing causal relations and building scientific constructs. Only a small part of it is relevant here. Behavior is an action (Befriedigungshandlung) that is determined by two variables, need and valence (Aufforderungscharakter). Need can be described as the desire for some end state. Valence is attached to objects or events and can be positive (attracting) or negative (repelling). According to McClelland (1987) phrasing, valence is the reward value of the end state. Valence determines the direction of behavior: Positive valence produces approaching behavior while negative valence induces avoidance or withdrawal behavior. Objects or events that possess valence are a *direct means* of satisfying needs and are called *autonomous valence* (selbständiger Aufforderungscharakter). Related, but different, to autonomous valence are derived valences (abgeleitete Aufforderungscharaktäre), which are only momentarily important as a means to an end for satisfying needs. Valences may change depending on the person's actual need or on the environmen-

[1] Lewin first published his work in German. His original expressions are added in parentheses.

tal circumstances. The psychological environment, different from the physical and social environments, refers to the internal and external situation in which a person is situated (cf. Lewin 1926, 351; Lewin 1935, 78).

McClelland (1987) specifies Lewin's Field Theory equation with respect to motivational forces in a psychological field: An intent, or psychological force, to perform an act is the product of two person variables (need and valence) divided by an environmental variable, psychological distance, which refers to all the difficulties in performing the task or in adopting the means necessary for reaching the goal (McClelland 1987, 7), i.e.,

$$B = f(P, E)$$
$$\text{Force towards an action} = \frac{\text{Need} \times \text{Valence}}{\text{Psychological distance}}. \quad (3.1)$$

Need and psychological distance are measured on positive scales. Valence may be positive or negative, resulting in approaching or avoidance behavior.

3.2.2 Murray's Need-Press Model

Murray (1938, 124), whose main interest was in clinical and personality psychology, defines need, which is undistinguishable from drive, as "a construct (...) which stands for a force (...) in the brain region, a force that organizes perception, apperception, intellection, conation and action in such a way as to transform in a certain direction an existing, unsatisfying situation." The counterpart of need is press, defined as a kind of effect an object or situation is exerting or could exert upon the individual (cf. Murray 1938, 748). Press may be positive or negative (and mobile or immobile, cf. Murray 1938, 120); positive press is beneficial and negative is harmful. A combination of need and press is called thema and describes a dynamic structure of individual-environmental interaction. Needs are divided into primary (viscerogenic) needs and secondary (psychogenic) needs (cf. Murray 1938, 76), the first referring to physiological/biological needs and the second to psychological needs.

Murray (1938) postulates a catalogue of about 30 unique psychogenic needs, including achievement need (to overcome obstacles; to exercise power; to strive to do something difficult as well as quickly and possible), acquisition need (to gain possessions and property; to grasp, snatch or steal things; to bargain or gamble), dominance need (to influence or dominate others; to persuade, prohibit, dictate; to lead and direct; to restrain; to organize the behavior of a group) and to understanding need (to analyze experience; to abstract; to discriminate among concepts; to define relations; to synthesize ideas). These needs are distinguished from needs involving other people and ideologies, or may be combinations of unique needs such as the superiority need, which is a combination of achievement and recognition (Murray 1938, 743–750). Further distinctions between types of needs include positive (approach) versus negative (avoidance) needs, and manifest versus latent needs (Scheffer and Heckhausen 2010, 53). Obviously, the classification of needs can easily be criticized with respect to the independence assumption between the needs proposed in the catalogue (Scheffer and Heckhausen 2010, 54, for examples). Nevertheless, Murray's (1938) Thematic Apperception Test (TAT), based on the theory and catalogue, has become one of the most important measurement instruments in the field of motivational psychology.

3.2.3 Maslow's Hierarchy of Needs

One of the most influential approaches of needs in the last century is Maslow's (1943) theory of human motivation, which still gets a lot of attention outside psychology. The theory postulates a need hierarchy with physiological needs at the bottom, then safety, belonging, esteem, and self-actualization needs at the top. Each group of needs consists of further specified needs. The lower the need in the hierarchy the stronger it is. That is, the physiological needs are stronger than the safety needs, which are stronger than the belonging needs (belongings and love, Maslow 1987), and so on (Maslow 1948). Physiological needs, which are ordered in a sub-hierarchy, have to be met before safety needs can be addressed, and so forth. Maslow (1948, 1987) identified several differences (altogether 16) between lower and higher needs. For instance:

1. The higher the need, the less imperative it is for sheer survival, the longer gratification can be postponed, and the easier it is for the need to disappear permanently.
2. Living at a higher need level means greater biological efficiency, greater longevity, less disease, better sleep, increased appetite, and so on.
3. Higher needs are less urgent subjectively.
4. Higher needs require better outside conditions to make them possible.
5. A greater value is usually placed upon the higher need than upon the lower by those who have satisfied both.
6. The pursuit and the gratification of the higher needs have desirable civic and social consequences (Maslow 1948).
7. Lower needs are far more localized, more tangible, and more limited than higher needs (Maslow 1987).

There have been several attempts to test the hierarchy of needs model. A common procedure was to employ questionnaire items and extract the categories via factor analysis (see Mitchell and Moudgill 1976 and Wahba and Bridwell 1976 for an overview of studies). Williams and Page (1989) developed the Maslowian Assessment Survey (MAS), a multidimensional measure considering only three needs: safety, belonging, and esteem levels. For each of the three needs they include the following subscales: need gratification, need importance, need salience, and self-concept. The latter measures how much an individual is like a prototypical person at a given level in the hierarchy. Lester (1990) proposes the *Need Satisfaction Inventory* with 50 items, ten for each need in the hierarchy, which measures on a seven-point Likert scale the degree to which an individual has satisfied each need category. For all these measures, the focus is mainly on identifying the hierarchy of the (five) needs rather than identifying the needs themselves.

3.2.4 Alderfer's E.R.G. Theory

Several modifications of Maslow's hierarchy of needs have been proposed. Alderfer (1969), for example, has developed a threefold conceptualization of human needs that includes existence, relatedness, and growth (E.R.G.). The model does not assume lower level satisfaction as a prerequisite for the emergence of higher order needs.

Relatedness needs include all the needs that involve relationships with significant other people, such as family members, superiors, coworkers, subordinates, friends, but also enemies (Alderfer 1969). They correspond to Maslow's (interpersonal) safety needs, (social) belongingness needs, and (interpersonal) esteem needs (Schneider and Alderfer 1973). Growth needs include all the needs that involve a person making creative or productive effects on himself or herself and the environment (cf. Alderfer 1969, 146). They correspond to Maslow's (self-confirmed) needs and self-actualization needs. The existence needs are of special interest here. They include physiological desires, like the previous theories, but also all kinds of material needs such as income, fringe benefits, and good physical working conditions. They correspond to Maslow's physiological needs and (material) safety needs. Importantly, Alderfer links existence needs to quantifiable necessities that satisfy them. Furthermore, an individual's satisfaction is relative to what another individual receives:

> One of the basic characteristics of existence needs is that they can be divided among people in such a way that one person's gain is another's loss when resources are limited. (…) This property of existence needs frequently means that a person's (or group's) satisfaction, beyond a bare minimum depends upon the comparison of what he gets with what others get in the same situation. However, this comparison is not "interpersonal" in the sense of necessitating comparison with known significant others. The interpersonal aspect of equity is not an issue for existence needs. The comparison process for material goods is simply among piles of goods, without necessarily attaching the added dimension of knowing who the others are who would obtain smaller or larger shares. (Alderfer 1969, 145f).

Alderfer provides seven major propositions to test the theory. Three of them are related to existence needs:

1. The less existence needs are satisfied, the more they will be desired.
2. The less relatedness needs are satisfied, the more existence needs will be desired.
3. The more existence needs are satisfied, the more relatedness needs will be desired (Alderfer 1969, 148).

Need frustration (i.e., lack of satisfaction) should motivate the person to take action to satisfy the needs. To measure satisfaction Alderfer (1969) proposes a questionnaire with six-point Likert-scale items in a working environment context. Need intensity measures are ratings of desire with five categories. For example, the "desire" items for existence needs with respect to "Pay" are 1. good pay for my work, and 2. frequent raises in pay. Those for "Fringe benefits" are 1. a complete fringe benefit program, and 2. frequent improvement in fringe benefits (Alderfer 1969, 160). The questionnaire items to measure existence needs satisfaction include the following:

Pay:

1. Compared to the rates for similar work here my pay is good.
2. Compared to similar work in other places my pay is poor.
3. I do not make enough money from my job to live comfortably.
4. Compared to the rates for less demanding jobs my pay is poor.
5. My pay is adequate to provide for the basic things in life.
6. Considering the work required, the pay is what it should be.

Fringe Benefits:

1. Our fringe benefits do not cover many of the areas they should.
2. The fringe benefit program here gives nearly all the security I want.
3. The fringe benefit program here needs improvement.
4. Compared to other places, our fringe benefits are excellent.

3.2.5 Other Need Theories in Psychology

There are at least two more need theories in psychology that receive considerable attention and include need as a reason for action. However, they are less important in this chapter because they propose only higher, psychological needs. McClelland's need theory assumes three needs: achievement, affiliation, and power. All of them are acquired over time and are shaped by the person's life experiences (McClelland 1987).

A more recent theory of motivation, called Self-Determination Theory (SDT), has been proposed by Deci and Ryan (1987, 2000) and Ryan and Deci (2000). They define a basic need, whether it be a physiological need or a psychological need, as an energizing state that, if satisfied, is conducive to health and well-being but, if not satisfied, contributes to pathology and illness (Ryan and Deci 2000, 74). They have identified three such needs: the need for competence, which refers to a person's need to have some control over his or her environment; relatedness, which refers to a person's need to feel a sense of belonging in a community; and autonomy, which refers to a need to freely integrate his or her experiences with his or her sense of self. According to Deci and Ryan (2000), the three needs are psychological and innate rather than learned. They also appear to be essential for optimal functioning of the natural propensities for growth and integration, as well as for constructive social development and personal well-being. SDT provides some explanation for the development of intrinsic motivation rather than extrinsic motivation.

3.2.6 *Evaluation*

What do these theories contribute to the identification of relevant needs? The majority distinguishes physiological needs, which are innate, from psychological needs, which may be innate or acquired. Several instruments are developed to identify specific needs (via factor or cluster analysis) and to measure the strength of the identified needs (via inventories and tests). Almost none of them, however, investigates how much of an entity is required to satisfy the needs. To express it in the current notation, needs in the sense of wants and desire to satisfy (subjectively) experienced deficiencies are identified and categorized; needs in the sense of demands, i.e., the concrete, quantifiable requirement to satisfy the wants are not. To bridge this gap, we focus on basic needs such as physiological needs and, in Maslow's and Alderfer's terminology, safety needs and existence needs, respectively. Within each need group we further limit our attention to those needs that can be satisfied by entities that can easily be quantified such as specific food items, housing items, health care items, and so on. In Alderfer's questionnaire the item "My pay is adequate to provide for the basic things in life" points in that direction. Furthermore, some propositions made by Maslow and Alderfer relate needs to each other and express some degree of needs satisfaction.

This allows—in principle—for two things: (1) Establishing the minimum need for each want and (2) comparing needs across different needs. The latter in particular is interesting when need can be converted into a common unit. Furthermore, Lewin's valence is attached to objects and represents the value to meet the end state of some desire, i.e., need. Using the field-theoretical equation proposed by McClelland, valence (value of the need) can be expressed by a person's need, his or her actions (or intention), and his or her difficulty in performing a task related to the needs.

3.3 Need as Justice Principle

In the context of distributive justice, need appears as one principle for the fair allocation of resources. Need is to be understood as neediness. Unlike philosophical approaches to justice, which focus on norms, definitions of distribution principles, allocation rules, and distribution procedures,[2] psychological perspectives are interested in how people judge justice, think and feel about it, and how and why they act accordingly. People may judge the result or outcome of an allocation process or judge the procedures that lead to the outcome. The first case is called 'distributive justice', the second "procedural justice". However, both processes are closely related

[2]Normative theories are not considered here. Jost and Kay (2010) provide a brief history of distributive justice, from the Aristotelian perspective, to the Marxian, to the liberal-progressive tradition, including utilitarianism and deontological approaches, and conservative perspectives.

and sometimes interdependent.[3]

Although social psychology has been concerned with related topics of social justice such as prejudice, intolerance, or outgroup hostility (e.g., Allport 1954; Lewin 1951), social justice only became a subfield in its own right in the 1970s, mainly shaped by Morton Deutsch, a doctoral student of Kurt Lewin, Melvin J. Lerner, and Gerald S. Leventhal. Many of their ideas (discussed later) have influenced not only research in psychology but have also been well received in today's (behavioral) economics.

3.3.1 *Justice and Allocation Principles*

According to Deutsch (1975), distributive justice is concerned with the fairness of distributions of goods and resources ("benefits and harms, rewards and costs, or other things which affect individual well-being", 138) among members of a group or of a society. In social psychology, early models and empirical work primarily focus on equity as the sole distribution principle (Adams 1965; Homans 1958; Walster et al. 1973). Deutsch (1975) and others, however, point out that other principles (which he calls "values") may well play a role when distributing outcomes. For example, a fair allocation of resources may also occur according to people's needs, ability, efforts, and accomplishments; according to the principle of reciprocity, so that none falls below a specified minimum (Deutsch 1975, 139); and other principles. Deutsch (1975) focuses on three main principles, equity, equality, and need, which are considered *equally* important. The equity principle has also been called the *contribution* principle. Although considered equally important, equity receives by far the most research attention. In particular, formal models have been developed solely for equity; need has become an add-on. We present the models on equity in more detail in order to evaluate their usefulness for identifying and measuring need.

3.3.1.1 Equity

In social psychology, equity theory emerged out of Homans' social exchange theory (Homans 1958), Adams' Inequity theory (Adams 1965), and Walster et al.'s (1973) modifications of inequity theory. It has become the most influential approach in social justice research. Not only has it triggered numerous empirical applications, it also represents one of the few formal models in social psychology. Equity theory assumes that distributions of resources are based on proportional relationships between a person's inputs, I, and his or her outcomes, O, and inequality arises if one person, *A*, *comparing* him/herself to another person, *B*, when one of the following inequalities

[3]Deutsch (1975) refers to the application of justice principles as distributive justice, whereas Mikula (1980) and Liebig (1997) refer to it as procedural justice.

holds (Adams 1965):

$$\frac{\mathrm{O}_A}{\mathrm{I}_A} > \frac{\mathrm{O}_B}{\mathrm{I}_B} \text{ or } \frac{\mathrm{O}_A}{\mathrm{I}_A} < \frac{\mathrm{O}_B}{\mathrm{I}_B}.$$

A condition of equity for two people[4] A and B exists if

$$\frac{\mathrm{O}_A}{\mathrm{I}_A} = \frac{\mathrm{O}_B}{\mathrm{I}_B}. \tag{3.2}$$

Input is broadly defined as education, intelligence, experience, training, skill, seniority, age, sex, ethnic background, social status, degree of effort, and more (Adams 1965, 277). Outcomes may be positive (e.g., rewards, payments) or negative (e.g., punishments, costs). Most empirical studies have taken place in the context of payment scenarios in the laboratory and wage plans in companies (see Liebig 1997 for an overview).

Although not obvious from Eq. (3.2), O and I are conceptualized as weighted sums of the individual outcomes (y_i) and individual inputs (x_j) (Adams 1965, 281). This implies that input and outcome are numbers leading to

$$\mathrm{O} = \sum v_i y_i \text{ and } \mathrm{I} = \sum w_j x_j.$$

Adams emphasizes the individual perceptions of each person involved, which may or may not be shared by the others. "The values of outcomes and inputs are, of course, as perceived by Person" (Adams 1965, 280). Indeed, Adams (1965) refers to the utility of outputs, that is $\mathrm{O} = \sum v_i u(y_i)$, but does not elaborate on it further. He is silent about the function concerning the inputs.

Assuming here a function g for inputs, which may be the identity function, Eq. (3.2) then becomes

$$\frac{\mathrm{O}_A}{\mathrm{I}_A} = \frac{\mathrm{O}_B}{\mathrm{I}_B} \Leftrightarrow \frac{\sum v_i u(y_{Ai})}{\sum w_j g(x_{Aj})} = \frac{\sum v_i u(y_{Bi})}{\sum w_j g(x_{Bj})}. \tag{3.3}$$

For an expression like Eq. (3.2) to be meaningful, the involved scales must satisfy specific properties. Meaningfulness of a proposition, according to Roberts (1979), requires that its truth value remains invariant under admissible transformations of the scale. An admissible transformation in this case is functions of the form $\phi(\mathrm{O}) = \alpha \mathrm{O}^\beta$ and $\phi(\mathrm{I}) = \alpha' \mathrm{I}^\beta$ with $\alpha, \alpha', \beta > 0$, which implies a *log-interval* scale. Note that log-interval scales correspond to exponential transformations of interval scales.

For example,

$$\phi(\mathrm{O}) = \begin{cases} \mathrm{O}^\alpha & \text{if } \mathrm{O} \geq 0 \\ -\lambda|\mathrm{O}|^\beta & \text{if } \mathrm{O} < 0 \end{cases} \tag{3.4}$$

[4]The person judging the situation may be one of the participants involved or an external observer.

describes a function for positive and negative outcomes (analogously for inputs I) and is the most popular parameterization of prospect theory (Kahneman and Tversky 1979; Tversky and Kahneman 1992). For $\alpha(\beta) < 1$ the curve becomes increasingly concave (convex); for $\lambda > 1$ the steepness of the convex part increases. In decision-making research, often $\alpha = \beta$ (Tversky and Kahneman 1992) or is close in magnitude (see Fox and Poldrack 2009 for an overview of studies). For equity theory, negative inputs and outcomes have a larger impact on the perceived proportional relationship between inputs and outcomes than positive ones.

Walster et al. (1973) have modified Eq. (3.2) to account for negative inputs, which, according to them, cannot be handled by the original model. A relationship is perceived and judged as fair or "equitable" when

$$\frac{O_A - I_A}{|I_A|} = \frac{O_B - I_B}{|I_B|} \tag{3.5}$$

holds. $|I|$ here is merely a scaling factor. Obviously, this argument is invalid when psychological functions, like in the prospect theory example, have been specified. Furthermore, the Walster et al. model is more restrictive with scale types than the Adams model. First, assuming a difference in the nominator implies that the scales for measuring outcomes and inputs need to be the *same*. Second, the admissible transformation is αO, which is an *absolute* scale. In psychology measurements, hardly any scale reaches a level beyond an interval scale (e.g., intelligence) or a log-interval scale (e.g., psychophysical scales). However, it is not clear from the Walster et al. (1973) paper whether or not they consider input as psychological (scaled) values at all.

Walster and Walster (1975) further extend their model by adding two exponents, one for each denominator, to Eq. (3.5), i.e., k_1 and k_2. The exponents take on the value $+1$ or -1, depending on the sign of A and B's inputs and the sign of their gains (Outputs–Inputs), defined as $k = sign(I) \times sign(O - I)$. The exponent's effect is to change the way relative outcomes are computed. Obviously, if $k = +1$, then $(O - I)/|I|$, and if $k = -1$, then it results in $|I|(O - I)$. This extension makes no sense. However, similar notations have been used in later versions of the influential model by Jasso (see Sect. 3.3.4, Jasso 1996, and Liebig 1997).

What happens if a person perceives inequality, i.e., Eq. (3.2) to be violated? In accordance with Festinger's theory of cognitive dissonance (Festinger 1957), Adams (1965, 283) proposed several means of reducing inequality or restoring equity. These include (a) the person altering his/her input (283); (b) the person altering his/her outcomes (288); and (c) the person distorting his/her inputs and outcomes cognitively (290). This means (a) and (b) apply when person i is one of the actors in Eq. (3.2), and that (c) applies both to actors and an observing person.

Intuitively, the larger the difference in the perceived relationship between outcome and inputs (i.e., $O_1/I_1 - O_2/I_2$), the larger is the perceived inequality and injustice. Furthermore, a positive difference indicates that person 1's outcomes is larger than deserved compared to person 2, whereas a negative value indicates that person 1 is underrewarded. To evaluate the magnitude of the perceived injustice, a reference is needed, which is naturally 0 in this case.

3.3.1.2 Equality

In psychology, equality is studied rarely on its own and usually in combination with the equity principle. In philosophy, however, equality receives the most attention, particularly because of the influence of Rawls (1971). In its simplest form, the principle dictates that every person should have the same level of material goods and services (Encyclopedia 2013). Equality will not be discussed here; instead, see Jost and Kay (2010) and Chap. 2 of this volume for details.

3.3.1.3 Need

Need in distributive justice is also rarely studied by itself and is mostly considered as one principle in a multidimensional approach, either competing with equity and equality or ignored altogether. Schwinger (1986) identifies several reasons for the lack of attention paid to the need principle, mainly pointing to its imprecise definition and its conceptualization. Different from the equity (contribution) principle, the need principle applies to interpersonal relationships with strong positive feelings toward the members of the group (cf. Deutsch 1975). This affective relationship is not required, or is even impedimental, when the equity principle determines the distribution. Because the choice of an allocation principle depends on the emotional relationship between group members, the three principles are difficult to link and a uniform theoretical integration impossible. The need principle has not been studied in the context of a justice approach, but rather in research about helping behavior, separating it even further from the other principles. Third, as a consequence of the previous issues, need has not been operationalized as an allocation mode like equity and equality, and has, therefore, not qualified for an economic exchange principle.

Thirty years later, need and the need principle are still theoretically underresearched in psychology.

3.3.1.4 Need as Input in Equity Theory

Equity theory is not only the most developed model in distributive justice, but is also considered the fundamental justice criterion in a multi-principle approach. Equity theorists argue that all other principles could simply be integrated into the model by specifying inputs and outcomes with respect to the principles under consideration (Austin and Hatfield 1980; Farkas and Anderson 1979; Jasso and Rossi 1977; Walster and Walster 1975). Assuming that need is a partial input, a person with a (greater) need should receive more than a person with no (less) need (Schwinger 1986).

Assume that person A has a greater need than person B, i.e., $x_{A_{need}} > x_{B_{need}}$. To restore equity, and for the Eq. (3.3) to hold, the output of person A needs to increase by some amount $y_{A_{need}}$. Depending on the perceived need, which is part of the input, the (evaluated) outcomes may substantially differ but the distribution is still judged as fair. Note that, if weights are scaled or normalized a rescaling is unavoidable when adding or deleting new input. Missing input for one person is set to zero. To the best of my knowledge, this approach has not been pursued in a systematic way. Besides scaling of different inputs, the cognitive process of evaluating, for example, need may also be different from evaluating aspects of equity as well. Furthermore, advocates of the multi-principle approach would strongly disagree with incorporating different principles into the equation for reasons of formal unification. They argue that this provides a theoretical parsimony but does not serve the needs of a psychological theory of justice.

3.3.2 A Facet Approach to Structure Social Justice Judgment

Sabbagh et al. (1994) believe that it is an empirical question whether evaluations of multidimensional inputs are complementary to or competing with the equity principle when performing social justice judgments. They provide a framework for analyzing distributive rules derived from the three main principles and refrain from evaluations. The framework is rather complex and comprises the three principles of justice (equality, equity, and need) and eight distributive rules, four social resources (money, learning opportunities, power, prestige) and, when making a judgment, Likert-type response categories (called range). From the need principle, two distributive rules are derived: primary and secondary needs, of which the descriptions are in line with Murray's (1938).

Each distributive rule is described by seven attributes with bipolar characteristics, e.g., the level of distribution is described either as microjustice or macrojustice, and perspective involves either self-interest or the interest of others. Primary and secondary needs are described by almost identical characteristics (microjustice level of distribution to individuals; explicit relevance of personal traits, e.g., mother of several children; neutral status determination, e.g., no special treats for needy people; others' interest perspectives; implicit or disregarded performance; and moral responsibility). Both need types differ with respect to entitlement. For primary needs the distribution rule is a simple outcome-focused rule aimed at immediate gratification, whereas for secondary needs the distributive rule is an elaborate entitling procedure aimed at long-term gratification (Sabbagh et al. 1994, 247). Using the attribute descriptions, Sabbagh et al. order the distributive rules along a spectrum, ranging from egalitarian (low differentiation, based on arithmetic equality) on one end and equitarian (high differentiation, based on ability) on the other end.

Need judgments are situated between these extremes. The ambiguity of the need principle may be resolved by interpreting it, on the one hand, as a principle of radical equality (increasing needy people's access to eligible goods) and, on the other hand, as a principle of equity (unequal distributions according to the persons' requirements, Sabbagh et al. 1994, 249). The approach also takes into account the kinds of resources allocated: prestige, power, learning opportunities, or money. Naturally, money (convertible resource) is associated with primary needs (people in greater need should receive more money) whereas power and learning opportunities are associated with secondary needs (people from weaker groups that have less influence should be given more opportunity to speak out; those with fewer opportunities should be given preference).

3.3.3 *Justice Judgment Model and Allocation Preference Theory*

Rather than integrating need into equity theory, Leventhal (1976) considers, in his theory of justice judgment, deserved outcomes for a person as the weighted sum of separate principles. A person's perception of a receiver's deservingness is

$$\begin{aligned}\text{Deserved outcomes} &= w_c D_{\text{by contribution}} + w_n D_{\text{by needs}} \\ &\quad + w_e D_{\text{by equality}} + w_0 D_{\text{by other rules}},\end{aligned}$$

where *deserved outcomes* is the person's overall estimate of the receiver's deserved outcomes; $D_{\text{by x}}$ is the person's estimate of the receiver's deserved outcome based on distribution rule x, $x \in \{\text{contribution, need, equality, other}\}$; and w_x is the weight by which rule x contributes to the overall estimated deserved outcome (Leventhal 1976, 214). The weights are normalized, i.e., they add up to 1. Note that Leventhal (Leventhal 1976) refers to the equity principle as the contribution rule. He also points to *other rules* such as the *promise rule* and the *legality rule* in a footnote but does not discuss them any further. Also note that different from the equity theory and its possible generalizations, no comparison between persons is required.

How to determine the weights and the estimated outcomes according to each distribution rule is specified in the justice judgment sequence. The person decides on the specific weights. The rule weights are influenced by both general and specific factors. General factors are those that affect all rules in the same manner: self-interest, for instance, favors the rule that is best for the judging person; conformity and imitation lead to a higher weight of the rule exercised by the majority or induced by obedience; and availability of reliable information about the receivers' behavior and outcomes. Specific factors, on the other hand, are those that affect the weights of only one distribution rule. Determinants for applying specific rules include situational and personal circumstances. Furthermore, the weighting of justice rules may depend on whether they are applied in cooperative settings (cf. Deutsch 1975), families, friendships, or other contexts. The judgment processes and estimations of $D_{\text{by x}}$ occur in computational subroutines, which process in parallel, are highly automatic, almost simultaneous, fast, and largely unconscious. The computational subroutine to determine $D_{\text{by contribution}}$ follows Adams (1965) equity theory, i.e.,

$$D_{\text{by contribution}} = \frac{\mathrm{O}_{units}}{\mathrm{C}_{units}} \times \text{total contribution},$$

where *total contribution* represents the person's perception of all relevant contributory behaviors and characteristics of the receiver (e.g., effort, appearance, loyalty, education, intelligence); C_{units} indicates the units of distributions and O_{units} is the matching units of outcomes. The ratio represents the person's overall estimate of a fair rate of exchange (according to Homans) of outcomes for contribution. Unfortunately, the examples provided by Leventhal are not illustrative of how the evaluation or estimation of D actually occurs, or how multiple factors adding to the overall estimation of D are determined. The lack of proper formalism, equations, and scaling methods makes it difficult to evaluate the entire approach and may be one explanation for why the model has not been well received outside of social psychology.

Leventhal (1980) and Leventhal et al. (1980) have generalized the justice judgment model, which focuses mainly on the process by which judgments of fairness are made, to allocation preference theory, which considers all determinants of allocation preferences. Allocation preference theory tries to combine the moral, cognitive, and motivational aspects of fairness judgments.

According to the theory, a distribution situation produces a family of distribution preferences (fdp) in the judging person, formalized as

$$fdp = \sum_{d}^{D} \left(\sum_{m}^{M} I_m E(dist_d \rightarrow goal_m) \right), \tag{3.6}$$

where D refers to the number of distribution types (principles); M to the number of goals a person pursues; goal_m is the mth goal; I_m the importance of the goal (weights, always sum up to 1); dist_d the dth distribution; and $E(dist_d \rightarrow goal_m)$ the expectancy or the person's belief that distribution d will either facilitate, interfere with, or be irrelevant to the attainment of goal m. The $\rightarrow$ indicates a perceived instrumental link between distribution d and goal m and takes on values $+1$, -1, and 0, respectively. Obviously, the expressions in Eq. (3.6) need numerical values. How they are achieved and on what scales they are measured remains open.

3.3.4 *Evaluation*

According to Liebig (1997, 142), multi-principle approaches are mainly concerned with (1) identifying relevant distribution and justice principles, (2) analyzing conditions of their scope, and (3) describing behavioral and attitudinal consequences when applying the distribution principles in different social contexts.

The problem with the approach is that hardly any *predictions* are derived from *theoretical* assumptions. As will be shown in Sect. 3.4, there are quite a few determinants of justice principles listed, however, they seem to be ad hoc or after the evidence. Furthermore, to be useful for identifying needs the approach requires more formal analysis. Scaling is a problem and functions of combining input and outcome do not go beyond a (generalized) linear model.

Jasso's (1978) *distributive justice force*, the most influential approach outside of psychology to measure justice, at least incorporates basic concepts of psychological functions, tapping on Fechner[5] and Stevens,[6] but does not say much about the measurement and scaling of actual reward, A, and just reward, C, when determining justice evaluation, J, of person k:

$$J_k = \ln\left(\frac{\mathrm{A}_k}{\mathrm{C}_k}\right). \tag{3.7}$$

Note that, different from the social exchange approaches, justice evaluation occurs not in comparison to *others* but only within person k. $J_k = 0$ represents the point of justice, person k is justly rewarded. When actual award exceeds just award, $J_k > 0$, person k is unjustly overrewarded. When just award exceeds actual award, $J_i < 0$, person k is unjustly underrewarded. Due to the mathematical properties of a logarithmic function, overrewarding is evaluated as less unjust than underrewarding. Furthermore, note that the logarithmic functions require both A and C to be positive or both to be negative. Different from psychophysics where the givens (right-hand side of Eq. (3.7)) are objectively measurable entities (e.g., physical stimuli) the fraction has objective (A) and subjective (C) parts. The function has been extended several times (e.g., Jasso 1996; Liebig 1997; Eriksson 2012).[7]

Sabbagh et al.'s (1994) approach provides a structure between the three distributive principles. The distinction between distribution principles and distribution rules is unclear. Rules are ordered along a differentiation continuum (related to the characteristics of the eight attributes), which remains fuzzy. An evaluation of the principles is omitted.

---

[5]Fechner's (1860) law of indirect scaling states that the perceived magnitude of a stimulus, P, equals the logarithm of stimulus intensity, S, relative to a standard stimulus (comparison stimulus), S_0, multiplied by constant c, i.e., $P = c \log \frac{S}{S_0}$. S and S_0 are physically measurable (objective) stimuli; the function mapping the physical stimuli intensities onto a psychological scale of perceived stimulus magnitudes is called a psychophysical function.

[6]According to Stevens' (1957) power law, the *perceived* magnitude of a stimulus P is the objective (physical, chemical, etc.) stimulus intensity S raised to the power of a, where a is characteristic for specific stimuli (e.g., light, tone, odor, etc.), multiplied by constant c, i.e., $P = cS^a$. For $0 \leq a \leq 1$ $(a \geq 1)$ the function is concave (convex). The scale is obtained by magnitude estimation. In the current context, the actual reward A is transformed according to Stevens' law.

[7]The definition of the justice evaluation function has changed considerably over the years, with even Jasso sometimes going back and forth between versions. One extensive form has been, e.g., $J_i = signum(\theta)[\|\theta\|] \ln(\alpha \mathrm{A}^{\beta}_{obj,i}/\mathrm{C})$, for person i.

There is no theory or model of justice based solely on the need principle. Need is either integrated into the equity theory or is merged with the just and actual reward in Jasso's model. In the multi-principle approach, need is one among several principles and is never studied in isolation. The focus there lies on weighting the principles without being specific. However, measuring aspects and scaling are (partly) considered. The facet approach is too unspecific and provides no means of identifying need, but it may be a start in the right direction.

3.4 Determinants of Justice Principles

In the following, we summarize determinants that may influence the preference for choosing one justice principle over another or influence the weights for different principles. Most determinants are situational ones, including social context and general goals of a distribution situation. Some studies highlight individual differences in justice principle preferences. In particular, demographic variables such as sex, age, and nationality have been extensively studied. Psychological variables have also been investigated in more recent studies. Few studies focus on cognitive determinants, for example, the way in which a distribution problem is presented. Most follow a social psychology approach, i.e., they propose hypotheses mostly unrelated to theories. The focus will be, if possible, on the need principle. However, with regard to theory development, need has received the least attention in empirical studies when compared to equity and equality.

3.4.1 Situational and Social Determinants

Deutsch (1975) has hypothesized under which conditions a specific principle will become a dominant one for distributing outcomes in cooperative settings. (1) When productivity is a primary goal, equity is more important than equality and need. (2) When the fostering and maintenance of good social relations is the goal, equality becomes the dominant distribution principle. (3) When the fostering of personal development and personal welfare is the goal, need becomes the dominant distribution principle (Deutsch 1975, 143).

Leventhal (1976) specifies the circumstances that influence the weights of the three principles: The contribution rule receives higher weights when the receiver's primary responsibility is to perform effectively (Leventhal 1976, 216). The need rule's weight is higher when there is affinity between the judging person and the receiver (close, friendly relationships) but also when there is a direct sense of responsibility for the receiver's welfare. Other factors that influence the weight for the need rule are success, failure, mood, and self-concern of the judging person. Successful people, competent people, and people in a good mood are more responsive to a receiver's needs and give higher weights to that rule. People who experience failure and preoccupation with self may reduce the weight of the need rule (lack of empathy). Sometimes failure may show the opposite effect, i.e., increase the responsiveness to others' needs: an unsuccessful person may bolster self-esteem or public image by displaying generosity (Leventhal 1976, 217). Finally, excessive demand by the receiver may be overwhelming for the judging person and threaten the person's independence and freedom of action and, therefore, reduce the weights of the need rule. The equality rule may receive high weights when maintenance of harmony and solidarity and prevention of conflicts among receivers is important. Furthermore, the equality rule is the simplest rule of all distributive justice rules and giving it high weights may reduce cognitive effort and complexity.

With an interest in the presentation of the distribution problem, i.e., the frames in which the problems are embedded, Törnblom (1988) proposes a framework within which the allocation process is explicated in terms of positive and negative outcome allocations, labeled the sign of the outcome allocation. Each of the two outcome allocations includes different forms, which may reflect the intention of the allocator or may be intention neutral. For instance, reward, benefaction, punishment, and revenge may imply certain underlying motives of the distributor, whereas gain, profit, gratification, loss, cost, or burden may not. The forms of allocation outcomes, in turn, may be accomplished in different ways. Törnblom distinguishes three such modes: delivery, withholding, and withdrawal. Delivery means presenting, transferring, handing, or giving something; withholding is refraining from presenting something; and withdrawal refers to taking away or removing something that the target person possesses (Törnblom 1988, 149).

Any specific form of outcome allocation may be accomplished in any one of the three accomplishment modes. The consequences, i.e., benefits or harms, depend on specific combinations of outcomes and accomplishment modes. For example, positive consequences or benefits may be obtained by delivering desirable outcomes and by withholding or withdrawing aversive outcomes. Negative consequences or harms can be obtained by delivering aversive outcomes, by withholding positive outcomes, and by withdrawing positively valued resources. Consequences may be material or nonmaterial and include status, affect, information, goods, money, and more.

Depending on the sign of the outcome allocation people may prefer to use identical or different justice principles. Unfortunately, Törnblom (1988) considers only the equality (E) and contribution (C) (equity) principles and ignores need altogether. He defines two consistent patterns, [E+ E−] and [C+ C−], which means that both under positive (+) and negative (−) outcomes the equality and the contribution principle, respectively, are preferred. The two inconsistent patterns are [E+ C−], indicating that the equality principle is preferred under a positive outcome allocation and the contribution principle under a negative outcome allocation, and [C+ E−], which indicates that the contribution principle is preferred under a positive outcome allocation and the equality principle under a negative outcome allocation. Which of the four choice patterns is more likely to be taken in a choice situation depends on three more variables: (1) on the individual's orientation (self-advantage, other-advantage); (2) on the recipient's perspective (responsible, non-responsible); and (3) on group-orientation (socio-emotional, task). Each choice pattern has advantages and disadvantages for a given person and therefore produces intra- and interpersonal conflict. For a model to analyze such conflicts, see Törnblom (1988).

Because Törnblom's framework on effects of positive and negative outcome allocation focuses on the allocation problem itself rather than on goals and situation variables, it could represent a first step in identifying needs from a cognitive perspective. What he is using is a framing setup, although he is obviously not aware of the literature. Tversky and Kahneman (1981) introduce the notion of a *decision frame*, which refers to the decision maker's conceptions of choice options among which he or she has to choose, the possible outcomes and conditional probabilities associated with a particular choice.

Whereas framing effects have been explored in numerous experiments across many disciplines with a variety of decision scenarios (for reviews see, e.g., Gächter et al. 2009; Gilovich et al. 2002; Kahneman et al. 1982; Kühberger 1998; Levin et al. 1998; Traub 1999), only a few studies have been conducted in the context of justice.

Sabbagh and Schmitt (1998) extend the conceptual framework by Sabbagh et al. (1994) for analyzing the dynamics of relations between positive and negative justice judgments. In addition to the justice principles and distribution rules (Facet A) and the social resources (Facet B: material, symbolic) (see Sect. 3.3.2), two more facets are added. Facet C describes the sign of the outcomes (positive, negative), similarly to Törnblom's approach while social context (Facet D: economic-competitive, educational-fostering) explicitly refers to the social determinants in justice judgments. As for the Törnblom framework, it does not allow for the deriving of hypotheses with respect to the selection of distribution principles, but at least need is part of the framework (see Sect. 3.3.2).

Lerner (2003), concerned with the justice motive, distinguishes two situations, in which justice judgments are investigated. In a "low impact" experimental situation, which involves role-play with minimal incentives, questionnaires, and interviews, no emotional and motivational engagement of the decision maker is required. This merely measures social preferences. However, judgments of (in)justice are revealed in high-impact situations, with emotionally compelling and personally engaging situations for the participants (Lerner 2003, 389). Lerner also distinguishes two ways in which people react to a justice-relevant event. One reaction happens automatically and intuitively (heuristic reaction) while the other reaction precedes a goal-directed assessment and evaluation of the available information (systematic reaction). The concepts and terminology are borrowed from the numerous dual process theories in social psychology (e.g., Chaiken and Trope 1999; Evans 2008).

3.4.2 Individual Determinants

Personality psychology in justice research is concerned with justice feelings as a personal trait, often labeled *social value orientation* (SVO, e.g., van Lange 1999). For any given situation, different people perceive and evaluate justice differently, and it is assumed that this variation in behavior is caused by relatively stable personality characteristics. For instance, self-oriented behavior coincides with the underlying assumption of equity theory that "(…) man is selfish" (Walster et al. 1973, 151) and seeks to maximize his or her self-interest. Other-oriented behavior, on the other hand, may be one specification of an underlying justice motive (Lerner 1975) that is expressed in the just world hypothesis that "Individuals have a need to believe that they live in a world where people generally get what they deserve. The belief that the world is just enables the individual to confront his physical and social environment as though they were stable and orderly" (Lerner and Miller 1978, 1030).[8] Several personality dimensions have been proposed, of which some apply to social behavior in general. For instance, the SVO distinguishes prosocial, individualistic, and competitive orientations. The latter two combine into the concept of pro-self orientation, which predicts behavior in social dilemmas.

To measure social behavior in justice situations, several scales (tests) have been developed, e.g., the Social Justice Scale (SJS) (Prilleltensky 2001; Torres-Harding et al. 2012) with four subscales: Attitudes toward social justice, perceived behavioral control, subjective norms, and behavioral intentions. Starting with Rubin and Peplau (1973, 1975), researchers have developed several beliefs in a just world (BJW) scales measuring the strength of the justice motive. For example, Dalbert et al. (1984) have developed a related six-item scale with a six-point response scale for Germany, called Allgemeiner Gerecht-Welt-Glaube (GWAL). The Global BJW scale (Lipkus 1991) consists of a 7-item scales with a 6-point Likert-type response scale. The items are: (1) I feel that people get what they are entitled to have. (2) I feel that a person's efforts are noticed and rewarded. (3) I feel that people earn the rewards and punishments they get. (4) I feel that people who meet with misfortune have brought it on themselves. (5) I feel that people get what they deserve. (6) I feel that rewards and punishments are fairly given. (7) I basically feel that the world is a fair place (see Hafer and Sutton 2016 for a review). None of the items is directly related to need (although item 1 may be interpreted as such). Baumert and Schmitt (2016) criticize the measure on several grounds, in particular that people with a strong belief in a just world do not necessarily restore justice when confronted with injustice but rather use cognitive strategies (biases) to interpret the situation. Schmitt and colleagues developed a justice sensitivity construct that measures how strongly people react to experienced (befallen) injustice. It is based on a self-report questionnaire with four types of indicators: (1) the frequency of perceived unjust events; (2) the intensity of anger invoked by an unjust event; (3) the intrusiveness of thoughts about the event; and (4) the punitivity, i.e., the desire to punish the victimizer (Schmitt 1996; Schmitt et al. 1995a. For more recent developments of the measure and inclusions of injustice perspectives such as victim, observer, beneficiary, and perpetrator, see Baumert and Schmitt 2016).

Some scales have been developed explicitly for distributive justice. For example, Schwinger and Winterhoff-Spurk (1984) propose the Rasch scales for measuring

---

[8]For a recent discussion on justice and self-interest see Montada and Maes (2016). For a review of past and current research on the justice motive see Ellard et al. (2016).

attitudes toward equity and equality. Unfortunately, need is not considered. The scaling approach is theoretically well founded but is, to the best of my knowledge, not further pursued in the justice research. Davey et al. (1999) offer the Preference for the Merit Principle (PMP) Scale, which measures people's preference for allocating outcomes on the basis of the distributive justice principle of merit. Again, need is not considered.

3.4.3 Evaluation

Situational, social, and personal factors play a role when evaluating justice principles. There is substantial research on framing effects in decision-making but far less research on their effect in justice judgments. Besides situational and social determinants, other frames may be employed. Levin et al. (1998) propose a typology for valence framing (the same critical information is either presented in a positive or negative light), which distinguishes between three different types of framing: (1) Risky-choice framing, (2) attribute framing, and (3) goal framing. The three framing types differ with respect to their operational definition, their typical results, and their underlying cognitive processes. In a risky-choice framing, the decision maker has the choice between two options, which are often presented in the form of lotteries. One choice option is typically a degenerated lottery, i.e., the outcome is certain; the other choice option is a risky lottery, with outcome probabilities unequal to 1 or 0. Possible outcomes of the lottery are framed as gain (positive frame) or loss (negative frame). Typical results are that, in a positive frame, decision makers more often choose the sure option, whereas in a negative frame, persons more often choose the risky gamble. That is, the risk preference changes depending of the framing.

In an attribute framing, one attribute within a given context is manipulated. Objects or events are described with attributes or characteristics that have a positive or negative connotation, or in terms of success and failure rates. The focus here is on item evaluation. Typical results are that positively described objects or events receive higher attractiveness ratings than negatively described ones. In a goal framing, the goal of an action or behavior is framed. A particular action may lead to positive consequences and refraining from the action may have negative consequences. A framing effect in this situation has occurred when the rates of adopting one or the other behavior differs.

Goal framing is mainly investigated in the context of health-related behavior, such as prevention of illness or drug use (see Levin et al. 1998 for variations of goal framing). Further kinds of framing include presentation modus (graphics, video, written information), origin of information, including case examples, and reporting from different perspectives (self or others) (see Winterbottom et al. 2008 for a review).

Personality also plays an important role when evaluating justice. Scales measuring individuals' disposition have been developed to determine attitudes towards justice per se rather than attitudes towards distributive justice or the need principle specifically. To validate the scales measuring disposition, further personality scales are included such as the Big Five Inventory. Depending on the correlation between the scales, those personality traits may explain some of the observed variance. Note, that these are ad hoc associations.

There are very few *theories* on justice and personality. One attempt has been made by Colquitt et al. (2006), who draw on three integrative theories to identify personality traits that explain the variations in individuals' reaction to fair and unfair treatment: fairness heuristic theory, uncertainty management theory, and fairness theory.

From fairness heuristic theory, which describes a heuristic to decide whether to cooperate with authorities, they conclude that trust propensity is a personality variable that could moderate justice effects.

Uncertainty management theory is related to the fairness heuristic. According to the theory, fairness can remove trust-related uncertainty and mitigate the discomfort associated with other forms of uncertainty (Colquitt et al. 2006, 113). Therefore, risk aversion may be another personal trait that can moderate justice evaluations. In particular, risk aversion should be associated with increased sensitivity to justice concerns (115). Fairness theory assumes that individuals engage in counterfactual thinking to determine the fairness of a particular event. Morality is the associated moderating personal trait. Colquitt et al. relate the derived personality traits to three forms of justice: procedural, interactional, and distributive. Only risk aversion is assumed to be a moderator for distributive justice. It predicts counterproductive behavior. Need as a justice principle is not considered.

3.5 Empirical Studies Investigating the Need Principles

There are numerous empirical studies on (distributive) justice, many of them related to work situations and organizations. However, there are only a few that focus explicitly on need. We concentrate on those studies that seek to test the determinants of justice principles, as in Sect. 3.4, with a focus on need.

3.5.1 Studies for Situational and Social Determinants

Schwinger and colleagues (Schwinger and Lamm 1981; Lamm and Schwinger 1980; 1983) test the hypothesis that the need principle is applied primarily under strong interdependence among the people involved and on high interpersonal attraction among recipients in several experiments. Keeping the inputs (e.g., amount of effort put into an essay) constant, the relationship between person 1 and 2 (close friends versus superficial acquaintance) and the cause of need (external cause versus internal cause) varies in a 2×2 factorization.[9] The dependent measure is the amount of money allocated to the needier person. Using analysis of variance on mean allocation

[9]Sex of the judging participant is another design factor. See Sect. 3.5.2.

scores, Lamm and Schwinger (1980) find that relationship has an effect on the amount allocated to the person. Specifically, the amount given to friends is larger than that given to acquaintances. No effect is observed for the cause of the need, however. They conclude that relationship is not a necessary condition for need considerations. Unfortunately, they do not include a neutral description, i.e., they leave out any information on relationship and cause.

To explore the impact of the sign of the outcome (good versus bad) and the mode of achieving the outcome (delivering versus withholding) on distributive justice, Törnblom and Ahlin (1998) conduct a vignette study describing a nuclear test that may result in danger from radiation exposure. Four frames with a combination of the following positive and negative outcomes and distribution modes are constructed: delivering a benefit (providing information), withholding harm (not providing misinformation), delivering harm (providing misinformation), and withholding a benefit (not providing information). Each scenario includes three solutions for allocating information about the possible danger, which are related to equity (informing army personnel, who contribute time and effort), need (informing children and the elderly, who are most vulnerable), and equality (informing everyone) distribution principles. Participants must rate the fairness of distribution principles on a 7-point Likert scale and select the allocation principle they would follow if they were to act as fairly as possible for the given scenario.

Törnblom and Ahlin (1998) perform a very detailed analysis (including two test sites, United States and Russia, which has no effect). The equality principle receives the highest ratings for positive outcome allocation for both modes of accomplishing outcomes but is considered unfair for negative outcome allocation for both modes. The equity and need principles are rated unfair for all four combinations. For the selection task the need principle receives the highest endorsement in the negative and the lowest in the positive outcome condition, compared to the remaining two principles. Specifically, when positive outcomes are accomplished by withholding harm, the equality principle seems to be the most just. When negative outcomes are accomplished by withholding a benefit, the need principle is seen as the most just. When positive outcomes were accomplished by withholding a harm, the equality principle is considered most just. Finally, when negative outcomes are accomplished by delivering a harm, the equality and need principles are considered most just.

Comparing the judgments within a principle given a specific mode or given a specific outcome shows mixed results inconsistent with the framework. Törnblom and Ahlin (1998) conclude that their findings may be irrelevant to distributive justice but rather relevant to procedural justice. Positive and negative outcomes are accomplished by delivering or withholding, which are two different procedures, and the participants' justice rating may be affected by procedural rather than distributive concerns.

Utilising Törnblom's classification framework, Gamliel and Peer (2006) show framing effects on justice judgments in three vignettes scenarios related to working environments: Old/new computer allocations (deliver), professional training programs with salary increase perspectives but with limited seats available (deliver/withhold), and overtime distributions (withhold). Participants rate the fairness of positive and negative frames with respect to the five allocation principles, ability, effort, tenure, need, and equality, using a six-point rating scale. In the deliver-new-versus-old-computer scenario, need receives, on average, the highest ratings, both for positive and negative frames; the second highest after effort for delivering or withholding the training program; the highest for withholding overtime (positive); and the second highest after equality for delivering overtime. Significant framing effects with respect to the need principle are observed for the training program resource and the overtime scenario. In healthcare resource allocation scenarios, Gamliel and Peer (2010) observe that need, equity, and tenure principles are evaluated as fairer in positively framed situations (i.e., to deliver health care resources to certain patients) than negatively framed situation (i.e., to not deliver healthcare resources to other patients).

3.5.2 Studies for Individual Determinants

There are numerous studies of individual differences in justice assessments, particularly measuring the feelings and reactions toward victims (self and other) when participants act as observers, beneficiaries, or perpetrators (see Baumert and Schmitt 2016; Gollwitzer and van Prooijen 2016; Hafer and Bègue 2005; Hafer and Sutton 2016 for summary and review). Here we highlight a few studies that focus on distributive justice, in particular those that include the need principle.

Major and Deaux (1982) investigate individual differences in two areas of justice behavior: reward distributions and reactions to injustice. Reward distribution is defined as the fair allocation of resources, either to others, to themselves or among themselves, and to others. Reaction to injustice is how a person reacts when he or she is treated unfairly by others, i.e., the reactions of victims or recipients of injustice. The latter is not considered here. Three individual characteristics, sex, age, and nationality, are included in their study, but no psychological variables. Based on a literature review, Major and Deaux find no sex differences when women and men allocate rewards to others and are not involved as corecipients (Major and Deaux 1982, 46). Women allocate less to themselves than men do (at least up to the year 1982).

Using a correlational approach between response items and justice principle scales, Schmitt et al. (1995b) find that endorsing the equity principle positively correlates with justifying one's own privileges; allegations of self-infliction of the deprived; trivializing differences between one's own privileges and the disadvantages of others; pity for deprived people; satisfaction with one's own privileges; anger at self-inflicted misfortune; despair when considering the situation of deprived people; and more. Endorsing the equity principle negatively correlates with the judgment that differences between one's own privileges and the disadvantages of others are unfair; perceiving no causal relationship between one's own privileges and the disadvantages of others; feeling no guilt toward deprived people; and lack of commitment to deprived people's concerns. Endorsing the need principle positively correlates with judging differences between one's own privileges and the disadvantages of others as unfair; perceiving a causal relationship between one's own privileges and the disadvantages of others; feeling guilt toward deprived people; showing outrage at the injustice suffered by deprived people; and willingness to get involved in deprived people's concerns. Endorsing the need principle negatively correlates with fending off the responsibility for needy people.

Törnblom and Ahlin (1998) include sex and age as covariates in the study described above. They find mixed results for sex and one main effect for age in the case of the need principle, but only for positive outcome allocations. The oldest group (36–66 years) rate the need principle as significantly more unfair than the youngest group (18–23 years).

3.5.3 Evaluation

Situational and social factors, some of them identical to frames, may influence the judgment and evaluation of justice (statements). There is little systematic research on their effect on specific distribution principles. That is, what is the influence of a situation and frame on a justice scale value? Do importance weights in a multi-principle approach change as a function of those factors and, if so, how? Personal determinants may account for some variance observed in individual justice or fairness judgments. However, often, questionnaire items are very closely related to a situation and it is not entirely clear what the interaction between situations and personal traits are. Often, it is not even clear what the personal trait is. Gender and age as covariates have been included mainly in sociological and political studies on justice, which are not covered here in detail. The results are mixed. Some studies find that women are more sensitive to needs than men while other studies do not.

3.6 Conclusion and Outlook

What is the psychological perspective on identifying needs? Can psychology contribute to an informed normative theory of needs and, if so, how? Normative theories, on one side, and psychological theories and models, on the other side, seem to be antipodes. For example, (subjective) expected utility theory is a normative theory on how a rational decision maker should ideally make decisions. But experiments have shown that each axiom proposed by expected utility theory is violated. In response, psychologists developed descriptive theories on how a decision maker actually makes a choice, the most prominent one being prospect theory. However, normative theories often serve as benchmarks to compare the ideal to real observed behavior, thereby allowing psychologists to model the deviations from the standard in order to derive a psychological model of behavior. A normative theory of needs, however, does not yet exist.

What can psychology contribute to the development of such a theory? As this chapter demonstrates, need in psychology is used in different contexts with different meanings. In the context of psychological theories on motives and motivation, need is a felt deficiency that drives the individual to goal-directed behavior. Here, we can draw on those theories that have identified specific needs by various means and also developed measures of need strength. Classifying needs as primary (physiological and basic) and secondary (all others) might be reasonable, but only if the classification makes no demands that lower needs must be satisfied before higher needs. In psychological motivation theories, the focus is on secondary psychological needs (e.g., achievement, power, competence, cognitive and affective), particularly in more recent theories. In this chapter, however, the focus lies more on primary needs (e.g., existence, including food, housing, safety) because the requirements to satisfy the needs are concrete and quantifiable. This is relatively new terrain for psychologists. How much food a person needs to still her hunger or how much space she needs to live comfortably are not questions psychologists are usually interested in. However, psychologists are interested in what happens, for example, when one person gets a certain quantity and another person receives double or half of it.

Social exchange theory in social psychology assumes that social behavior is based on mutual give-and-take of material and immaterial goods. In particular, the theory proposes that mutual exchange is formed by using a subjective cost–benefit analysis (e.g., Homans 1958; Thibaut and Kelley 1959). These theories, also absorbed in psychological theories on motivation (Keller 1981), are the forerunners of theories on justice in psychology. Typically, the input and output amounts associated with the hypothetical persons are given and the participant is asked to evaluate a statement by comparing at least two recipients. There are hardly any tasks where the participant has to come up with a demand, i.e., needs, that a hypothetical person might have. Judging a distribution as fair or just or rating the fairness of a statement are measurement and scaling problems.

Measurement and scaling are very important areas in psychology and much advanced in perception. For instance, psychophysical theories and methods allow for the mapping of physical scales onto psychological scales (e.g., intensity to loudness; see Fechner, Stevens, above); or response frequencies to psychometrical scales (e.g., the weighting function τ in prospect theory). The majority of approaches on justice in psychology, however, rely on Likert-type scales to measure justice judgments, which are ordinal scales only. That is, the distance between two rating values is meaningless in a measurement theoretical sense. Furthermore, amounts allocated to recipients on which judgments are made are not varied systematically. Therefore, identifying the absolute amount of need (demand) is impossible. One way to more directly judge the amount of need a person might have is to design a conjoint measurement approach (e.g., Hensher et al. 2005; Krantz et al. 1971; Louviere et al. 2000) in which amounts are systematically varied. However, this cannot be done in isolation but only in conjunction with other characteristics that describe the person. This could include the situational, social, or personal circumstances of the person in need, or may even involve a tradeoff between those factors. That is, identifying a person's need may well depend on circumstances outside the pure demand to satisfy the wants. An informed normative theory of need must be aware of this. From a psychological perspective, preferences and judgments of the decision maker are constructed and are, therefore, variable. That is, different from economic theory, preferences in psychology are not elicited, inherently invariable within the decision maker, and description-invariant.

A wealth of research, however, has shown that judgments are prone to all kinds of cognitive biases. For example, decision makers respond in different ways to different but objectively equivalent variations of the same problem (i.e., framing). A few studies on justice judgments include frames (e.g., Törnblom) but there is no general *theory* on how frames may affect the justice judgments and, in particular, no theory on the effect on need judgments.

Finally, almost no link to cognitive processes has been made. However, as Lerner (2003, 389) recognizes

> the heuristic-based justice appraisals often take the rather primitive form of simple univalent associations of outcomes, personal characteristics, emotions, and restorative acts—for example, bad things happen to bad people, bad outcomes are caused by bad people, similar people deserve similar outcomes—whereas, the systematic appraisals and subsequent responses reflect conventional rules of thought, including the normatively appropriate rule for determining deserving, blame, and the reestablishment of justice, for example, merit, equality, and norm-based entitlements. Second, although the heuristic responses occur automatically, the person must have an incentive with sufficient time and cognitive resources to engage in systematic thought processes.

There are no general theories yet on how all this is linked together to identify need, let alone a formal model. This, however, is indispensable to any contribution to an informed normative model.

Acknowledgments This chapter has been written as part of DFG Research Group 2104 "Needs-based Justice and Distribution Procedures", Project A1 "Framing in Need-identification: Data an Models" (DI 506/13 − 1). This funding is gratefully acknowledged. I thank an anonymous reviewer for his/her comments.

References

Adams, J. S. (1965). Inequity in social exchange. In L. Berkowitz (Ed.), *Advances in experimental social psychology* (Vol. 2, pp. 267–299). New York: Academic.

Alderfer, C. P. (1969). An empirical test of a new theory of human needs. *Organizational Behavior and Human Performance, 5*, 142–175.

Allport, G. W. (1954). *Nature of prejudice*. Cambridge: Addison-Wesley.

Austin, W., & Hatfield, E. (1980). Equality, power, and social justice. In G. Mikula (Ed.), *Justice and social interaction* (pp. 25–61). Bern: Hans Huber Publishers.

Baumert, A., & Schmitt, M. (2016). Justice sensitivity. In C. Sabbagh & M. Schmitt (Eds.), *Handbook of social justice theory and research* (pp. 161–180). Heidelberg: Springer.

Chaiken, S., & Trope, Y. (1999). *Dual process theories in social psychology*. New York: Guilford.

Colquitt, J. A., Scott, B. A., Judge, T. A., & Shaw, J. C. (2006). Justice and personality: Using integrative theories to derive moderators of justice effects. *Organizational Behavior and Human Decision Processes, 100*, 110–127.

Dalbert, C., Montada, L., Schmitt, M., & Schneider, A. (1984). *Existentielle Schuld: Ergebnisse der Item- und Skalenanalysen*, Trier: P.I.V.-Bericht Nr. 16, http://psydok.psycharchives.de/jspui/bitstream/20.500.11780/307/1/beri0124.pdf.

Davey, L. M., Bobocel, D. R., Son Hing, L. S., & Zanna, M. P. (1999). Preference for the merit principle scale: An individual difference measure of distributive justice preferences. *Social Justice Research, 12*(3), 223–240.

Deci, E. R., & Ryan, R. M. (1987). The support of autonomy and the control of behavior. *Journal of Personality and Social Psychology, 53*(6), 1024–1037.

Deci, E. R., & Ryan, R. M. (2000). The "What" and "Why" of goal pursuits: Human needs and the self-determination of behavior. *Psychological Inquiry, 11*(4), 227–268.

Deutsch, M. (1975). Equity, equality, and need: What determines which value will be used as the basis of distributive justice? *Journal of Social Issues, 51*(3), 137–149.

Encyclopedia (Stanford Encyclopaedia of Philosophy). (2013). Distributive justice. http://plato.stanford.edu/entries/justice-distributive/.

Evans, J. S. B. (2008). Dual-processing accounts of reasoning, judgment, and social cognition. *Annual Review of Psychology, 59*, 255–278.

Ellard, J. H., Harvey, A., & Callan, M. J. (2016). The justice motive: History, theory, and research. In C. Sabbagh & M. Schmitt (Eds.), *Handbook of Social Justice Theory and Research*. Heidelberg: Springer.

Eriksson, K. (2012). The accuracy of mathematical models of justice evaluations. *Journal of Mathematical Sociology, 36*(2), 125–135.

Farkas, A. J., & Anderson, N. H. (1979). Multidimensional input in equity theory. *Journal of Personality and Social Psychology, 37*, 879–896.

Fechner, G. T. (1860). *Elemente der Psychophysik*. Leipzig: Breitkopf & Härtel.

Festinger, L. (1957). *A theory of cognitive dissonance*. Stanford: Stanford University Press.

Fox, C. R., & Poldrack, R. A. (2009). Prospect theory and the brain. In P. W. Glimcher, E. Fehr, C. Camerer, & R. A. Poldrack (Eds.), *Neuroeconomics: Decision making and the brain*, (pp. 145–173). London: Academic.

Gächter, S., Orzen, H., Renner, E., & Starmer, C. (2009). Are experimental economists prone to framing effects? A natural field experiment. *Journal of Economic Behavior and Organization, 70*, 443–446.

Gamliel, E., & Peer, E. (2006). Positive versus negative framing affects justice judgments. *Social Justice Research, 19*(3), 307–322.

Gamliel, E., & Peer, E. (2010). Attribute framing affects the perceived fairness of health care allocation principles. *Judgment and Decision Making, 5*(1), 11–20.

Gilovich, T., Griffin, D., & Kahneman, D. (2002). *Heuristics and biases. The psychology of intuitive judgment*. Cambridge: Cambridge University Press.

Gollwitzer, P. M., & Moskowitz, G. B. (1996). Goal effects on action and cognition. In E. T. Higgins & A. W. Kruglanski (Eds.), *Social psychology. Handbook of basic principles* (pp. 361–399). New York: Guildford Press.

Gollwitzer, M., & van Prooijen, J.-W. (2016). Psychology of justice. In C. Sabbagh & M. Schmitt (Eds.), *Handbook of social justice theory and research*. Heidelberg: Springer.

Hafer, C. L., & Bègue, L. (2005). Experimental research on just-world theory: Problems, development, and future challenges. *Psychological Bulletin, 131*(1), 128–167.

Hafer, C. L., & Sutton, R. (2016). Belief in just world. In C. Sabbagh & M. Schmitt (Eds.), *Handbook of social justice theory and research*. Heidelberg: Springer.

Heckhausen, J., & Heckhausen, H. (Eds.). (2010). *Motivation and action*. Cambridge: Cambridge University Press.

Hensher, D. A., Rose, J. M., & Greene, W. H. (2005). *Applied choice analysis: A primer*. Cambridge: Cambridge University Press.

Homans, G. C. (1958). Social behavior as exchange. *American Journal of Sociology, 63*(6), 597–606.

Jasso, G. (1978). On the justice of earnings: A new specification of the justice evaluation function. *American Journal of Sociology*, *83*(6), 1398–1419.

Jasso, G. (1996). Exploring the reciprocal relations between theoretical and empirical work. The case of the justice evaluation. *Sociological Methods & Research*, *24*(3), 253–303.

Jasso, G., & Rossi, P. H. (1977). Distributive justice and earned income. *American Sociological Review*, *42*, 639–651.

Jost, J. T., & Kay, A. C. (2010). Social justice. In S. T. Fiske, D. T. Gilbert, & G. Lindzey (Eds.), *Handbook of social psychology* (5th ed., pp. 1122–1165). New York: Wiley.

Kahneman, D., Slovic, P., & Tversky, A. (1982). *Judgment under uncertainty: Heuristics and biases*. Cambridge: Cambridge University Press.

Kahneman, D., & Tversky, A. (1979). Prospect theory: An analysis of decision under risk. *Econometrica*, *47*, 263–291.

Keller, J. A. (1981). *Grundlagen der Motivation*. München: Urban und Schwarzenberg.

Konow, J. (2003). Which is the fairest one of all? A positive analysis of justice theories. *Journal of Economic Literature*, *XLI*, 1188–1239.

Krantz, D. H., Luce, R. D., Suppes, P., & Tversky, A. (1971). *Foundations of Measurement. Additive and Polynomial Representations* (Vol. 1). New York: Academic.

Kühberger, A. (1998). The influence of framing on risky decisions: A meta-analysis. *Organizational Behavior and Human Decision Processes*, *75*(1), 23–55.

Lamm, H., & Schwinger, T. (1980). Norms concerning distributive justice: Are needs taken into consideration in allocation decisions? *Social Psychology Quarterly*, *43*(4), 425–429.

Lamm, H., & Schwinger, T. (1983). Need consideration in allocation decisions: Is it just? *Journal of Social Psychology*, *119*, 205–209.

Lerner, M. J. (1974). The justice motive: "Equity" and "Parity" among children. *Journal of Personality and Social Sciences*, *29*(4), 539–550.

Lerner, M. J. (1975). The justice motive in social behavior: Introduction. *Journal of Social Issues*, *32*(3), 1–20.

Lerner, M. J. (2003). The justice motive: Where social psychologists found it, how they lost it, and why they may not find it again. *Personality and Social Psychology Review*, *7*(4), 388–399.

Lerner, M. J., & Miller, D. T. (1978). Just world research and the attribution process: Looking back and ahead. *Psychological Bulletin*, *83*(5), 1030–1051.

Lester, D. (1990). Maslow's hierarchy of needs and personality. *Personality and Individual Differences*, *11*(11), 1187–1188.

Leventhal, G. S. (1976). Fairness in social relations. In J. W. Thibaut, J. T. Spence, & R. C. Carson (Eds.), *Contemporary topics in social psychology* (pp. 211–239). Morristown: General Learning Press.

Leventhal, G. S. (1980). What should be done with equity theory? In K. J. Gergen, M. S. Greenberg, & R. H. Willis (Eds.), *Social exchange: Advances in theory and research* (pp. 27–55). New York: Plenum Press.

Leventhal, G. S., Karuza, J, Jr., & Fry, W. R. (1980). Beyond fairness: A theory of allocation preferences. In G. Mikula (Ed.), *Justice and social interaction: Experimental and theoretical contributions from psychological research* (pp. 167–218). Bern: Hans Huber Publishers.

Levin, I. P., Schneider, S. L., & Gaeth, G. J. (1998). All frames are not created equal: A typology and critical analysis of framing effects. *Organizational Behavior and Human Decision Processes*, *76*(2), 149–188.

Lewin, K. (1926). Vorsatz, Wille und Bedürfnis. *Psychologische Forschung*, *7*, 330–385.

Lewin, K. (1935). *A dynamic theory of personality*. New York: McGraw-Hill.

Lewin, K. (1943). Defining the "Field at a Given Time". *Psychological Review*, *50*(3), 292–310.

Lewin, K. (1951). *Field theory in social science*. New York: Harper and Row.

Liebig, S. (1997). *Soziale Gerechtigkeitsforschung und Gerechtigkeit in Unternehmen*. München: Hampp Verlag.

Lipkus, I. (1991). The construction and preliminary validation of a global belief in a just world scale and the exploratory analysis of the multidimensional belief in a just world scale. *Personality and Individual Differences, 12*, 1171–1178.
Louviere, J. J., Hensher, D. A., & Swait, J. D. (2000). *Stated choice methods: Analysis and application*. Cambridge: Cambridge University Press.
Major, B., & Deaux, K. (1982). Individual differences in justice behavior. In J. Greenberg & R. L. Cohen (Eds.), *Equity and justice in social behavior*. New York: Academic.
Maslow, A. H. (1943). A theory of human motivation. *Psychological Review, 50*, 370–396.
Maslow, A. H. (1948). "Higher" and "Lower" needs. *Journal of Psychology, 25*, 433–436.
Maslow, A. H. (1987). *Motivation and personality* (3rd ed.). New York: Addison-Wesley.
McClelland, D. C. (1987). *Human motivation*. Cambridge: Cambridge University Press.
Metz-Göckel, H. (2014). Bedürfnis. In M. A. Wirtz (Ed.), *Dorsch – Lexikon der Psychologie* (18th ed., p. 255) Bern: Hogrefe.
Mikula, G. (1980). Introduction: Main issues in the psychological research on justice. In G. Mikula (Ed.), *Justice and social interaction: Experimental and theoretical contributions from psychological research* (pp. 167–218). Bern: Hans Huber Publishers.
Mitchell, V. F., & Moudgill, P. (1976). Measurement of Maslow's need hierarchy. *Organizational Behavior and Human Performance, 16*, 334–349.
Montada, L., & Maes, J. (2016). Justice and self-interest. In C. Sabbagh & M. Schmitt (Eds.), *Handbook of social justice theory and research*. Heidleberg: Springer.
Murray, H. A. (1938). *Explorations in personality*. New York: Oxford University Press.
Prilleltensky, I. (2001). Value-based praxis in community psychology: Moving towards social justice and social action. *American Journal of Community Psychology, 29*(5), 747–778.
Rawls, J. (1971). *A theory of justice*. Harvard: Harvard University Press.
Roberts, F. S. (1979). *Measurement theory with applications to decisionmaking, utility, and the social sciences*. London: Addison-Wesley.
Rubin, Z., & Peplau, A. (1973). Belief in a just world and reactions to another's lot: A study of participants in the national draft lottery. *Journal of Social Issues, 29*(4), 73–93.
Rubin, Z., & Peplau, A. (1975). Who beliefs in a just world? *Journal of Social Issues, 31*(3), 65–89.
Ryan, R. M., & Deci, E. L. (2000). Self-determination theory and the facilitation of intrinsic motivation, social development, and well-being. *American Psychologist, 55*(1), 68–78.
Sabbagh, C., & Schmitt, M. (1998). Exploring the structure of positive and negative justice judgments. *Social Justice Research, 11*(4), 381–396.
Sabbagh, C., & Schmitt, M. (Eds.). (2016). *Handbook of social justice theory and research*. Heidelberg: Springer.
Sabbagh, C., Dar, Y., & Resh, N. (1994). The structure of social justice judgments: A facet approach. *Social Psychology Quarterly, 57*(3), 244–261.
Scheffer, D., & Heckhausen, H. (2010). Trait theories of motivation. In J. Heckhausen & H. Heckhausen (Eds.), *Motivation and action* (pp. 42–70). Cambridge: Cambridge University Press.
Schmitt, M. J. (1996). Individual differences in sensitivity to befallen injustice (SBI). *Personality and Individual Differences, 21*(1), 3–20.
Schmitt, M. J., Neumann, R., & Montada, L. (1995a). Dispositional sensitivity to befallen injustice. *Social Justice Research, 8*(4), 385–407.
Schmitt, M., Maes, J., & Schmal, A. (1995b). *Gerechtigkeit als innerdeutsches Problem: Einstellungen zu Verteilungsprinzipien, Ungerechtigkeitssensibilität und Glaube an eine gerechte Welt als Kovariate*, Berichte aus der Arbeitsgruppe "Verantwortung, Gerechtigkeit, Moral" Nr. 82, Trier: Universität Trier, Fachbereich I – Psychologie
Schneider, B., & Alderfer, C. P. (1973). Three studies of measures of need satisfaction in organizations. *Administrative Science Quarterly, 18*(4), 489–505.
Schwinger, T. (1986). The need principle of distributive justice. In H. W. Bierhoff, R. L. Cohen, & J. Greenberg (Eds.), *Justice in social relations* (pp. 211–225). New York: Plenum Press.

Schwinger, T., & Lamm, H. (1981). Justice norms in allocation decisions: Need consideration as a function of resource adequacy for complete need satisfaction, recipients' contributions, and recipients' interpersonal attraction. *Social Behavior and Personality*, *9*(2), 235–241.

Schwinger, T., & Winterhoff-Spurk, P. (1984). Gleichheits- vs. Leistungsprinzip: Rasch-Skalen zur Messung dispositioneller Einstellungen zu zwei Prinzipien der Gerechtigkeit. *Diagnostica*, *30*(2), 125–143.

Stevens, S. S. (1957). On the psychophysical law. *Psychological Review*, *64*(3), 153–181.

Thibaut, J. W., & Kelley, H. H. (1959). *The social psychology of groups*. New York: Wiley.

Törnblom, K. Y. (1988). Positive and negative allocations: A typology and a model for conflicting justice principles. In E. J. Lawler & B. Markovsky (Eds.), *Advances in group processes* (Vol. 5, pp. 141–168). London: JAI Press.

Törnblom, K., & Ahlin, A. (1998). Mode of accomplishing positive and negative outcomes: Its effect on fairness evaluations. *Social Justice Research*, *11*(4), 423–442.

Torres-Harding, S. R., Siers, B., & Olson, B. D. (2012). Development and psychometric evaluation of the social justice scale (SJS). *American Journal of Community Psychology*, *50*, 77–88.

Traub, S. (1999). *Framing effects in taxation. An empirical study using the german income tax schedule*. Heidelberg: Physica.

Tversky, A., & Kahneman, D. (1981). The framing of decisions and the psychology of choice. *Science*, *211*(4481), 453–458.

Tversky, A., & Kahneman, D. (1992). Advances in prospect theory: Cumulative representation of uncertainty. *Journal of Risk and Uncertainty*, *5*(4), 297–323.

van Lange, M. A. M. (1999). The pursuit of joint outcomes and equality in outcomes: An integrative model of social value orientation. *Journal of Personality and Social Psychology*, *77*(2), 337–349.

Wahba, M. A., & Bridwell, L. G. (1976). Reconsidered: A review of research on the need hierarchy theory. *Organizational Behavior and Human Performance*, *4*, 142–175.

Walster, E., Berscheid, E., & Walster, G. W. (1973). New directions in equity research. *Journal of Personality and Social Psychology*, *25*(2), 151–176.

Walster, E., & Walster, G. W. (1975). Equity and social justice. *Journal of Social Issues*, *31*(3), 21–43.

Williams, D. E., & Page, M. M. (1989). A multi-dimensional measure of Maslow's Hierarchy of needs. *Journal of Research in Personality*, *23*, 192–213.

Winterbottom, A., Bekker, H. L., Conner, M., & Mooney, A. (2008). Does narrative information bias individual's decision making? A systematic review. *Social Science and Medicine*, *67*, 2079–2088.

Chapter 4
Need-Based Justice: A Sociological Perspective

Bernhard Kittel

Abstract This chapter analyses the structural conditions and behavioral consequences of individual justice attitudes, values, and beliefs. The first part develops a sociological concept of need-based justice. The forms of social relations characteristic of different modes of societal integration refer to context-specific principles of justice that dominate interactions between individuals. People motivate their behavior by framing it in terms of the justice principle considered appropriate for the relevant form of societal integration. Need-based justice is considered appropriate for solidary communities, in contrast to hierarchies, networks, and markets. In the next step, need-based justice is characterized as a norm that, more than other principles of justice, depends on social agreement, because it necessarily has to consider particular circumstances and, thus, cannot be operationalized in terms of a universal prescription. The second part discusses sociological research on need-based justice at the individual, relational, and aggregate level of analysis. Research in these three traditions highlights the relevance of need in popular attitudes, the close association between solidarity and adherence to the need principle, and the institutionalization of a focus on need satisfaction in liberal welfare regimes. In the third part, the various implications of the proposed conceptualization of a sociological view for the study of need-based justice are discussed.

4.1 Introduction

A sociological account of justice is situated between the ideational level discussed in philosophy and the behavioral level studied in psychology and economics (Miller 1999; Liebig 2001; Konow 2003). While the former distinguishes different princi-

B. Kittel (✉)
Department of Economic Sociology & FOR 2104, University of Vienna,
Oskar-Morgenstern-Platz 1, A-1090 Wien, Austria
e-mail: bernhard.kittel@univie.ac.at

S. Traub and B. Kittel (eds.), *Need-Based Distributive Justice*,
https://doi.org/10.1007/978-3-030-44121-0_4

ples of justice and their relative merits, the latter focuses on fairness as a form of human behavior deviating from the orthodox assumption of narrow, short-term, self-regarding utility maximization. Sociology, in turn, places reciprocal relationships and structures center stage. Contextualized notions of distributive justice developed in political philosophy, such as "spheres of justice" (Walzer 1983) or "local justice" (Elster 1992) relate the concept to the condition that people "have a certain relationship to one another" (Miller 2013, 150). Different social contexts are characterized by different types of relationships and different institutions, in which different principles of justice are generally considered relevant. A sociological perspective, therefore, emphasizes the importance of the particular social structure in which individuals take their decisions.

Hence, such a perspective focuses on the mutual dependency of structural conditions and individual actions. On the one hand, individual attitudes and actions are embedded in structural, institutional, and cultural contexts that condition, restrict, and incentivize specific perceptions, understandings, perspectives, and modes of behavior. On the other hand, these social phenomena are manifestations of the social interactions of individuals and thus depend on the way individuals conceptualize their world (Liebig and Sauer 2016).

Previous state-of-the-art reports on the sociology of justice have discussed the whole range of principles of justice potentially legitimizing allocations and distributions, as well as the distinctions one can draw with respect to other forms of justice (Arts and van der Veen 1992; Müller 1992; Liebig and Sauer 2016). Building on these summaries, the aim of this chapter is more circumscribed. I intend to explore the social conditions under which the satisfaction of *needs* is invoked as an adequate principle to generate a just situation, and to study the conditions under which societal allocation rules refer to needs. Although this restriction seems to produce a rather narrow focus, compared to the broad range of justice research, need can rightly be considered the most fundamental, albeit also the most contested, concern of justice (Müller 1992, 21–22).

I will, first, discuss possible foundations of justice principles in sociological theory more generally. In Sect. 4.3, I will elaborate on the need principle and separate needs from related concepts Sect. 4.2. Section 4.4 serves to present an overview of the sociological literature on need-based justice. The section is divided into three parts, following a popular differentiation of sociological approaches focusing on the individual, the relational and the collective level of sociality. Section 4.5 brings together the various elements and proposes a way to systematize efforts to develop a sociological account of need-based justice. The conclusion then highlights some implications for empirical research.

4.2 Distributive Justice and Social Integration

As has been repeatedly noted previously, classical sociological theory has been remarkably silent on the notion of justice, despite the fact that core topics of sociology, such as inequality, social stratification, or social institutions, have profound implications for justice perceptions and attitudes (Arts and van der Veen 1992; Lengfeld and Liebig 2002). The only notable exception among the classics is Émile Durkheim, whose complete work can be read as an attempt to understand the moral foundations of society (Müller 1992).

For Durkheim (1964 [1893]), "justice sentiments" and legal institutions—as manifestations of societally dominant conceptions of justice—are inherently related to the type of solidarity on which a society is built (Garland 2013). Mechanical solidarity is based on penal law, or retributive justice, which maintains social cohesion by punishing deviations from "common consciousness." Organic solidarity is characterized by the idea of restitution that fosters exchange among individual members of a society: "Every contract (...) assumes that behind the parties who bind each other, society is there, quite prepared to intervene and to enforce respect for any undertakings entered into" (Durkheim 1964 [1893], 71). This conception thus points to a twin logic in which justice bolsters social cohesion: while individuals may develop subjective "justice sentiments," that is, perceptions and attitudes, societies institutionalize specific concepts of justice in relation to the specific concepts of solidarity underlying the bonds between their members.

Extending Durkheim's classification, Müller (1992, 25–26) suggests to distinguish four forms of justice: *Commutative* justice refers to justice in exchange relations, *contributive* justice is a concern in the determination of relative contributions to a common good, *distributive* justice is related to the allocations to group members, and *constitutive* justice is the right of group membership that underlies the three other forms of justice. Relative endowments or allocations become relevant if their size is conceptualized in terms of rights and comparisons are made between the actual share and the share that one believes one is entitled to (Arts and van der Veen 1992, 148–149). In contrast to Durkheim's notions of retribution and restitution, which establish a direct link between an individual act and a collectively imposed sanction, redistribution refers to a more generalized idea of justice. Distributive justice is about the general principles that should guide allocations and endowments, and redistribution is a collective mechanism for balancing relative fortunes that is backed by the threat of legitimate force.

4.2.1 Dimensions of Distributive Justice

There is much disagreement about the exact list of principles underlying various aspects of distributive justice (Lamont and Favor 2016; Konow 2003). Nevertheless, a consensus seems to have emerged in sociology to distinguish four principles: equality, equity, entitlements, and need (Liebig and Sauer 2016). These principles are rooted in an *elective affinity* (Weber 1949) with a classification of different forms of sociality, or relational models (Fiske 1992). These models—*communal sharing*, *authority ranking*, *equality matching*, and *market pricing*—are motivated by the measurement level involved in comparisons between individuals, being nominal, ordinal, interval, and ratio scales, respectively. Fiske claims that individuals assess their social relationships in terms of these four scales and adjust their behavior to the standards involved in these comparisons. In a solidary community, the heterogeneity of individuals is acknowledged. Authority establishes an ordinal ranking between individuals and equality requires consideration of countable differences between individuals. Finally, market relations are based on an assessment of relative values with respect to a common point of reference.

Liebig and Sauer (2016, 50) use this largely inductive analytical framework for a discussion of homologies between forms of sociality and justice principles that are proper to the form of sociality in an ideal typical sense. They attribute the need principle to solidary communities, equality to networks and cooperatives, equity to the market, and entitlements to hierarchical relationships. The first three of these conceptual matches constitute the classical trio of fundamental justice principles (Miller 1999; Sen 2009). Moreover, these three principles can also be linked to another classical typology differentiating forms of the economic integration of a society (Polanyi 1957). From this perspective, *reciprocity* is a constitutive element of symmetric relationships, *redistribution* presupposes a center in a community empowered to take allocative decisions, and *market exchange* presupposes the existence of an anonymous market in which prices are set as a result of the interplay of supply and demand. The justice principles salient in allocations according to these forms of integration are need, equality, and equity, respectively, whereby each constitutes a specific form of mutual recognition appropriate for the sphere of social interaction (Honneth 2014).

In these contexts, status- or power-dependent entitlements stand apart and need further explication. The concept does not appear as a topic of serious discussion in political philosophy,[1] which starts from "a first fundamental question about political justice in a democratic society, namely what is the most appropriate conception of justice for specifying the fair terms of social cooperation between citizens regarded as free and equal" (Rawls 2005, Lecture 1). The consideration of justice in hierarchical structures is thus an original sociological contribution that is based on the premise that "actual" societies do not conform to the Rawlsian ideal (Honneth 2014; Lengfeld 2008). Allocations correlating with status differences may be the consequence of the recognition of individual merit by others and thus be derived from the equity principle. However, whether the power to make decisions for a collectivity is obtained by descent, force, or democratic election, and whether this rule is legitimized by reference to tradition, charisma, or rationality, does not exclude the possibility that it may be considered just by at least some of those exposed to it, which makes the entitlement principle empirically relevant. If the principles of freedom and equality of human beings are rejected, variation in entitlements unrelated to individual merit may be considered just even by those manifestly deprived of their fair share according to other justice principles.

Liebig and Sauer sort the four justice principles in a 2×2 matrix, but do not elaborate on the rationale for the placement of types into cells. Nevertheless, they give a few clues as to a possible interpretation of their conceptualization, which

[1] For example, the term does not appear in the indexes of Miller (1999) and Sen (2009). Konow (2003, 1206) discusses entitlements only in the context of meritocratic systems.

Table 4.1 Forms of sociality and justice principles

		Relation to resource	
		Instrumental	Consummatory
Referent	External (system integration)	Adaptation Market exchange Equity Pricing	Goal attainment Hierarchy Entitlement Ranking
	Internal (social integration)	Latency Solidary community Need Sharing	Integration Networks and cooperatives Equality Matching

Notes Cell entries: 1st row: social function; 2nd row: social relationship; 3rd row: justice principle; 4th row: relational model. Source: Adapted and extended from Liebig and Sauer (2016, 51)

will be used here for rooting the typology in a more fundamental theoretical argument. First, quoting Törnblom (1992), they suggest that both need and equality are related to "long-term, strong-tie relationships" (Liebig and Sauer 2016, 50), whereas equity structures short-term, weak-tie relationships, leaving entitlements to hierarchies. Second, they suggest that a solidary community should be interpreted in terms of shared origin and identity.

These considerations imply interpreting the four forms of sociality in a slightly adapted fashion in terms of the $AGIL$ scheme (Parsons 1951). Table 4.1 illustrates this idea. Parsons differentiated societal functions with reference to the relation of agents toward resources (instrumental vs. consummatory) and the definition of a boundary between an agent ('system') and her context ('environment') (external vs. internal). A, adaptation, is the realm of market exchange in which social relationships rest on short-term and anonymous interactions, which are characterized by the invocation of the principle of equity. According to this line of thought, terms of exchange reflect relative scarcity and a just distribution is realized if all demands are met by supply. Adaptation to changing environments is thus effectuated through Adam Smith's *invisible hand* as a by-product of the anonymous interaction between individuals satisfying their aspirations.

G, goal attainment, is the dimension of decision-making. Different social entities organize and legitimize the making of decisions obligating all members of the collectivity in different ways. For example, in firms decision power is legitimized by ownership, in democratic polities representation is grounded in free elections. The power differentials, which constitute at least temporary hierarchical relationships, generate entitlements, which are regarded as just to the extent that the principles underlying legitimate rule are accepted by the ruled. Entitlements entail a backward-looking and a forward-looking component. The difference between higher ranking and lower ranking individuals has been traditionally legitimized by a trade of protection against loyalty and tribute between power holders and subordinates. Although this principle is at odds with the fundamental premises underlying modern republican and democratic rule, it may still be at work in the acceptance of societal stratification and the formation of an economic, political, and cultural elite due to, for example, inheritance (Beckert 2008). Hence, for example, while modern, democratic political systems formally apply the principle of equality to individual voting weights in elections, the probability of actually being selected is vastly unequally distributed in the population (Stiglitz 2015). The entitlement principle of justice entails the claim to specific allocations that are not based on merit of position holders but are merely connected to the social position of an office.

I, integration, in turn, is conceptualized as the dimension of societal harmony in the sense of a shared and convergent set of norms and values held by a group of formally equal agents. This is the realm of voluntary cooperation in peer groups, as manifested in the "civil society." The most fundamental justice principle in this respect is equality. Equal access to public resources and equality before the law are core elements of justice that foster the acceptance of the existing social order and the willingness to stay part of the community. People experience the continuous violation of the norm of equality as relative deprivation, which is a frequent cause of violent unrest and revolt (Runciman 1966; Gurr 1970).

L, latency, refers to the maintenance of integrative and solidary elements of the society, most fundamentally the continuing existence of its members, or at least their descendants, and mutual ties. According to Hechter (1987, 18), "solidarity is a function of two independent factors: first, the extensiveness of its corporate obligations, and, second, the degree to which individual members actually comply with these obligations. Together, these provide the defining elements of solidarity. The greater the average proportion of each member's private resources contributed to collective ends, the greater the solidarity of the group." Garland (2013, 35) adds, "[s]olidarity will be greater where groups exert more control (including the internalized controls of socialization) and individuals are more dependent on the group for needed resources (including identity) that are otherwise unavailable." Thus the satisfaction of individual needs becomes prominent in this dimension. Other than in the dimension of integration, solidarity "need not be a warm, communitarian experience of fellowship and mutuality: for many individuals, the strong solidarity of the pre-industrial family was largely a matter of power, dependency and subservience" (Garland 2013, 35). Most notably, need is considered as the core allocative principle in families, whereby transfers are justified by the notion of belonging. As Garland's remark suggests, however, the satisfaction of need does not predetermine how a solidary group such as a family deals with surplus: To the extent that hierarchical structures, relative performance or the individuality are salient, other principles may be added to the satisfaction of needs. At the societal level, the idea of giving to the needy extends into charity as an element of the civil society, but again, other principles may be relevant for the allocation of surplus. Historically, deficiencies in the provision of basic needs to large societal strata has given rise to the welfare state, which, however, depends on the notion of community in the context of politically defined societies. In that sense, redistribution requires both a defined border between an inside and an outside and at least some inequality among insiders.

Focusing on the difference between the columns of the matrix, the principles of equity and need share their instrumental nature in equalizing allocations to some externally set standard of differentiation. In the case of equity, the allocation accounts for the relative contribution of resources, while the consideration of needs accounts for the relative absence of resources. In contrast, the principles of entitlement and equality share the reference to a given set of individuals and their relationship, which is hierarchical in the former and equal in status in the latter.

The contrast between external and internal referents of action in the rows of the $AGIL$ scheme has been conceptualized in sociological theory as the distinction between society (*Gesellschaft*) and community (*Gemeinschaft*) (Tönnies 1957 [1887], Weber (1968) [1921]), system integration and social integration (Lockwood 1964), or between system and lifeworld (Habermas 1984). Both market exchange and hierarchy are embedded in formal institutions that confront individuals as social facts (Durkheim 1982 [1895]), constituting purely functional relationships independent of mutual empathy and solidarity. In contrast, both solidary communities and networks or cooperatives generate a notion of belonging based on reciprocal relations between the members of society, thus producing a boundary between insiders and outsiders. Relationships are established between particular individuals or with reference to a particular group constituted by some grounds of commonality.

Besides differentiating rows and columns, there is also an observation to make about the diagonals of the matrix. According to Elster (1992, 68), allocative principles "fall into two major groups: those that do not make any reference to properties of the potential recipients and those that do." The justice principles in the two cells on the main diagonal, equity and equality, are abstract concepts which are potentially universally applicable. Equity posits a simple relationship of merit or desert between an individual contribution and a connected claim on a share in the common good or an exchange rate between two goods. The principle contains equality as both a boundary case and a default case in which there is no reason for differentiating between individual allocations. The two off-diagonal cells, in contrast, refer to particularistic claims. Neither needs nor entitlements invoke an unequivocal abstract justice principle, but require some notion of appropriateness. Claims about needs or entitlements are specific to the individual in two different senses. In a hierarchical structure, agents are entrenched in a particular power relation with denotable individuals in specific societal positions. Given the lack of a universal yardstick, entitlements are up to the beholder. In a solidary community based on mutual acquaintance, all members are expected by all other members to support those who lack a particular resource. In this sense, and seemingly paradoxical, we can differentiate needs from entitlements by their universalism in the application of a particularistic concept of allocation: Every member of the society is granted the right to the satisfaction of the same set of fundamental needs, whereas entitlements allow for a differentiation of needs according to status.

4.2.2 Diagnostics of Modern Societies

From a sociological point of view, most notably in its functionalist stream, the dominance of universalistic principles is the hallmark of modernity in comparison to the particularistic views of traditional societies (Arts and van der Veen 1992). Societal integration in systems characterized by democracy and capitalism relies on the notions of equality and equity, respectively, whereas the more traditional social integrative bonds of family and authority, with their associated principles of justice—need and entitlement—are considered archaic remnants of obsolete forms of integration. Universal principles of justice provide a normative yardstick for rational–legal legitimacy (Weber 1968 [1921]), thereby allowing for the disengagement of societal practices and interactions from concrete relational bonds (Polanyi 1944). However, universal principles necessarily target some average, which means that they disregard specific individual needs. Moreover, as Durkheim (1964 [1893], 289) has argued, the more abstract a norm is formulated, the more difficult is its application in a particular situation (Lindenberg 2008). Their application may thus generate conditions that conflict with other societal values, such as, in particular, humanity, solidarity, and care for less fortunate members of society.

With the increasing "disembedding" of the market from social contexts (Polanyi 1944), that is, the development of an own distinctive logic of economic interactions and the hegemony of economic thinking, the "neoliberal idea of the free-market individual" and "[t]he ideological notion of the self-sufficient individual ultimately implies the disappearance of any sense of mutual obligation—which is why neoliberalism inevitably threatens the welfare state" (Beck and Beck-Gernsheim 2002, xxi). Against this atomized view of the individual, the concept of *institutionalized individualism* entails the awareness of the "fundamental incompleteness of the self" that is a "product of complex, contingent and thus high-level socialization." Further, "[i]n developed modernity (...) human mutuality and community rest no longer on solidly established traditions, but, rather, on a paradoxical collectivity of reciprocal individualization" (Beck and Beck-Gernsheim 2002, xxi).

For Honneth (2014), the dominance of proceduralism that is mandated by the emphasis on formal equality in modern theories of justice following Rawls (1971) has a paradoxical side effect. The overarching postulate of equality marginalizes other principles of justice and thus undermines relationships of recognition. Mutual recognition is not a good that can be divided and allocated to group members, but is historically constituted as a relationship and based on the appreciation of each others' subjectivity. In that sense, the focus on equality in modern society fosters what Habermas (1984) has described by the metaphor of the "colonization of the lifeworld." While "modernization" is characterized by an increasing dominance of equity and equality, leaving aside as a societal norm the claim to entitlement by mere status, there seems to be a limit to the possibility to organize society according to universal principles of justice, implying an ongoing, or even increasing, relevance of the need principle. While in modern societies markets rely on equity and politics on equality of vote, both social spheres, that dominate both societal life and public discourse, ultimately rest on notions of justice that focus on the input side of the processes constituting their reproduction. From this perspective, differences in outcomes are irrelevant as long as the principle of equality of opportunity is met. Such a perspective, however, ignores power differences, societal stratification, and inequality in access to resources, which predetermine differences in outcomes despite formal equality of opportunity.

Another variant of the same diagnosis, which is informed by an empirical analysis based on extensive longitudinal data, discusses the subjugation of the "lifeworld" under the logic of economic thinking in terms of the "disintegration" of society: "The combination of bad socio-economic conditions and strong democratic deficits is usually perceived as a double injustice" (Imbusch and Heitmeyer 2012, 327 [transl. author]). If large sections of the population experience relative deprivation as unjust and consider core norms of society as unattainable, they either articulate discontent as support for right-wing parties or disappear from the public sphere in political apathy (Klein and Heitmeyer 2011, 380).

These diagnoses of modern society share the observation that different logics prevail in different societal spheres and that one logic, which emphasizes formal and anonymous modes of interaction and which requires a universal principle of justice, dominates other forms of interaction. This development, these authors claim, impairs mutual recognition and solidarity and thus gradually erodes the normative foundation of society, that is the perception of society as just.

4.3 The Need Principle as a Social Norm

The need principle has been the object of substantial dispute in political philosophy (Miller 1999; Brock 2013). Most notably, five arguments have been raised against the acceptance of needs as a foundation of justice. Needs have been said to conflict with justice because no universal list of needs can be generated, needs are difficult to distinguish from mere desires or wants, the satisfaction of needs interferes with other principles of justice, the principle may be abused in authoritarian ways, and needs are expensive to satisfy (Brock 2013, 445). While these criticisms have been refuted on philosophical as well as sociological grounds (Miller 1999; Brock 2013; Müller 1992), this list of concerns makes clear that need-based justice is a sociological problem in a more fundamental sense than the other principles of justice. The acceptance of a claim invoking a need must rely on a social process involving the collective recognition of individual wants and desires as legitimate grounds of allocation under scarcity.

4.3.1 The Concept of Need

Humans have heterogeneous needs and needs are inherently instrumental: A particular agent claims to need *X* in order to do *Y*. Both *X* and *Y* are open to challenges: The necessity of doing *Y* and the requirement of *X* for doing *Y* may be disputed by others. Allocation claims referring to needs thus are not unconditional rights derived from an abstract principle, but the acceptance of demands or wants as needs depends on a prior agreement about what is considered a legitimate need claim that is always up for renegotiation.

In everyday life, humans are capable of distinguishing veritable needs from mere desires or wants: "It is the belief that the satisfaction of basic needs has normative *precedence* over the satisfaction of wants that generates condemnation when such needs are not satisfied" (Doyal and Gough 1991, 3 [emph. orig.]). An attempt to identify a set of general needs based on the notion of "quality of life" has been developed by the "capabilities approach" (Sen 1973, 2000). In this vein, and abstracting from differences between individuals and cultures, Nussbaum (2000, 2011) has introduced the concept of *thresholds* for a set of human "functionings" that are required for a dignified life: "[A]ll should get above a certain threshold level of combined capability, in the sense not of coerced functioning but of substantial freedom to choose and act" (Nussbaum 2011, 24). This idea is operationalized into ten "central capabilities" (Nussbaum 2011, 33–34), being "life," "bodily health," "bodily integrity," "senses, imagination, and thought," "emotions," "practical reason," "affiliation," "other species," "play," and "control over one's environment." She then insists on the attribution of these capabilities to individual persons instead of groups, but acknowledges the possibility of deriving group capabilities from the individual ones (Nussbaum 2011, 35).

Apart from a core of "intrinsic" needs, a wide range of "instrumental" needs, which go beyond the capabilities described above, may be articulated (Miller 1999, 206–213). With respect to "instrumental" needs, however, Miller rejects both such an objective standard and a particularistic option deriving the concept of need from subjective preferences. Instead, he suggests that consensus about legitimate "instrumental" needs is generated by reference to social norms defining a "minimally decent life" in a particular society (Miller 1999, 210). Depending on the natural and social environment of the society, such norms may vary. Thus, the only relevant criterion for need to count is that "members of the society have agreed that it should count" (Miller 1999, 225). Once more, as Hegtvedt (2005, 25) formulates, "[j]ustice is not simply in the eyes of an individual beholder, but it is in the eyes of a community, however defined."

The instrumentality of needs implies that, at least to some extent, the concept of need-based justice depends on other principles of justice: the postulate of equality implies that those subjects who have less than the equal share have a legitimate claim to an allocation equalizing the shares. In other words, they are in need of the difference between the actual and the ideal state. In the above formulation, *Y* would be an equal share and *X* would be an additional allocation. Thus, it is the idea of outcome equality under the condition of heterogeneous endowments that motivates the need principle (Eckhoff 1974). Similarly, the equity principle implies that all endowments lower than the deserved share have to be amended by additional allocations. However, the need principle differs from equality and equity in the sense of referring to an exogenous standard that is neither related to relative performance nor to a universal sharing norm. A need-based claim generates a right of relief irrespective of prior contributions. Needs vary over time and across individuals and are unrelated to earlier effort (Sen 1973, 104). The invocation of needs thus departs from the "objective" conception of equality in taking into account different starting conditions of group members in a specific situation. In this sense, need-based justice relies on a particular and subjective notion of equality: "Allotments need not here be objectively the same size but they must, in some manner, be subjectively equal from the recipient's point of view" (Eckhoff 1974, 36).

Reflecting particular conditions, the invocation of needs offers a compromise between the principles of equity, which, in its pure form, is likely to produce starvation of those who cannot contribute to the common good, and equality, which curtails individual incentives to contribute to the common good. This argument has been popularized as "Boulding's principle" (Traub et al. 2005): "We face the dilemma (...) that if everyone gets his deserts, some may be driven from the table, and if everyone comes to the table, some may not get their deserts. In practice, this seems to be resolved by the establishment of a social minimum as reflected for instance, in the poor law, in social security and various welfare services. The principle of desert may come into play above this social minimum. That is to say, society lays a modest table at which all can sup and a high table at which the deserving can feast" (Boulding 1962, 83).

As a principle, need-based justice is a distinct type of justice. When it comes to its practical specification, however, it does not only depend on, but can also be expected to appear in combination with other principles of justice. It specifies the minimum allocation that an individual can legitimately claim.

4.3.2 The Social Recognition of Needs

These reflections raise the question of how a community recognizes need claims as legitimate. If justice is the manifestation of autonomy, which is a relational concept, then it is realized through respect, that is, the mutual recognition of each others' needs, persuasions, and capabilities (Honneth 2012, Chap. 4). By its relational nature, recognition presupposes "parity of participation": "If and when such patterns constitute actors as peers, capable of participating on a par with one another in social life, then we can speak of reciprocal recognition and status equality. (...) From this perspective, misrecognition is (...) an institutionalized relation of social subordination" (Fraser 2000, 113–115).

Any social order entails a particular distribution of access to, and participation in, collective decision-making. Needs must be articulated in public, require interpretation in a given context, and are contested between different agents who may struggle over the political status of particular needs, over their interpretation, and over their satisfaction by the provision of specific resources (Fraser 1989, 294). Needs may be articulated "from below" by advocacy groups or "from above" by policy-makers and experts, giving rise to different types of public discourses. Claims may be raised in opposition to the hegemonic discourse, may be shifted into the realm of experts, or may be "reprivatized" (Fraser 1989, 303), hence silenced. Building on this emphasis on discourses about needs, we can thus distinguish two phases in the societal articulation of needs that are separated by a collective decision in which needs are collectively recognized: in the first phase, particular need claims are articulated and generalized into a demand for a universal rule establishing a right, in the second phase the general rule is applied in the assessment of individual claims (Tranow 2013).

The emphasis on social norms is important for understanding the relationship between need-based justice and humanitarianism. Both target the relief from suffering. A social norm stating need as a principle of justice establishes both a right of the recipient to obtain the resources to satisfy the need and an obligation on the part of others to support the needy person (Miller 1999, 76). A humanitarian act, instead, is purely voluntary and grounded in a moral of benevolence (Barnett 2011). The type and amount of humanitarian support is determined by the donor, whereas the potential recipient cannot claim a right to the relief of a specific need. Humanitarian support thus depends on a benevolent person to address the need. As soon as humanitarianism becomes a social norm, however, it entails the promise and expectation that each member of the community will benefit from others' adherence to the norm. It is thus difficult in practice to distinguish a humanitarian motive of need-based justice from a norm of reciprocity promising mutual insurance against certain specified forms of hardship (Schwartz 1975, 132).

The crux is in the double conditionality entailed in the mutuality principle: For one, members of a community expect help from the other members, including current recipients of support, in case of their own potential need at a later point in time (Sinn 1995). But in addition, support is conditional on the willingness of welfare recipients to do their best to leave their condition (Goodin 2002). These mutual expectations, which can be seen as an instance of weak reciprocity, are perfectly compatible with the assumption of self-interest under conditions of uncertainty about others' behavior. Collectivities thus have to balance the benefit of the public good of an insurance system against the danger that this will provide incentives to free-ride on the others' contributions.

Bowles and Gintis (2000, 37 [emph. orig.]) propose that societies solve this problem by relying on reciprocity. The claim that "*strong reciprocity*, along with *basic needs generosity*, not unconditional altruism, better explains the motivations that account for the political success of the welfare state." However, in a thorough reflection of the behavioral economics literature on reciprocity, Guala (2012) argues that the evidence supporting the existence of the strong version of reciprocity, which relies on costly punishment, in natural environments is still unconvincing. Instead, he suggests, the empirical literature finds that societies develop means of sustaining cooperation that rely on local, cheap, and coordinated institutions, which are characteristic of weak reciprocity. Similarly, doubts about the very existence of a preference for fairness continue to abound, given that prosocial behavior declines as soon as some "moral wiggle room" is present in anonymity or no reputational gains can be obtained from fair behavior (Dana et al. 2007; Franzen and Pointner 2012). Berger (2013) concludes from the existing evidence that strong, or—in his terms—altruistic, reciprocity may indeed be a genetic disposition acquired by humans in the course of evolution (Fehr and Fischbacher 2003), and thus a fundamental human motivation, in *targeted* reciprocal relationships. In undirected constellations, however, strong reciprocity seems to be at work only in low-cost situations. This may explain the observable patterns of altruistic behavior and the restriction of its empirical observation to either small, solidary communities based on emotional ties in which members have extensive information about each other, or to laboratory experiments.

Thus, transforming humanitarianism into a principle of need-based justice, requires collective recognition of a need as a legitimate claim (Schwartz 1975), which is conditional on mechanisms to avoid free riding. While small groups rely on intimate knowledge about each other and mutual observance, or, to put it in Durkheim's terms, "mechanical solidarity," larger groups need institutional mechanisms to prevent reciprocal behavior from being crowded out by exploitation (Olson 1965). It is this dilemma which explains why the principle of need-based justice is rooted in solidary communities and why it risks degenerating into a system of means-tested transfers while pushing welfare recipients into labor market activity in larger societies.

4.3.3 Social Conditions of Need Recognition

As was argued above, need-based justice entails the idea that all members of a society are entitled to the consumption of a certain basket of goods, or, put otherwise, a certain standard of living. At this point, it is important to explicitly address the distinction between needs and entitlements. Although needs materialize in social interaction as entitlements, they are distinguished from the latter by referring to some quasi-universal standard derived from a common understanding of what constitutes a "minimally decent life." There is thus a universal foundation in the recognition of needs. Entitlements, in contrast, reflect position-based needs in the sense of a societal acceptance of a specific endowment related to the holder's position in a societal hierarchy. All members of society have a legitimate claim on the means of subsistence, but a chief may be legitimately entitled to a larger share of the prey because of his social status. This is a variant of Boulding's principle, wherein merit is replaced by status.

Need generates a power differential in which a person requiring a resource is at a disadvantage with respect to an endowed person. Fulfilling the needs of others by a humanitarian act is a gift and thus generates a power asymmetry between giver and taker. If the expression of needs is bidirectional, the mutual satisfaction of need establishes a symmetric and reciprocal relationship among equals (Gouldner 1960;

Blau 1964). If it is unidirectional, the implied transfer of power generates a hierarchical relationship, in which the poorer partner trades a resource at her disposition, such as loyalty, for need satisfaction. The recipient of the gift satisfying the need will thus carry an obligation to repay the incurred debt in any currency available to that person (Mauss 1968 [1902–03]). In this way, the principle of need-based justice may foster the establishment of a hierarchical relationship: Different societal strata may be attributed socially recognized claims to entitlements of different size, which are legitimized by accumulated "credit" from earlier occasions in which richer people have supported poorer members of the community (Simmel 1989 [1900]).

More than the other principles of justice, the acceptance of need-based justice depends on the legitimacy of procedures. For the criteria to be acceptable to all in societies larger than small-scale groups such as families or clans, or, for that matter, the one-hour "societies" in experimental laboratories, some mechanism of mutual verification of adherence to the principle of justice defining individual relations must be in place.

Most famously, Habermas (1996) has emphasized the importance of publicly exchanged honest arguments that are freely stated and based on good reasons referring to potentially universal justifications as a precondition for a just society. Such an ideal discourse can be used as a yardstick for the evaluation of actual practices, although it is, as he himself admits, unrealistic to expect it to be established in the "real world" (Steiner et al. 2004). Nevertheless, this argument clearly links the justice of outcomes to the procedures leading to the outcome. Procedural justice with respect to the distribution of resources according to needs has been most extensively discussed in the field of health care (Landwehr 2013). Daniels and Sabin (1997, 323) have proposed four conditions of procedural justice that "capture the essential elements in achieving legitimate and fair coverage decisions (...)," these being (1) public accessibility, (2) reasonableness, (3) mechanisms for the revision of decisions, and (4) regulations ensuring that these three conditions are met. Whereas the latter two conditions require formal procedural rules, conditions (1) and (2) have implications for the procedure leading to the recognition of needs: "Condition 1 requires openness or publicity, that is, transparency about reasons for a decision. Condition 2 involves some constraints on the kinds of reasons that can play a role in the rationale: it recognizes the fundamental interest all parties have in finding a justification all can accept as reasonable" (Daniels and Sabin 1997, 323).

Summing up, the present literature suggests that need-based justice is a social norm that relies on a collective consensus about the eligibility criteria that extends beyond humanitarian support by constituting a legitimate claim that is based on reciprocal expectations to get one's needs fulfilled. The need principle goes beyond equity and equality by recognizing individual particularities as a reason for departing from strict proportionality. It is a formally unconditional right, but, at the same time, it generates a duty of the recipient toward the community at the informal level. Other members of the community expect any form of reciprocation, such as some effort to overcome the condition of need or the willingness to support others at a later point in time. The satisfaction of needs is thus embedded in exchange relationships. In addition, given the high demands on the recognition of individual need claims by the group, some procedural conditions may facilitate the establishment of recognized allocation principles, in particular as groups become larger.

These considerations motivate some expectations that can serve as broad, guiding hypotheses for empirical research. First, reference to the need principle should be observed in solidary communities, not in markets, hierarchies, networks, or cooperatives. It should also vary with the extent to which social relations are defined as solidary. Second, reference to the need principle should be more frequently observed in long-term, proximate relations and it should decline with rising social distance. And third, a need claim *X* will be satisfied if a need *Y* is socially recognized as a right.

4.4 Three Perspectives on Need-Based Justice

Fehr and Gintis (2007, 44) have noted, in one of the very few discussions of sociological thought by economists, that

> sociological theory has not developed a coherent, broadly accepted framework that facilitates cumulative scientific progress and explains the emergent aggregate patterns of social behavior in terms of individuals' preferences, their beliefs, and the social and economic constraints they face. Nor has sociological research developed a parsimonious, empirically grounded view of the basic motivational driving forces of human behavior, which may be due to the limited role that controlled experiments played in the development of the discipline.

As a cure, they suggested the "Beliefs, Preferences, and Constraints" (BPC) approach, which happens to be closely related to the "Desires, Beliefs, and Opportunities" (DBO) approach introduced a few years earlier by analytical sociology (Hedström 2005).

Fehr and Gintis (2007, 46) acknowledge the sociological theory of social value internalization but argue that this approach "neither explains how individuals adjudicate between satisfying personal material needs and social obligations nor clarifies the conditions under which individuals accept and reject alternative normative principles." In particular, Fehr and Gintis (2007) elaborate on the conditions under which self-regarding and other-regarding preferences dominate individual action. Core elements of their proposal include the concepts of conditional cooperation, reciprocity, and fairness. These traits are conceptualized as properties of individual preferences and the resulting behavior.

In a response to this expansion of economics into core topics of sociology Diekmann (2008) and Simpson and Willer (2015, 45) argue that cooperation and prosocial behavior are promoted by "three broad classes of social mechanisms—rules, reputations, and relations." These mechanisms help to induce otherwise self-regarding individuals to conform to other-regarding norms in a community, by prescribing certain behaviors and sanctioning their violation either institutionally or by means of collective disapproval and reputation loss, or by embedding individuals in a closer knit network of mutually reinforcing trust relations.

While the two perspectives converge with respect to the elements highlighted in the analytical framework, they diverge with respect to the relative emphasis of individual agency and social conditions (Pointner and Frantzen 2015, 745). Most notably in the present context, in behavioral economics reciprocity is conceptualized as a specific type of behavior: "Reciprocity is a behavioral response to perceived kindness and unkindness" (Falk and Fischbacher 2006, 294). The source of reciprocity is thus believed to reside within the individual as part of the natural endowment of humans. Whether it is an internalized social norm or a genetically inherited constant of human nature may be subject to some controversy (Fehr and Fischbacher 2003; Richerson and Boyd 2005). In any case, from this perspective the crucial agent, and thus object of analysis, is the individual. In stark contrast, a sociological perspective views reciprocity as a structural property of a relationship: "Reciprocity, the giving of benefits to another in return for benefits received, is a defining feature of social exchange" (Molm et al. 2007a, 199). From this perspectives, the source agency is external to the individual: the normative power, or "social fact," of the rule of reciprocity induces individuals to behave reciprocally in a context mandating this behavior irrespective of the exact individual source of motivation.

Within the framework of a multilevel view of society (Coleman 1986; Hedström and Swedberg 1996; Liebig and Sauer 2016) sociological analyses of justice can take three different perspectives derived from the three social mechanisms identified above. This distinction echoes the classical philosophical approach to think in terms of three stages—thesis, antithesis, and synthesis (Hegel 1986 [1820])—and the fundamental psychological classification of the self into the individual, the relational, and the collective self (Sedikides and Brewer 2001) in terms of different levels of aggregation in the social sciences. At the individual level, attitudes toward justice and motivations to adhere to particular principles of justice in specific situations are the main object of interest. At the relational level, the focus is on actual behavior in interaction with other people in mostly small groups. The question is, which justice principles guide interactions and under which conditions does the need principle become relevant? Finally, at the collective level, the way societal institutions operationalize principles of justice becomes the main topic of interest. I will discuss each level in turn, thereby broadening the view to contributions from neighboring disciplines, although maintaining the specifically sociological three-level framework.

4.4.1 *The Individual Perspective: Attitudes Toward Need-Based Justice*

Individual attitudes toward justice have been studied in two ways (Gaertner and Schokkaert 2012; Clark and D'Ambrosio 2015). Mostly psychologists and economists have used decision experiments to explore choices in hypothetical or incentivized situations involving trade-offs between different principles of justice. Sociology has a stronger tradition in survey research on the perception of and attitudes towards inequality and justice.

Any evaluation of distributive justice can be framed in the abstract as a statement about the relationship between the actual share and the share that is considered just by whatever criterion the evaluator considers relevant. This idea has been framed by Jasso (1980) in terms of a general formula, $J = \ln(A/C)$, where J denotes the subjective justice evaluation, A the actual share, and C the share that is regarded as just. The problem here is in the determination of the C term. The definition of the just share is left unspecified in this general model and can actually be filled by any conception of distributive justice.

The need principle appears to play a considerable role in individual allocation decisions in hypothetical distribution tasks entailing differentiation (Törnblom and Foa 1983). Typically, vignettes describe the profiles of two persons and vary a criterion invoking a need, such as the price of a required good or some biological capacity. Respondents participating in such questionnaire experiments depart from equal allocations as soon as they are informed about relative need levels. In an impartial observer setting where subjects are asked to divide a hypothetical sum of money between two recipients with different need levels, Lamm and Schwinger (1980, 427) observe three focal distributions: an equal one disregarding needs, one exactly covering the need level of the other person and allocating all excess to self, and a third one satisfying both need levels while allocating the excess equally to both. Further studies showed that the extent to which needs are taken into account depends on the social proximity of the involved persons, on relative contributions, and the sufficiency of the available resource to meet all needs (Schwinger and Lamm 1981; Lamm and Schwinger 1983). In a similar experimental design, allocations typically closely match the need level, although there is some variation depending on the exact formulation of the decision problem with respect to the allocation mechanism applied (Yaari and Bar-Hillel 1984). In a vignette study, Scott and Bornstein (2009) show that framing a hypothetical allocation decision in terms of an exogenous disaster such as a flood, need becomes the most prominent principle for distributing resources irrespective of the type of resource, although the effect is more pronounced for medicine and food than for money. A similar finding is reported in Kause et al. (2018).

A second line of research relevant to the study of justice preferences uses monetary incentives and implements need in the context of dictator games. It shows that needs are considered by at least some of the dictators. For example, both the characterization of the recipient as "poor" and the information that the recipient lives in a poor country raise the amount transferred to the recipient (Brañas-Garza 2006; Cappelen et al. 2013). However, given that these needs are not conceptualized as a right, these experiments do not address need as a principle of justice, but as a humanitarian act. Further studies compare the relative popularity of payoff distributions representing different principles of justice before and after lifting the Rawlsian veil of ignorance (Frohlich and Oppenheimer 1992). The task of the participants is to rank a set of proposed distributions individually and in groups. Although none of the selected distributions raises the issue of needs directly, one of them comes close to this principle by combining a floor income for all group members with a distribution that maximizes average income. As transcripts of the experimental chat sessions show, participants interpreted this distribution rule in terms of need (Frohlich and

Oppenheimer 1992, 61–64). But as soon as basic needs are covered, other principles become more prevalent.

Subsequent work in this tradition added nuance to the original findings. Women and liberals appear to be more sensitive to need concerns than men and conservatives (Scott et al. 2001; Michelbach et al. 2003). Herne and Suojanen (2004) find that the floor constraint is the most popular distribution only behind the veil of ignorance. In the informed control condition, a less efficient Rawlsian distribution maximizing the lowest payoff obtains the most votes. Similarly, Traub et al. (2005, 305) observe: "The impressive performance of Boulding's standard of behavior illustrates that people exhibit a propensity to trade off the chances of admitting more inequality against the risk of being among the worst off in society." This finding is particularly suggestive for the analysis of the need principle because it points to the importance of the insurance motive under uncertainty. Similarly, d'Anjou et al. (1995) observe that self-interest and ideology, next to age, help to predict justice attitudes. Attitudes toward distributive justice may be motivated by merit and need. Merit is invoked as a justification for reward heterogeneity related to effort, while need is tied to the motive to honor investment even if the intended contribution failed to materialize (d'Anjou et al. 1995, 377).

In contrast to these approaches using measures of intention or behavior in circumscribed situations and using a restricted sample of mostly students, sociologists have used items in large-scale cross-national surveys to measure justice perceptions and attitudes. Most notably, the *International Social Justice Project* (ISJP) has fielded four waves over the period 1991–2007 in several, though varying, countries (Wegener and Mason 2002; Wegener 2006, 2015) and became the seed of a strong sociological tradition of empirical justice research at the Humboldt University in Berlin (Wegener 1987; Jasso and Wegener 1997; Müller and Wegener 1995). Next to other dimensions of justice, the questionnaire contains several items evaluating aspects of need-based justice, covering the extent to which household income meets needs, the relevance of the size of the family an employee supports in the judgment of normative and actual determinants of pay, and the role of the government in guaranteeing a minimum standard of living for everyone. Furthermore, respondents are confronted with an item directly relating to the perception of need ("In COUNTRY, people get what they need.") and one on the normative attitude toward need as a principle of justice ("The most important thing is that people get what they need, even if this means allocating money from those who have earned more than they need"). Several of these items are also administered as part of the social inequality module of the *International Social Survey Programme* (ISSP), and some are also used in the *European Social Survey* (ESS).

Initial studies of the ISJP data suggest that need is one of three core criteria that are actually used for the evaluation of justice: "[O]ur results point toward respondents articulating established attitudes to distributive justice, although rather broad ones; namely, those of equality of outcome, justified inequalities, and need" (Swift et al. 1995, 34). In addition, the importance attributed by respondents to need as a principle of justice affects the support for government intervention for redistribution (Kluegel and Miyano 1995). The individual evaluation of the justice of relative income levels also reflects, among other factors, the relevance of needs: the less need, operationalized as family size, is considered relevant, the higher is the income that a respondent considers just for a chairman or managing director of a large corporation (Arts et al. 1995, 143).

The populations of formerly communist countries appear to diverge with respect to the extent of their normative adjustment to market systems. While a trend toward market-oriented justice norms is observed in the Czech Republic and former East Germany, public opinion in Bulgaria, Hungary, and Russia remained largely in the socialist normative framework (Kluegel et al. 1999). Nevertheless, in all mentioned countries, positional differences became more important as determinants of justice attitudes from 1991 to 1996 (Verwiebe and Wegener 2000).

The German ISJP data show that, despite initial indications to the contrary, justice perceptions in the Eastern and Western part have not converged (Wegener and Liebig 2000, 2010). Gerlitz et al. (2012) show that the perceived justice of the distribution system has declined between 1991 and 2006, in particular, though starting from a generally higher level than in the formerly communist part, in the Western part of the country. This holds for the observation of equal opportunities as well as for perceived justness of rewards for effort and skills. An exception to this overall declining trend, however, is the largely stable, although somewhat fluctuating, evolution of the perception that the consideration of needs is just. In particular, a substantial increase in average appreciation of the need-satisfying nature of the distribution system is observed between 1996 and 2001. Unfortunately, the authors do not elaborate on this specific aspect of popular justice perceptions in Germany.

Further results from these comparative surveys underscore the popularity of the Boulding principle. Averaged over the countries participating in this project, the equity principle is supported by a large majority of the respondents, the need principle by about half, and the equity principle by less than a quarter (Aalberg 2003, 44). Thus, merit is an uncontroversial foundation of justice perceptions, but many people wish to attenuate the implications of this principle for those who fail to attain a sufficient allocation for survival by a floor constraint. This finding is robust across surveys, countries, and time (Aalberg 2003, 47–50). In this vein, in-depth interviews reveal that both higher and lower class individuals perceive inequality due to merit a moral imperative but deplore, at the same time, the injustice of both poverty and extreme wealth (Sachweh 2012). Further studies emphasize the core position of the meritocratic principle in modern Western societies, and suggest that individual support for the equity principle also depends on the extent to which a country has adopted a distribution system based on meritocratic principles (Kunovich and Slomczynski 2007; Sachweh and Olafsdottir 2012).

A study using ESS data for 24 European countries finds that preferences depend on individual achievement. Wealthier strata of the population tend to favor either the equity or the equality principle, conditional on welfare programs and institutional design: "[E]quality prevails for provisions that cover less predictable and controllable social risks, whereas equity tends to matter more in the case of provisions that cover social risks that can be foreseen and are regarded as personal responsibility" (Reeskens and van Oorschot 2013, 1190). In contrast, people with low income do not differentiate that much between equity and equality, but instead are considerably more concerned about establishing and maximizing minimum standards in accordance with the need principle.

Turning to attitudes toward need as a criterion of allocations, research has primarily addressed healthcare services. For example, according to ISSP data, popular attitudes toward the use of person-based priority criteria such as age, care responsibilities, and health-related behavior, for access to health care vary considerably between countries, but in only few countries a majority would be in favor of differentiating with respect to these criteria (Rogge and Kittel 2016).

Further recent work in this tradition has focused on developing more precise measures of justice attitudes by using factorial surveys (Liebig et al. 2015) and by introducing the Basic Social Justice Orientations (BSJO) scale that is based on an item battery easy to build into population surveys (Hülle et al. 2017). Both approaches include elements referring to needs. The *European Social Survey* Round 9 (2018) includes a module on justice and fairness in Europe that has been coordinated by Stefan Liebig.[2]

Finally, a few studies have approached the analysis of justice-related welfare attitudes with qualitative methods. Using focus groups, Dwyer (2000) has explored opinions on welfare rights in the United Kingdom, one of the countries that has most strongly engaged in market-oriented public management reforms. He concluded: "What they [the respondents] objected to were the principles and practices of the market being imposed on public welfare provision. These are seen as being incompatible with both the substantive social rights and the notions of social justice that the users view as integral to their vision(s) of citizenship" (Dwyer 2000, 194). Most notably, in their evaluation of welfare rights, citizens clearly distinguish between areas: "[W]hen comparing the three areas of welfare that are under scrutiny in this study (healthcare, housing, and social security), it is apparent that the degree to which the users are willing to accept the principle of conditional welfare rights depends extensively on the context of their imposition" (Dwyer 2000, 194). Whereas unconditional health care is almost unanimously supported, housing and financial support for persons in need is typically made dependent on good behavior and prior contributions.

The results of a similar study on social attitudes based on focus groups in the UK are summarized as follows: "People appear to apply separate principles of 'fairness' and 'mutuality' to the structures of taxation and public spending. Fairness in taxation may involve more progressivity than the current system, and those with low incomes may need more help. The support this implies for the redistributive impact of government does not appear to be primarily motivated by concerns about making incomes more equal, but rather the outcome of belief in a system in which everyone can get help when they need it, and everyone contributes according to their means" (Hedges 2005, iv).

---

[2]The data are available at http://www.europeansocialsurvey.org/data/.

The findings from the *British Social Attitudes Survey* suggest that these sentiments and attitudes can be generalized: "[M]ost people support the principles of social justice, but have reservations when it comes to paying more tax, particularly if it is intended primarily to help the poor. Views are complex, and support for greater fairness, a social minimum and more equal opportunities appears to be much stronger in relation to some groups than others. The extent of need is relevant—those with children are more likely to be supported—but, at the same time, groups which are seen to be contributing to society in some way, rather than just being passive recipients of welfare are also likely to be favoured" (Taylor-Gooby 2005, 2).

With respect to the individual level of justice attitudes, which are mostly studied in experiments and surveys, the evidence suggests that adherence to the principle of need-based justice is indeed dependent on emotional proximity. It is most prominently evoked in close, solidary relationships and communities, although there seems to be broad consensus that societies should provide the means for some sort of "minimally decent life," which, however, may be restricted to accepted members of the society and which may be perceived as being conditional on prior behavior and mutuality. The need principle is thus bounded by some criterion of membership. Moreover, in surveys need is more important to respondents with a higher risk of being in need. In that sense, the invocation of the need principle may be less driven by humanitarianism than by the insurance motive, which is ultimately based on self-interest.

4.4.2 The Relational Perspective: Need-Based Justice in Social Interaction

In the literature on social exchange networks, research has focused on the distribution of assets and endowments conditional on the structure of the network (Neuhofer et al. 2015). In contrast to the studies on hypothetical decisions and attitudes discussed in Sect. 4.4.1, this section focuses on actual behavior in interaction situations involving distributive and allocative decisions. Although relative allocations in distributive tasks have thus been the core research topic in this field, neither the attitudes underlying the decisions nor the implications for justice have been a major area of study. Nevertheless, in an ongoing stream of studies justice-related aspects of exchange networks have been explored (Cook and Hegtvedt 1983; Hegtvedt and Markovsky 1995; Hegtvedt 2005). Typically, need-based justice is discussed as one of several principles that are relevant under specific conditions only.

A prime condition of the applicability of the concept of justice is that social relations involve "a minimal degree of actual, normatively expected or potential cooperation" (Deutsch 1975, 141). In line with the typology elaborated in Sect. 4.2, different aims of cooperation—enhancing productivity, fostering enjoyable social relations, and fostering personal development and welfare—are associated with different justice conceptions. Whereas the first two aims refer to equity and equality, respectively, the reference to need-based justice is the dominant principle in the latter context (Deutsch 1975, 146). The clause that mutual help in case of need is a "natural duty" of the members of a group (Rawls 1971) "is intensified in relation to those for whose personal development and welfare we are responsible, such as those who are legitimately dependent upon us," which is observed, for example, in families, schools, or hospitals (Deutsch 1975, 146).

These fundamental insights have been further elaborated in two different directions. One line of thought, which has its roots in social psychology, takes the notion of responsibility as a point of departure and interprets the need principle not only as an individual attitude, but "as a norm ruling all transactions of resources in interpersonal relationships of identity, high interdependence, and intimacy" (Schwinger 1986, 216). Given the low potential for conflict over resources, interdependent and intimate relations based on affection provide the most appropriate context for equalizing heterogeneous endowments by reference to need (Greenberg and Cohen 1982; Törnblom 1992). According to this view, mutually taking responsibility for the other is a manifestation of social cohesion: "When we feel identified with others, our typical justice preference will be based in the entitlements of need" (Ellard et al. 2016, 130).

The other line of thought, which is more specifically a product of sociology, focuses on the notion of structural dependency. The idea that the need principle entails a situation of power-dependency has been most explicitly elaborated by Stolte (1987). After differentiating power-balanced from power-imbalanced networks, Stolte argues that the latter may give rise to either predatory or protective coalitions. A predatory coalition is characterized by the exploitation of the subordinate by the powerful, who consensually develop a status-preserving conception of entitlement-based justice legitimizing the inequality in endowments and profits benefiting the powerful. A protective coalition, instead, aims at redistributing resources from the richer to the poorer, "taking from actors who previously have enjoyed a structural advantage and exchange-ratio privilege, giving to those who have previously suffered structural disadvantage and exchange-ratio deprivation" (Stolte 1987, 781). He then argues, without further explication but alluding to Marx' famous statement, that this redistribution will be framed in terms of a justice norm of "consummatory need": "From each actor in the exchange network according to her accumulated privilege, to each actor in the structure according to her (subsistence) need" (Stolte 1987, 781).

Experimental studies on power structures in networks have consistently shown that individuals make use of the power assigned to them in order to extract a larger share in exchange relations, but they are restrained if the interaction is framed in terms of solidary community (Cook et al. 2013; Molm 2014). Nevertheless, the position of an individual in the social structure strongly influences the willingness to redistribute endowments (Cabrales et al. 2011; Esarey et al. 2012, Kittel et al. 2015), and self-interest remains the decisive motivating factor of decisions (Durante et al. 2014; Kittel et al. 2017).

Note the difference in perspective underlying the two notions of need-based justice: Whereas Deutsch (1975) conceptualizes redistributive allocations as voluntary transfers echoing the humanitarian conception in an affectionate environment (Schwartz 1975), Stolte (1987) additionally brings in a revolutionary impetus of forced extraction from the well-endowed group members. Given that the satisfaction of needs is a fundamental requirement of survival, the failure to provide the means of a "minimally decent life" breeds unrest and revolution in a society. Thus, adherence to the principle of need-based justice entails an element of preservation of the given societal order. As a principle, it defines minimal allocations required for the maintenance of the social structure and thus may serve to stabilize inequality.

Need-based justice thus seems to become prevalent at the extreme ends of the continuum between consensual and conflictual social relations. Although Stolte (1987, 781) refers to other justice principles, such as equity and equality, in this context, he does not specify a reason for his claim that a revolutionary coalition will emphasize need as the dominant principle underlying the internal distribution of resources extracted from the better-off. If the first line of reasoning discussed above is correct, Stolte's "protective coalition" in its revolutionary form must also develop some amount of internal cohesion for need to be accepted as a criterion for the distribution of resources. In that sense, this coalition must constitute a new "society" based on interdependence and intimacy to allow for need to become a legitimate principle of justice.

Although social exchange theory has not focused specifically on issues relating to justice, various findings are pertinent to the sociological study of need-based justice. Most notably, structural conditions of reciprocity and solidarity (Molm et al. 2007a, 2013; Thye et al. 2011) and affective relationships and relational cohesion in networks (Lawler 2001; Lawler et al. 2008) are important correlates of justice perceptions that may particularly inform work on need-based justice. Nevertheless, this literature has developed ideas about the structural preconditions for the establishment of affective relationships in a group that may form the fundament of justice perceptions. Defining social solidarity as "the integrative bonds that develop between persons, and between persons and the social units to which they belong" (Molm et al. 2007a, 207), the concept is further elaborated into the dimensions trust, affective regard, social unity, and feelings of commitment. In all four dimensions group solidarity increases when shifting from a negotiated form of exchange to a reciprocal form, and further to a generalized form (Molm et al. 2007a, 231). Thus, successful interaction under less controllable—and thus more risky—conditions fosters the evolution of solidarity in a group. The "gift" of trust as a "first step" generates an obligation to adhere to the norms of reciprocity and fairness (Adloff and Mau 2006, 109), which may set in motion a virtuous cycle in which reciprocity and solidarity reinforce each other. In turn, one can hypothesize, both the emotional proximity of solidary relationships and trust-enhancing structures of interaction foster the acceptance of need as a criterion of justice.

The literature focusing on the relational level, which is predominantly experimental, is very explicit in its insistence on social proximity and relational cohesion as a precondition for the consideration and satisfaction of needs in small groups. Perhaps the most important addition to the discussion of attitudes at the individual level is the introduction of structure in the sense of dependency relationships. Being needy means depending on others for subsistence, which gives those others power that they can use either in a benevolent or exploitative manner. With an eye to the typology presented in Sect. 4.2, this consideration leads to an important further aspect of need-based justice: Lacking reciprocity, the need principle may well degenerate into power- and status-dependent entitlements.

4.4.3 The Collective Perspective: Justice in Welfare Regimes

Turning to the societal level, issues of distributive justice turn up with respect to the organization of the welfare state. Systems of alleviating the consequences of poverty by a redistributive mechanism can be conceptualized as public goods aimed at avoiding popular unrest or criminality (De Swaan 1988). Historically, poor relief has been the source of the modern conception of the welfare state. For example, the alleviation of the lot of those who can barely survive by providing basic needs was the main motivation of the English Speenhamland system installed in 1795, which established wage supplements funded by local landowners and the parish and which aimed at mitigating the disruptions of the economic changes involved in the rapid industrialization of England, although the system turned out not to be sustainable and the British poor law of 1834 reinstalled workhouses as a means of keeping the poor off the streets (Thompson 1963; Polanyi 1944). Thus, although one cannot rule out the presence of altruistic motives in individual cases, the overall system has an important strategic component of containing potential threats to the established order and the rich strata of society.

Likewise, the introduction of the Bismarckian mandatory social security system in Germany from 1883 onwards has been explicitly aimed at preventing poverty-induced social unrest, but it was also meant to undermine voluntary insurance pools installed by trade unions and Christian workers organizations (Sigerist 1999 [1943]). Access to this contribution-based system is restricted to people in the labor force whose cash benefits are meant to be status-preserving, thus adding an element of entitlement to the need criterion. This contrasts with the social security system introduced in Britain by Lord Beveridge, which is a tax-funded system that provides uniform and flat-rate benefits to the whole population (van der Zee and Kroneman 2007; Rohwer 2008) and leaves any provision beyond the coverage of basic needs to the market. These two approaches have inspired the various systems installed in the European countries and worldwide (Pestieau 2006; Hu and Manning 2010).

Justice principles have been a core building block of the seminal classification of welfare regimes into three "ideal types," that is, the social-democratic, conservative, and liberal models (Sachweh 2016). Reference to de-commodification, which fosters equality, and stratification, which relates to entitlements, in the differentiation of these three regimes (Esping-Andersen 1990) underlines that the way institutions structure and influence the allocation and distribution of resources embodies specific principles of justice.

The universal social programs of the *social-democratic* welfare regime aim at equalizing both opportunities and outcomes and can thus be considered a "high road" variant of the Beveridge system. Citizens have equal access to a generous and strongly decommodifying public welfare system that is financed through high taxes.

In contrast, the hallmark of the *conservative* regime is its reliance on income replacement provided by a social insurance system of the Bismarckian type. Access to social benefits largely depends on prior contributions and payments are proportional to contributions, which, in turn, depend on prior income levels. Thus a strong element of equity is built into this regime, which, quite intentionally, results in a status-preserving effect of the system. Access thus does not depend on citizenship, but on usually mandatory insurance which, in turn, depends on participation in the labor market. This demarcation generates an insider–outsider distinction based on labor, which mandates a different solution for those not in formal paid employment. Access to social services for nonworking adult family members and children relies on their family relationship with an employed person, which generates specific dependencies and reinforces hierarchical structures both in the society and in the family.

Finally, in the *liberal* regime access to social services is provided in the market by private insurance companies and thus indirectly depends on some source of income to pay insurance fees. Neither citizenship nor employment are formal preconditions, although in modern societies the usual source of income will be work.

While the universal system in social-democratic regimes provides fairly generous services to all citizens, the conditionality on employment or work in conservative and liberal regimes generates among citizens a group of outsiders not covered by the social security system. Historically, this void has given rise to the establishment of a second, residual layer of social security that provides the means of survival to those not covered in any other way by the main system.

Such programs focus on covering needs, but not more. Given the residual conception of these systems, they are built to provide services only to those who are in "real" need, that is, in a state of poverty. While the mandatory social insurance system in conservative regimes shields the majority of the population from hardship, limiting the size and scope of gaps in coverage, for liberal regimes the principle of need becomes a primary concern of welfare provision (Torp 2011). In this context, programs targeted at the "certifiably needy" (Esping-Andersen 1990, 43) require a definition of "what counts as a necessary requirement of a "minimally decent life," and thus as a legitimate need" (Sachweh 2016, 298).

In small groups, the mutual observance of each others' sense of duty with respect to the articulation of need claims and the possibility to punish deviations feeds a virtuous cycle of reciprocity and solidarity. This control mechanism dissolves in the anonymity of large societies, meaning the recognition of need is shifted from an informal mutual understanding of legitimate and illegitimate need claims to a formal procedure (van Oorschot et al. 2017). The identification and definition of a "minimally decent life," from which collectively recognized needs are deduced, are delegated to appointed bodies of experts. The impartial and fair treatment of need claims by the social security administration is, at least conceptually, ascertained by the transparency of procedures with possibilities to appeal.

Social security is a public good and thus subject to the strategic dilemma characterizing these goods. In order to combat the exploitation of need-oriented programs by free riders, societies have developed mechanisms to restrict access to such programs. One mechanism is the installation of means-testing provisions intended to identify those who are in "real" need. Although this is a formal approach to institutionalizing the idea of a "minimally decent life," it targets the individual level and takes into account the particular situation of an applicant. Most European countries have installed provisions by which applicants must disclose their financial assets in order to gain access to the need-based minimum benefit systems. The humiliating nature of such controls serves as a disincentive to apply.[3] A second mechanism is the emergence of a public discourse on concerns of misuse, and obtaining access to means-tested services often entails a societal stigmatization of beneficiaries as socially inferior (Rothstein 1998, 158). The individual and the relational mechanisms mutually reinforce each other's effectiveness, but they marginalize beneficiaries: "The end result is often to add the insult of misrecognition to the injury of deprivation" (Fraser 1998, 9).

In the public discourse, whole neighborhoods are depicted as welfare-dependent (MacDonald et al. 2014), and confronted with their representation in the media, people dependent on welfare experience develop negative attitudes toward themselves (Fohrbeck et al. 2014). This mechanism thus aims at the relational level of social status. Roosma et al. (2016) analyze the perception of mis-targeting of benefits in the population. Using ESS data, they find perceptions of welfare state abuse mostly in liberal countries, while perceptions of underuse are widespread in Mediterranean and post-communist countries.

The conditionality and stigmatization of need satisfaction in welfare regimes at the societal level highlights an interesting turn in the meaning of need-based justice when comparing its connotation at the individual, relational, and aggregate level. In the context of individual attitudes and preferences, as well as in small-scale interactions, need is couched in terms of solidarity and intimate relations and it relies on mutual affection. In the welfare state context, it is a last, means-tested, resort intended to support individual failure to lead a self-sufficient life, which results in stigmatization and incapacitation.

The particularistic nature of needs conflicts with the universality required for a general societal rule, such as a law on social security. Poverty is thus typically operationalized in terms relative to a general standard in a society or in terms of some generally accepted criteria. An example of the former is the definition of poverty as a personal income below 50% of the median disposable income in a country (OECD 2015, 57). An example of the latter is a list containing the ability to buy

[3] A case in point is the reform trajectory of the Austrian social security system. In order to remove the humiliating aspects of the Austrian "social assistance," which entailed severe controls, the "minimum income benefit" has replaced this system in 2010, which formulates benefits as a right and lessened controls. The result was a decrease in the non-take-up rate of 53–30%, which, still, marks a considerable reluctance to apply for social benefits (Fuchs et al. 2019). In 2019, the then center-right government enacted a partial shift back to the previous system in order to increase pressure on beneficiaries to take up a job.

durable consumer goods, to eat fish or meat every second day, to go on a 1-week annual holiday away from home, to avoid mortgage or rental arrears, to keep the home warm and to cope with unexpected expenses (Guio et al. 2012, 1). Western states perform differently with respect to the alleviation of poverty, and, somewhat ironically, countries characterized by the liberal regime, which set need at center stage of the welfare regime, fare considerably worse in combating poverty than the other two regimes (Sachweh 2016, 304). After a careful examination of various indicators of redistribution across OECD countries, Korpi and Palme (1998, 681–682) conclude: "The more we target benefits at the poor only and the more concerned we are with creating equality via equal public transfers to all, the less likely we are to reduce poverty and inequality," a finding which they term the "paradox of redistribution."

Welfare regimes appear to not only materialize specific conceptions of justice and generate distinct outcomes. They also produce variation in popular justice attitudes. According to ISSP data, the population in social-democratic regimes tends to hold egalitarian views and support welfare state intervention, while in conservative countries inegalitarian views are more widespread, although support for the welfare state is strong. In liberal countries, in turn, support for the welfare state is low and inegalitarian views are paramount (Svallfors 1997, 295). According to the same data source, however, equality and need appear to rank higher in the preferences of citizens of countries with a liberal welfare regime than in social-democratic regimes, but not compared to conservative regimes (Arts and Gelissen 2001, 295). In turn, these effects are not generally replicated in a study using more recent ESS data. The need principle neither appears to be more prevalent in liberal countries than in the other regimes, nor does equality turn out to be more popular in social-democratic countries (Reeskens and van Oorschot 2013, 1189). Instead, the findings point toward a more nuanced differentiation, according to which popular views on principles of redistributive justice in unemployment programs do not covary with the institutional logic of the welfare state, while they do with respect to old age pensions. So far, this literature suggests that welfare regimes frame popular views on what is considered just as much as they are the congealed outflow of those views. In a nutshell, institutions promote the justice conceptions on which they are built.

According to Roosma et al. (2014) people have opinions about the preferred role of the state in welfare provision and about the perceived performance of the welfare state. The preferred role of the state take the values "strong" and "weak"; the perceived performance can be either "good" or "bad." Combining the two dimensions, the authors hypothesize that empirically four clusters of combined opinions ("overall positive," "overall critical," "performance critical," and "role critical") should be observable, and that the distribution over opinions should vary over welfare regimes. Using ESS data, Roosma et al. (2014) show that the social-democratic regime engenders generally positive attitudes, a majority of citizens of Mediterranean and post-communist countries are performance critical, and those of countries with a conservative or liberal regime tend to be more role critical.

Nevertheless, despite its success as a heuristic device, the phenomenological approach to welfare regimes initiated by Esping-Andersen (1990) limits the possibility to describe and explain differences between regimes in the context of a more fundamental theoretical framework (Kasza 2002; Arts and Gelissen 2010). Instead, Mau (2004, 63) has developed an approach to systematically relate welfare regimes to principles of redistributive justice as "structures of mutual obligations" (Goodin 2002) by anchoring the concept in the "moral and social logic of welfare exchanges." His starting point is the idea of a "moral economy of welfare state institutions," which he defines as "the ongoing logic of social support for, and acceptance of, the redistributive nature of welfare provision whereby a commitment to the fate of the less well-off, the disadvantaged and people at risk is recognized" (Mau 2004, 59). Such a moral economy, he adds, depends on a "closed world" in which societies are considered "masters of justice," individuals reciprocally stand in for each other's fate, and regulatory institutions mediate individual demands, needs, and entitlements.

Mau distinguishes four ideal types of welfare regimes and argues that they are based on different conceptions of reciprocity. Phenomenologically, welfare regimes vary with respect to the comprehensiveness of and the conditionality involved in the provision of social services, which can be cross-tabulated in order to generate an analytical framework (Mau 2004, 65).[4] The first ideal type embraces universal, comprehensive welfare arrangements embedded in a solidary society which collectivizes responsibility for individual well-being by decommodifying labor as in the Scandinavian model (Esping-Andersen 1990). Reciprocity is generalized in the sense of individuals understanding themselves "as partaking in a collective arrangement of mutuality," in which "relationships between benefits and (...) 'repayments' are usually indeterminate" (Mau 2004, 64). Individual needs do not appear as a relevant criterion in ideal societies characterized by this type as long as the total amount of disposable resources is sufficient to cover all needs via redistribution.

The second type takes up the "Boulding principle" of the Beveridge tradition in the liberal regime by guaranteeing "uniform, flat-rate benefits or benefits that cover risks according to need criteria" (Mau 2004, 65), which define a "minimally decent" standard of life. In return for benefits, members of the society are expected to be willing in principle to repay the debt incurred by the benefits and to contribute meaningfully to the society, but no mechanisms of enforcing these expectations are installed. All society members take part in a uniform risk-sharing pool providing insurance against need-generating risks.

In the third type, the main idea underlying the conception of welfare is that individuals are expected to take responsibility for their own lives. The state, as the representative of the collectivity, merely steps in as a residual safety net after all other resources have been exhausted. This genuinely liberal, or residual, regime provides support only to those who demonstrate their neediness and who also enter an obligation to repay the received benefit in terms of "compliance with duties of a different kind" (Mau 2004, 66), such as norm-adherent behavior, a healthy lifestyle, or political quiescence. In this regime, the conditional nature of reciprocity is explicit, but undirected in the sense of being formulated as an obligation toward the collectivity.

[4] Note that this fourfold distinction is not connected to Parsons' *AGIL* scheme because of the different dimensionality underlying the table.

This is the world in which the need principle is the primary referent of redistribution, albeit not as an outgrowth of mutuality in a solidary community, but originating from a generalized humanitarian principle which is subsequently made conditional on good behavior.

Finally, the fourth type of welfare regime establishes a clear proportionality between prior contributions and entitlements, or even contractual rights, to benefits in the Bismarckian tradition. Although risks are pooled in collective insurance programs, the idea of reciprocity is individualized not only by the dependence of benefits on prior contributions, but also by the dependence of the size of benefits on the size of contributions. In that sense, reciprocity is "balanced" by the principle of equivalence of contributions and benefits. A concern for needs is not part of the logic of this regime.

Although Mau does not explicitly elaborate the differentiation in terms of need-based justice concerns, in his discussion of the different types of welfare regimes specific arguments for recognizing needs serve to motivate the distinction between different variants of the liberal regime (Mau 2004, 64–67). The focus on needs is at the core of two types of reciprocity as social structures, that echo Durkheim's forms of solidarity. On the one hand, a conditional form requires that every transfer is matched by a visible repayment in other currency. Close mutual observation generates transparency about behavior and immediate sanctions make deviations from the norm of reciprocity costly. On the other hand, an unconditional form rests on the assumption that those obtaining transfers develop a disposition to reciprocate by adherence to a norm mandating such behavior without actually controlling whether this disposition is present or directly sanctioning its absence. At the relational level of social interactions, the norm of group solidarity based on some shared characteristic ensures that group members internalize prosocial behavior and build up trust that others do the same.

At the collective level, need-based justice is often rhetorically embedded in a public narrative of solidarity. However, in contrast to the relational level, we have seen that the concept actually is not associated with the idea of a solidary community, but tends to be expressed as a means-tested residual that is characteristic of the liberal welfare regime. This shift in context, and connotation, is remarkable and points to a discontinuity in the comparison of small and large groups that resonates with the problem of free-riding in the provision of public goods (Olson 1965). The shift may well be explained by the increasing anonymity of social relations as the group size increases. In large groups, the possibilities of direct reciprocity between individuals are restricted and thus they have to rely on indirect reciprocity, which demands a higher level of generalized trust in the community. Absent generalized trust, groups can only maintain redistributive mechanisms if they fall back on institutional control and sanctioning mechanisms to confine potential exploitation (Ostrom et al. 1992; Fehr and Gächter 2000). This observation leads back to Durkheim's "organic solidarity" and the integrating effects of cross-cutting cleavages that avoid permanent subordination of particular individuals or groups: "In modern, pluralistic societies, welfare states depend not on strong, in-group solidarity, but instead upon the willingness of diverse groups to work with one another—a willingness that is facilitated where individuals simultaneously belong to many groups and are capable of bridging boundaries and sustaining coalitions" (Garland 2013, 35).

4.5 Sociological Contributions to a Theory of Need-Based Justice

Needs, their distribution in society, and their satisfaction are fundamental to many sociological research questions, in particular in the fields of social stratification, inequality, and welfare. In this respect, consequences and implications of heterogeneous needs have been at the core of a long tradition in sociology. Nevertheless, for a long time, the discipline has remained rather silent on questions of distributive *justice* in general and on the systematic elaboration of a theory of need-based justice in particular. Moreover, to the extent that needs have been in the focus of empirical research, scholars have mainly studied the relative importance of the principle and its dependence on socio-demographic and -economic factors in different institutional contexts. While some work in social theory and social psychology has explored the relational and relative aspects of needs, these questions seem to be a still largely uncharted area in social theory and empirical sociology. Furthermore, the expectations derived from Sects. 4.2 and 4.3 have been touched only partially. Thus, the need principle may still motivate further theoretical exploration and empirical research.

What does the emphasis on emergent social phenomena as the constitutive elements of an account of need-based justice imply for a sociological research agenda? I have argued that distributive justice rests on a shared understanding of the legitimate grounds for individual allocations from a shared resource. This perspective entails that the members of the society producing the shared resource must develop attitudes on justice principles in the context of shared distributive norms. They must elaborate these norms in a way that makes them acceptable to others. And they must recognize each other as autonomous subjects who can legitimately express justice claims. These three dimensions underlie what Fraser (2009) has denoted the "what" of justice, being redistribution, recognition, and representation.

What, then, is special about need-based justice? And what can sociology contribute to a better understanding of the conditions for needs to become salient in distributive justice? Based on the various and heterogeneous ideas that have been discussed in this chapter so far, I can only highlight some loose ends that might be usefully tied together without necessarily announcing a breakthrough in theory development.

In Sect. 4.2, justice principles were introduced as normative referents for the maintenance of legitimacy and order with respect to the fundamental dimensions of societies. The problems of situating social relations in a context and of defining the appropriate ideational reference points guiding the modes of interaction are thus identified as the core sociological contributions to the theory of need-based justice.

The notion of fairness at the behavioral level presupposes a conception of appropriateness in a given social context, which, in turn, relies on an adequate principle of justice. As long as allocation principles are considered just within the normative order of markets, hierarchies, peer groups, and solidary communities, each of which structures a specific social function of society, individual deviations from the relevant principle in personal interactions are sanctioned by others, thus reasserting the validity of the principle in a given context. At the collective level, perceptions of injustice undermine the legitimacy of the normative order.

Viewed from the perspective of redistribution, Fraser's first dimension, a need is the difference between a particular individual endowment of a resource and the amount of that resource that one believes one is entitled to. In contrast to mere wants or desires, needs cannot be framed in terms of individual preferences alone, but entail an implicit or explicit reference to a right, which is an inherently social condition. By being framed as a right, need-based justice goes beyond humanitarianism, but simultaneously the reference to such an entitlement makes the need claim dependent on the recognition of that claim by others who have the power to satisfy the need. The relationship between individual and community inherent in the notion of entitlement implies that need-based justice relies on a boundary separating those that are eligible from those that are not. Although none of the obvious criteria of legitimizing such a boundary—cooperative practice, political coercion, and common identity—can be considered satisfactory on normative grounds, jointly they cover societally observable restrictions in the scope of justice (Miller 2013, 151). From a sociological perspective, this scope restriction of communities has been framed in terms of a 'we-relationship' of consociates (Schütz 1967 [1932]).

This recognition, Fraser's second dimension, may be framed in terms of basic, or "intrinsic" needs that have a universal scope in the sense of being part of human nature. This is the line of argument suggested by a universalizing, normative theory mostly developed in political philosophy (Miller 1999; Sen 2009). In order to survive as a human being, individuals must have access to resources beyond some threshold reflecting basic needs (Nussbaum 2011). Notwithstanding the deep philosophical problems attached to the identification of basic human needs and the capabilities that human beings should be allowed to freely develop, the other frame in terms of "instrumental" needs seems to be more challenging for a sociological perspective. Instrumental needs depend on one of the other principles of justice, because the entitlement to need satisfaction requires an operational definition that serves as a reference point for the calculation of the amount of a resource needed. On the one hand, this reference point may be a universal principle such as equity or equality, which places need-based justice in a position that is dependent on some notion of proportionality. If, on the other hand, it is defined with respect to a social consensus about what is considered a "minimally decent life" in a specific community, the definitional problem undergoes a double shift. The first shift relates to the conception of a "decent life," which identifies the substantive scope of redistribution. Given the heterogeneity of living standards both within and between societies, subjective perceptions of need depend on the frame of reference in which the comparison is made. This comparison refers to the second shift, which addresses the personal scope of need-based justice. By restricting access to redistribution to members of a community, the subjective sense of entitlement is objectified as a principle of justice that excludes non-members despite their status of being in need. The need principle is then absorbed by the notion of justice as entitlement, which reproduces the stratification of society both within societies and between them. Within a community, needs are based on a common notion of a threshold that is generally accepted as a minimum requirement to take part in communal social life. Different notions of community based on different definitions of boundaries generate different entitlements.

On the one hand, need-based justice builds on universal proportional principles of justice (resource divided by either contribution or number of contributors) to capture relationships within the community. On the other hand, it builds on the particularistic principle of entitlement to define the boundaries of the community, meaning the needs of "others" may be recognized on humanitarian grounds but not as part of a reciprocal relationship. The recognition of needs rests on the formal and mutually confirmed eligibility of all community members to be supported in case of need. As a consequence, it is the invocation of the need principle as a justice norm that establishes a reciprocal relationship between the members, which, in turn, itself becomes the foundation of the justice norm, thereby reinforcing the mutual dependency of justice principles and types of reciprocity (Mau 2004). This norm serves as a reference for identifying and collectively recognizing individual claims in relation to those of other members of the society. All this happens within the confines of welfare state institutions that themselves consist of "congealed" justice conceptions.

The principle of need-based justice is unconditional at the level of normative theory. At the level of empirical observation, the findings are more convoluted. We have seen in Sect. 4.4 that (1) needs are indeed considered by people as a relevant criterion for distributing resources, that (2) the recognition of needs is particularly salient in small-scale relationships among members of solidary communities characterized by a close mutual monitoring of behavior, and that (3) adherence to the need principle is challenged in larger societies by the risk of fraud and exploitation, which has given rise to institutional provisions of conditionality and means-testing as well as the public stigmatization of welfare recipients. There is thus strong evidence that humans do not only restrict the scope of entitlements to members of a community, but that they also attach conditions to the recognition of needs. One important distinction that people make appears to be based on the attribution of responsibility. People who landed in their predicament through their own actions are less likely to receive help than those who fell prey to some accident, and if the former receive support, its continuation is more likely to be conditional on further behavior.

Needs are simultaneously manifested and ephemeral. In order to be recognized by the community, they have to be framed in universal terms in the sense of being accessible to all and obtain the status of an entitlement in a particular predicament. However, when it comes to formulating general conditions of need, the concept slips away in the labyrinthine details of particularities. In everyday life, humans have developed a good sense of evaluating need claims in particular contexts, but need-based justice has withstood any attempt at formalizing a general set of conditions.

For the recognition of needs to be generally accepted as a norm guiding relations in a specific societal realm, we have to refer to Fraser's third dimension and fall back on the procedural conditions mentioned in Sect. 4.3.3. First, both the principles underlying allocation criteria and the procedures of eligibility must be transparent. Second, considering that collective regulations constitute decisions about principles underlying the resolution of interest conflicts in a society, they cannot be left to a simple tug-of-war between social groups in a majority vote. Such a solution would cede the definition of needs to the powerful. Instead, decisions must be based on an impartial deliberation about the distribution of benefits and costs to different members of society. This provision requires some sort of delegation to a board of reputed experts entrusted with the preparation of reasonable allocation proposals. This solution, however, shifts the problem to the identification of experts. Again, since rules and procedures are not innocuous, any principle of justice may still be compromised by power relations.

4.6 Conclusion and Outlook

In this chapter, I have discussed the current state of the art in sociological research on need-based justice. After a discussion of some important classifications, the chapter contextualized the principle of need-based justice at the conceptual level and provided an overview of research discussing need-based justice at the levels of individual attitudes, relations, and collectivities. The analysis concluded with a few preliminary reflections on a potential sociological contribution to an empirically saturated theory of need-based justice.

Such a contribution faces several challenges that affect both theoretical reasoning and methodological perspectives. First, having identified boundaries of "we-relationships," stratifications into status groups, and power relations as important determinants of differentiation in the collective recognition of needs, an important next step is to theoretically spell out and empirically analyze the forms of differentiation and the substantive and personal scope restrictions that are attributed to the recognition of needs. While a broad range of theoretical approaches will be helpful in capturing various dimensions of need-based justice, conceptualizing attitudes and behavior in relation to justice norms in terms of beliefs, preferences, and opportunities, which are the foundation of analytical sociology, may offer tools for assessing the tension between rational action and normative orientations that feed the ambiguity of need-based justice. How does the social structure affecting the visibility of needs influence the willingness of individuals to take each others' needs into account? What effects result from differences in power and how are these effects transformed by individual perceptions, attitudes, and values? Under what societal conditions does self-interest trump normative persuasions?

Second, changing societal structures and ideologies engender shifts in justice perceptions and attitudes, reorganize relations in society, and reconfigure institutions. On all three levels, sociological research has produced valuable insights into various bits and pieces. Differences in attitudes are clearly related to individuals' positions in a stratified society, social distance reduces the salience of need as a principle of justice, and welfare regimes affect both the level of inequality in societal outcomes and individual attitudes. In particular, the social determination of individual attitudes has been studied to some extent, but a systematic attack on the tangled interrelationships between phenomena at the three levels of analysis is still on the agenda for future research.

A third challenge is the relevance of procedures for the identification and recognition of needs. While it is clear that every social group develops some minimum set of agreed-upon procedures, and, at least from a normative perspective, we have an understanding of the requirements for procedures to be accepted as just, there is still much to be done before we fully understand the possibilities and implications of deviations from the normative ideal. For example, while much effort has been invested into devising just procedures for the distribution of health goods, little practical guidance has resulted from this work due to the complexity of the problem.

With a view on current societal developments, a fourth challenge may be to situate need-based justice in terms of various sociological diagnoses of time. The distribution of systemic risks (Beck 1992), the distribution of rewards for effort (Frank and Cook 1995), or the rising inequality in wealth and life chances (Piketty 2014; Stiglitz 2015), to mention just a few, produce a wide array of justice-related problems. It will be a task of sociologists to summarize and interpret the results of empirical justice research in more general terms and to intervene in public debate.

Finally, sociological justice research is a first-rate example of the fruitfulness of using the whole methodological toolkit of the social sciences for producing robust findings that cumulate into a coherent narrative by mutually complementing the lacunae left by each approach. Survey-based observations on distributions of attitudes in the population are reinforced by experimental studies on the conditions of behavior and the mechanisms of interaction, and complemented by comparative assessments of institutional structures. While we can expect to learn much from using these methods in future research, one methodological perspective that might earn some more attention is the qualitative study of the ways individuals interpret their world in terms of justice. How do individuals make sense of their experiences? How do individuals relate to justice principles in their own motivations of their behavior? And how do individuals cope with the vicissitudes of life and what is the significance of justice in these accounts? Integrating insights that we can hope to obtain from such research into survey and experimental studies may help interpreting perceptions and attitudes that are stated in surveys and behavioral puzzles that are observed in experiments.

Confronting theoretical accounts saturated with empirical material with individual interpretations of the same phenomena may open new avenues for understanding need-based justice as a social phenomenon. There is little hope that this research program will offer quick and clear solutions to fundamental societal problems. But there is hope that the continuing and cumulative work on need-based justice will help us to identify and better understand these challenges.

Acknowledgments This chapter has been written as part of DFG Research Group 2104 "Needs-based Justice and Distribution Procedures," Project B1 "Distributive Preferences and Needs-based Justice in Networks," which is funded by the Austrian Science Fund (reference I 1888 G-11) in the DACH framework. This funding is gratefully acknowledged. I thank Sabine Neuhofer, Manuel Schwaninger, Georg Kanitsar, Stefan Traub, Frank Nullmeier and an anonymous reviewer for their comments.

References

Aalberg, T. (2003). *Achieving justice: Comparative public opinions on income distribution*. Leiden: Brill.

Adloff, F., & Mau, S. (2006). Giving social ties, reciprocity in modern society. *European Journal of Sociology*, *47*, 93–123.

Arts, W., & Gelissen, J. (2001). Welfare states, solidarity and justice principles: Does the type really matter? *Acta Sociologica*, *44*, 283–299.

Arts, W., & Gelissen, J. (2010). Models of the welfare state. In F. Castles, S. Leibfried, J. Lewis, H. Obinger, & C. Pierson (Eds.), *The Oxford handbook of the welfare state* (pp. 569–585). Oxford: Oxford University Press.

Arts, W., Hermkens, P., & van Wijck, P. (1995). Justice evaluation of income distribution in east and west. In J. R. Kluegel, D. S. Mason, & B. Wegener (Eds.), *Social justice and political change* (pp. 131–150). Berlin: De Gruyter.

Arts, W., & van der Veen, R. (1992). Sociological approaches to distributive and procedural justice. In K. R. Scherer (Ed.), *Justice: Interdisciplinary perspectives* (pp. 143–176). Cambridge: Cambridge University Press.

Barnett, M. N. (2011). *Empire of humanity: A history of humanitarianism*. Ithaca: Cornell University Press.

Beck, U. (1992). *Risk society. Towards a new modernity*. London: Sage.

Beck, U., & Beck-Gernsheim, E. (2002). *Individualization: Institutionalised individualism and its social and political consequences*. London: Sage.

Beckert, J. (2008). *Inherited wealth*. Princeton: Princeton University Press.

Berger, R. (2013). Altruistische Reziprozität. Theoretische Überlegungen und experimentelle Evidenz. *Kölner Zeitschrift für Soziologie und Sozialpsychologie*, *65*, 31–48.

Blau, P. M. (1964). *Exchange and power in social life*. New York: Wiley.

Boulding, K. E. (1962). Social justice in social dynamics. In K. E. Boulding, P. A. Freund, W. K. Frankena, A. Gewirth, & G. Vlastos (Eds.), *Social justice*. Englewood Cliffs: Prentice Hall.

Bowles, S., & Gintis, H. (2000). Reciprocity, self-interest, and the welfare state. *Nordic Journal of Political Economy*, *26*, 33–53.

Brañas-Garza, P. (2006). Poverty in dictator games: Awakening solidarity. *Journal of Economic Behavior and Organization*, *60*(3), 306–20.

Brock, G. (2013). Needs and distributive justice. In J. Gaus & F. D'Agostino (Eds.), *The routledge companion to social and political philosophy*. London: Routledge.

Cabrales, A., Nagel, R., & Rodrigues Mora, J. V. (2011). It is hobbes, not rousseau: An experiment on voting and redistribution. *Experimental Economics*, *15*, 278–308.

Cappelen, A., Moene, K. O., Sörensen, E. Ö., & Tungodden, B. (2013). Needs versus entitlements. An international fairness experiment. *Journal of the European Economic Association*, *11*, 574–598.

Clark, A. E., & D'Ambrosio, C. (2015). Attitudes to income inequality: experimental and survey evidence. In: A. B. Atkinson & B. Francois (Eds.) *Handbook of income distribution* (Vol. 2A, pp. 1147–1208). Amsterdam: Elsevier.

Coleman, J. S. (1986). Social theory, social research, and a theory of action. *American Journal of Sociology, 91*, 1309–1335.
Cook, K. S., Cheshire, C., Rice, E. R., & Nakagawa, S. (2013). Social exchange theory. In J. DeLamater & A. Ward (Eds.), *Handbook of social psychology* (pp. 53–76). Dordrecht: Springer.
Cook, K. S., & Hegtvedt, K. A. (1983). Distributive justice, equity, and equality. *Annual Review of Sociology, 9*, 217–241.
Dana, J., Weber, R. A., & Kuang, J. X. (2007). Exploiting moral wiggle room: Experiments demonstrating an illusory preference for fairness. *Economic Theory, 33*, 67–80.
Daniels, N., & Sabin, J. (1997). Limits to health care: Fair procedures, democratic deliberation, and the legitimacy problem for insurers. *Philosophy and Public Affairs, 26*, 303–350.
d'Anjou, L., Steijn, A., & Van Aarsen, D. (1995). Social position, ideology, and distributive justice. *Social Justice Research, 8*, 351–384.
De Swaan, A. (1988). *In care of the state: Health care, education and welfare in Europe and the USA in the modern era*. Oxford: Oxford University Press.
Deutsch, M. (1975). Equity, equality, and need: What determines which value will be used as the basis of distributive justice? *Journal of Social Issues, 31*(3), 137–149.
Diekmann, A. (2008). Soziologie und Ökonomie: Der Beitrag experimenteller Wirtschaftsforschung zur Sozialtheorie. *Kölner Zeitschrift für Soziologie und Sozialpsychologie, 60*(3), 528–550.
Doyal, L., & Gough, I. (1991). *A theory of human need*. Houndmills: Palgrave Macmillan.
Durante, R., Putterman, L., & van der Weele, J. (2014). Preferences for redistribution and perception of fairness: An experimental study. *Journal of the European Economic Association, 12*, 1059–1086.
Durkheim, E. (1964 [1893]). *The division of labor in society*. New York: The Free Press.
Durkheim, E. (1982 [1895]). *The rules of sociological method*. New York: The Free Press.
Dwyer, P. (2000). *Welfare rights and responsibilities: Contesting social citizenship*. Bristol: Policy Press.
Eckhoff, T. (1974). *Justice: Its determinants in social interaction*. Rotterdam: Rotterdam University Press.
Ellard, J. H., Harvey, A., & Callan, M. J. (2016). The justice motive: History, theory, and research. In C. Sabbagh & M. Schmitt (Eds.), *Handbook of social justice theory and research* (pp. 127–143). Heidelberg: Springer.
Elster, J. (1992). *Local justice: How institutions allocate scarce goods and necessary burdens*. New York: Sage.
Esarey, J., Salmon, T., & Barrilleaux, C. (2012). Social insurance and income redistribution in a laboratory experiment. *Political Research Quarterly, 65*, 685–698.
Esping-Andersen, G. (1990). *The three worlds of welfare capitalism*. Princeton: Princeton University Press.
Falk, A., & Fischbacher, U. (2006). A theory of reciprocity. *Games and Economic Behavior, 54*, 293–315.
Fehr, E., & Fischbacher, U. (2003). The nature of human altruism. *Nature, 425*, 785–791.
Fehr, E., & Gächter, S. (2000). Cooperation and punishment in public goods experiments. *American Economic Review, 90*(4), 980–994.
Fehr, E., & Gintis, H. (2007). Human motivation and social cooperation: Experimental and analytical foundations. *Annual Review of Sociology, 33*, 43–64.
Fiske, A. P. (1992). The four elementary forms of sociality: Dramework for a unified theory of social relations. *American Psychological Association, 99*(4), 689–723.
Fohrbeck, A., Hirseland, A., & Ramos Lobato, P. (2014). How benefits recipients perceive themselves through the lens of the mass media - some observations from Germany. *Sociological Research Online, 19*, 1–8.
Frank, R. H., & Cook, P. J. (1995). *The winner-take-all society: Why the few at the top get so much more than the rest of us*. New York: Penguin Books.
Franzen, A., & Pointner, S. (2012). Anonymity in the dictator game revisited. *Journal of Economic Behavior and Organization, 81*, 74–81.

Fraser, N. (1989). Talking about needs: Interpretive contests as political conflicts in welfare-state societies. *Ethics, 99*, 291–313.
Fraser, N. (1998). *Social justice in the age of identity politics: Redistribution, recognition, and participation*. WZB Discussion Paper, No. FS I 98-108, Berlin.
Fraser, N. (2000). Rethinking recognition. *New Left Review, 3*, 107–120.
Fraser, N. (2009). *Scales of justice. Reimagining political space in a globalizing world*. New York: Columbia University Press.
Frohlich, N., & Oppenheimer, J. A. (1992). *Choosing justice. An experimental approach to ethical theory*. Berkely: University of California Press.
Fuchs, M., Hollan, K., Premrov, T., & Scoppetta, A. (2019). *Falling through the social safety net? Analysing non-take-up of minimum income benefit and monetary social assistance in Austria*. Euromod Working Paper Series, EM9/19. https://www.euromod.ac.uk/publications/falling-through-social-safety-net-analysing-non-take-minimum-income-benefit-and.
Gaertner, W., & Schokkaert, E. (2012). *Empirical social choice. Questionnaire-experimental studies on distributive justice*. Cambridge: Cambridge University Press.
Garland, D. (2013). Punishment and social solidarity. In J. Simon & R. Sparks (Eds.), *The sage handbook of punishment and society* (pp. 23–39). New York: Sage.
Gerlitz, J.-Y., Mühleck, K., Scheller, P., & Schrenker, M. (2012). Justice perceptions in times of transition: trends in Germany, 1991–2006. *European Sociological Review, 28*, 263–282.
Goodin, R. E. (2002). Structures of mutual obligation. *Journal of Social Policy, 31*, 579–596.
Gouldner, A. W. (1960). The norm of reciprocity: A preliminary statement. *American Sociological Review, 25*, 161–178.
Greenberg, J., & Cohen, R. L. (1982). Why Justice? Normative and instrumental interpretations. In J. Greenberg (Ed.), *Equity and justice in social behavior* (pp. 437–466). New York: Academic.
Guala, F. (2012). Reciprocity: Weak or strong? What punishment experiments do (and do not) demonstrate. *Behavior and Brain Sciences, 35*, 1–59.
Guio, A.-C., Gordon, D., & Marlier, E. (2012). *Measuring material deprivation in the EU. Indicators for the whole population and child-specific indicators*, Eurostat.
Gurr, T. R. (1970). *Why men rebel*. Princeton: Princeton University Press.
Habermas, J. (1984). *Theory of communicative action*. Boston: Beacon Press.
Habermas, J. (1996). *Between facts and norms, contributions to a discourse theory of law and democracy*. Cambridge: MIT Press.
Hechter, M. (1987). *Principles of Group Solidarity*. Berkely: University of California Press.
Hedges, A. (2005). *Perceptions of redistribution: Report on exploratory qualitative research*, Casepaper 96. Centre for analysis of social exclusion, London school of economics.
Hedström, P. (2005). *Dissecting the social. On the principles of analytical sociology*. Cambridge: Cambridge University Press.
Hedström, P., & Swedberg, R. (1996). Rational choice, empirical research, and the sociological tradition. *European Sociological Review, 12*, 127–146.
Hegel, G. W. F. (1986 [1820]). *Grundlinien der Philosophie des Rechts*. Berlin: Suhrkamp.
Hegtvedt, K. A. (2005). Doing justice to the group: Examining the roles of the group in justice research. *Annual Review of Sociology, 31*, 25–45.
Hegtvedt, K. A., & Markovsky, B. (1995). Justice and injustice. In K. S. Cook, G. A. Fine, & J. S. House (Eds.), *Sociological perspectives on social psychology* (pp. 257–280). Boston: Allyn and Bacon.
Herne, K., & Suojanen, M. (2004). The role of information in choices over income distributions. *Journal of Conflict Resolution, 48*, 173–193.
Honneth, A. (2012). *The I in We. Studies on the theory of recognition*. Cambridge: Polity Press.
Honneth, A. (2014). *Freedom's right. The social foundations of democratic life*. Cambridge: Polity Press.
Hu, A., & Manning, P. (2010). The global social insurance movement since the 1880s. *Journal of Global History, 5*, 125–148.

Hülle, S., Liebig, S., & May, M. J. (2017). Measuring attitudes toward distributive justice: The basic social justice orientations scale. *Social Indicators Research*,. https://doi.org/10.1007/s11205-017-1580-x.
Imbusch, P., & Heitmeyer, W. (2012). Krisenzeiten – Desintegrationsdynamiken und soziale Konflikte. In: W. Heitmeyer & P. Imbusch (Eds.) *Desintegrationsdynamiken. Integrationsmechanismen auf dem Prüfstand* (pp. 319–338). Wiesbaden: Springer VS.
Jasso, G. (1980). A new theory of distributive justice. *American Sociological Review*, *45*(1), 3–32.
Jasso, G., & Wegener, B. (1997). Methods for empirical justice analysis: part I. Framework, models, and quantities. *Social Justice Research*, *10*, 393–430.
Kasza, G. J. (2002). The illusion of welfare regimes. *Journal of Social Policy*, *31*, 271–287.
Kause, A., Vitouch, O., & Glück, J. (2018). How selfish is a thirsty man? A pilot study on comparing sharing behavior with primary and secondary rewards. *PLOS One*, *13*(8), e0201358.
Kittel, B., Kanitsar, G., & Traub, S. (2017). Knowledge, power, and self-interest. *Journal of Public Economics*, *150*, 39–52.
Kittel, B., Paetzel, F., & Traub, S. (2015). Competition, income distribution and the middle class: An experimental study. *Journal of Applied Mathematics*, Article ID 303912.
Klein, A., & Heitmeyer, W. (2011). Demokratieentleerung und Ökonomisierung des Sozialen: Ungleichwertigkeit als Folge verschobener Kontrollbilanzen. *Leviathan*, *39*, 361–383.
Kluegel, J. R., Mason, D. S., & Wegener, B. (1999). The legitimation of capitalism in the post-communist tradition. Public opinion about market justice, 1991–1996. *European Sociological Review*, *15*, 251–283.
Kluegel, J. R., & Miyano, M. (1995). Justice beliefs and support for the welfare state in advanced capitalism. In J. R. Kluegel, D. S. Mason, & B. Wegener (Eds.), *Social justice and political change*. Berlin: De Gruyter.
Konow, J. (2003). Which is the fairest one of all? a positive analysis of justice theories. *Journal of Economic Literature*, *41*(4), 1188–1239.
Korpi, W., & Palme, J. (1998). The paradox of redistribution and strategies of equality: Welfare state institutions, inequality, and poverty in the western countries. *American Sociological Review*, *63*, 661–687.
Kunovich, S., & Slomczynski, K. M. (2007). Systems of distribution and a sense of equity: A multilevel analysis of meritocratic attitudes in post-industrial societies. *European Sociological Review*, *23*, 649–663.
Lamm, H., & Schwinger, T. (1980). Norms concerning distributive justice: Are needs taken into consideration in allocation decisions? *Social Psychology Quarterly*, *4*, 425–429.
Lamm, H., & Schwinger, T. (1983). Need consideration in allocation decisions: Is it just? *Journal of Social Psychology*, *119*, 205–209.
Lamont, J., & Favor, C. (2016). Distributive justice. In: E. N. Zalta (Ed.) *The stanford encyclopedia of philosophy*. https://plato.stanford.edu/archives/win2016/entries/justice-distributive.
Landwehr, C. (2013). Procedural justice and democratic institutional design in health-care priority setting. *Contemporary Political Theory*, *12*, 296–317.
Lawler, E. J. (2001). An affect theory of social exchange. *American Journal of Sociology*, *107*(2), 321–352.
Lawler, E. J., Thye, S. R., & Yoon, J. (2008). Social exchange and micro social order. *American Sociological Review*, *73*, 519–542.
Lengfeld, H. (2008). Was die Soziologie von John Rawls gelernt hat. *Soziologische Revue*, *31*, 17–24.
Lengfeld, H., & Liebig, S. (2002). Zwischen Normativität, Institutionenanalyse und Einstellungsforschung: Soziale Gerechtigkeit im Spiegel der Soziologie. *Soziologische Revue*, *25*, 22–34.
Liebig, S. (2001). Lessons from philosophy? Interdisciplinary justice research and two classes of justice judgments. *Social Justice Research*, *14*, 265–287.
Liebig, S., & Sauer, C. (2016). Sociology of justice. In C. Sabbagh & M. Schmitt (Eds.), *Handbook of social justice theory and research* (pp. 37–59). Heidelberg: Springer.

Liebig, S., Sauer, C., & Friedhoff, S. (2015). Using factorial surveys to study justice perceptions: Five methodological problems of attitudinal justice research. *Social Justice Research*, *28*, 415–434.
Lindenberg, S. (2008). Social norms: What happens when they become more abstract. In A. Diekmann, K. Eichner, P. Schmidt, & T. Voss (Eds.), *Rational Choice: Theoretische Analysen und Empirische Resultate* (pp. 63–82). Wiesbaden: Springer VS.
Lockwood, D. (1964). Social integration and system integration. In G. K. Zollschan & W. Hirsch (Eds.), *Explorations in Social Change*. London: Routledge.
MacDonald, R., Shildrick, T., & Furlong, A. (2014). Benefits street and the myth of workless communities. *Sociological Research Online*, *19*, 1–6.
Mau, S. (2004). Welfare regimes and the norms of social exchange. *Current Sociology*, *52*, 53–74.
Mauss, M. (1968 [1902-03]). *Essai sur le don. Forme et raison de l'échange dans les sociétés archaïques*. Paris: Presses universitaires de France.
Michelbach, P. A., Scott, J. T., Matland, R. E., & Bornstein, B. H. (2003). Doing rawls justice: An experimental study of income distribution norms. *American Journal of Political Science*, *47*(3), 523–539.
Miller, D. (1999). *Principles of social justice*. Cambridge: Harvard University Press.
Miller, D. (2013). *Justice for earthlings. Essays in political philosophy*. Cambridge: Cambridge University Press.
Molm, L. D. (2014). Experiments on exchange relations and exchange networks in sociology. In: M. Webster Jr. & J. Sell (Eds.) *Laboratory experiments in the social sciences* (2nd ed., pp. 199–224). Amsterdam: Elsevier.
Molm, L. D., Collett, J. L., & Schaefer, D. R. (2007). Building solidarity through generalized exchange: A theory of reciprocity. *American Journal of Sociology*, *113*(1), 205–242.
Molm, L. D., Melamed, D., & Whitham, M. M. (2013). Behavioral consequences of embeddedness: Effects of the underlying forms of exchange. *Social Psychology Quarterly*, *76*, 73–97.
Molm, L. D., Schaefer, D. R., & Collett, J. L. (2007). The value of reciprocity. *Social Psychology Quarterly*, *70*, 199–217.
Müller, H.-P. (1992). Durkheims Vision einer "gerechten" Gesellschaft. *Zeitschrift für Rechtssoziologie*, *13*, 16–43.
Müller, H.-P., & Wegener, B. (Eds.). (1995). *Soziale Ungleichheit und soziale Gerechtigkeit*. Opladen: Leske und Budrich.
Neuhofer, S., Reindl, I., & Kittel, B. (2015). Social exchange networks: A review of experimental studies. *Connections*, *35*(2), 34–51.
Nussbaum, M. (2000). *Women and human development. The capabilities approach*. Cambridge: Cambridge University Press.
Nussbaum, M. (2011). *Creating capabilities. The human development approach*. Cambridge: Belknap Press of Harvard University Press.
OECD. (2015). *In it together. Why less inequality benefits all*. Paris: OECD Publishing.
Olson, M. (1965). *The logic of collective action. Public goods and the theory of groups* (2nd ed.). Cambridge: Harvard University Press.
Ostrom, E., Walker, J. M., & Gardner, R. (1992). Covenants with and without a Sword: Self-governance is possible. *American Political Science Review*, *86*(2), 404–417.
Parsons, T. (1951). *The social system*. London: Routledge.
Pestieau, P. (2006). *The welfare state in the European Union: Economic and social perspectives*. Oxford: Oxford University Press.
Piketty, T. (2014). *Capital in the twenty-first century*. Cambridge: Harvard University Press.
Pointner, S., & Frantzen, A. (2015). Fairness. In N. Braun & N. J. Saam (Eds.), *Handbuch Modellbildung und Simulation in den Sozialwissenschaften* (pp. 743–771). Wiesbaden: Springer VS.
Polanyi, K. (1944). *The great transformation. The political and economic origins of our time*. Boston: Beacon Press.
Polanyi, K. (1957). The economy as instituted process. In K. Polanyi, C. M. Arensberg, & H. W. Pearson (Eds.), *Trade and market in early empires* (pp. 243–270). New York: The Free Press.

Rawls, J. (1971). *A theory of justice*. Cambridge: Belknap Press of Harvard University Press.
Rawls, J. (2005). *Political liberalism* (exp ed.). New York: Columbia University Press.
Reeskens, T., & van Oorschot, W. (2013). Equity, equality, or need? A study of popular preferences for welfare redistribution principles across 24 European countries. *Journal of European Public Policy, 20*, 1174–1195.
Richerson, P. J., & Boyd, R. (2005). *Not by genes alone. How culture transformed human evolution*. Chicago: University of Chicago Press.
Rogge, J., & Kittel, B. (2016). Who shall not be treated: Public attitudes on setting health care priorities by person-based criteria in 28 nations. *PLoS ONE, 11*, 1–15.
Rohwer, A. (2008). Bismarck versus Beveridge: Ein Vergleich von Sozialversicherungssystemen in Europa. *Ifo-Schnelldienst, 61*, 26–29.
Roosma, F., van Oorschot, W., & Gelissen, J. (2014). The preferred role and perceived performance of the welfare State: European welfare attitudes from a multidimensional perspective. *Social Science Research, 44*, 200–210.
Roosma, F., van Oorschot, W., & Gelissen, J. (2016). The achilles heel of welfare state legitimacy: Perceptions of overuse and underuse of social benefits in Europe. *Journal of European Public Policy, 23*, 177–196.
Rothstein, B. (1998). *Just institutions matter. The moral and political logic of the universal welfare state*. Cambridge: Cambridge University Press.
Runciman, W. G. (1966). *Relative deprivation and social justice: A study of attitudes to social inequality in twentieth-century britain*. London: Routledge.
Sachweh, P. (2012). The moral economy of inequality: Popular views on income differentiation, poverty and wealth. *Socio-Economic Review, 10*, 419–445.
Sachweh, P. (2016). Social justice and the welfare state: Institutions, outcomes, and attitudes in comparative perspective. In C. Sabbagh & M. Schmitt (Eds.), *Handbook of Social justice theory and research* (pp. 293–313). Heidelberg: Springer.
Sachweh, P., & Olafsdottir, S. (2012). The welfare state and equality? Stratification realities and aspirations in three welfare regimes. *European Sociological Review, 28*, 149–168.
Schütz, A. (1967 [1932]). *The phenomenology of the social world*. Evanstown: Northwestern University Press.
Schwartz, S. (1975). The justice of need and the activation of humanitarian norms. *Journal of Social Issues, 31*(3), 111–136.
Schwinger, T. (1986). The need principle of distributive justice. In H. W. Bierhoff, R. L. Cohen, & J. Greenberg (Eds.), *Justice in social relations* (pp. 211–225). New York: Plenum Press.
Schwinger, T., & Lamm, H. (1981). Justice norms in allocation decisions: Need consideration as a function of resource adequacy for complete need satisfaction, recipients' contributions, and recipients' interpersonal attraction. *Social Behavior and Personality, 9*(2), 235–241.
Scott, J. T., & Bornstein, B. H. (2009). What's fair in foul weather and fair? Distributive justice across different allocation contexts and goods. *Journal of Politics, 71*, 831–846.
Scott, J. T., Matland, R. E., Michelbach, P. A., & Bornstein, B. H. (2001). Just deserts: An experimental study of distributive justice norms. *American Journal of Political Science, 45*(4), 749–767.
Sedikides, C., & Brewer, M. B. (Eds.). (2001). *Individual self, relational self, collective self*. London: Routledge.
Sen, A. (1973). *On economic inequality*. Oxford: Oxford University Press.
Sen, A. (2000). Social justice and the distribution of income. In: A. B. Atkinson & F. Bourguignon (Eds.), *Handbook of income distribution* (Vol. 1, pp. 59–85). Amsterdam: Elsevier.
Sen, A. (2009). *The idea of justice*. Cambridge: Belknap Press of Harvard University Press.
Sigerist, H. E. (1999 [1943]). From bismarck to beveridge: Developments and trends in social security legislation. *Journal of Public Health Policy, 20*, 474–496.
Simmel, G. (1989 [1900]). *Philosophie des Geldes*. Berlin: Suhrkamp.
Simpson, B., & Willer, R. (2015). Beyond altruism: Sociological foundations of cooperation and prosocial behavior. *Annual Review of Sociology, 41*, 43–63.
Sinn, H.-W. (1995). A theory of the welfare state. *Scandinavian Journal of Economics, 97*, 495–526.

Steiner, J., Bächtiger, A., Spörndli, M., & Steenbergen, M. R. (2004). *Deliberative politics in action. Analysing parliamentary discours*. Cambridge: Cambridge University Press.
Stiglitz, J. E. (2015). *The great divide*. New York: Norton.
Stolte, J. F. (1987). The formation of justice norms. *American Sociological Review*, *52*(6), 774–784.
Svallfors, S. (1997). Worlds of welfare and attitudes to redistribution: A comparison of eight western nations. *European Sociological Review*, *13*, 283–304.
Swift, A., Marshall, G., Burgoyne, C., & Routh, D. (1995). Distributive justice: Does it matter what the people think? In J. R. Kluegel, D. S. Mason, & B. Wegener (Eds.), *Social justice and political change* (pp. 15–47). Berlin: De Gruyter.
Taylor-Gooby, P. (2005). *Attitudes to social justice*. London: Institute for Public Policy Research.
Thompson, E. P. (1963). *The making of the english working class*. London: Victor Gollancz.
Thye, S. R., Lawler, E. J., & Yoon, J. (2011). The emergence of embedded relations and group formation in networks of competition. *Social Psychology Quarterly*, *74*, 387–413.
Tönnies, F. (1957 [1887]). *Community and society*. East Lansing: Michigan State University Press.
Törnblom, K. Y. (1992). The social psychology of distributive justice. In: K. Scherer (Ed.) *Justice: Interdisciplinary perspectives* (pp. 177–236). Cambridge: Cambridge University Press.
Törnblom, K. Y., & Foa, U. G. (1983). Choice of a distribution principle: Crosscultural evidence on the effects of resources. *Acta Sociologica*, *26*, 161–173.
Torp, C. (2011). Social justice in the welfare state: From the perspective of the comparative history of institutions. In H.-W. Micklitz (Ed.), *The many concepts of social justice in European private law*. Cheltenham: Edward Elgar.
Tranow, U. (2013). Solidarität: Vorschlag für eine soziologische Begriffsbestimmung. *Analyse und Kritik*, *35*, 395–421.
Traub, S., Seidl, C., Schmidt, U., & Levati, M. V. (2005). Friedman, harsanyi, rawls, boulding or somebody else? An experimental investigation of distributive justice. *Social Choice and Welfare*, *24*, 283–309.
van der Zee, J., & Kroneman, M. W. (2007). Bismarck or beveridge: A beauty contest between dinosaurs. *BMC Health Services Research*, *7*, 94–105.
van Oorschot, W., Roosma, F., Meuleman, B., & Reeskens, T. (Eds.). (2017). *The social legitimacy of trageted welfare. Attitudes to welfare deservingness*. Cheltenham: Edward Elgar.
Verwiebe, R., & Wegener, B. (2000). Social inequality and the perceived social justice gap. *Social Justice Research*, *13*, 123–149.
Walzer, M. (1983). *Spheres of justice. A defense of pluralism and democracy*. New York: Basic Books.
Weber, M. (1949). *The methodology of the social sciences*. New York: Free Press.
Weber, M. (1968 [1921]). *Economy and society. An outline of interpretive sociology*. New York: Bedminster Press.
Wegener, B. (1987). The illusion of distributive justice. *European Sociological Review*, *3*, 1–13.
Wegener, B. (2006). *International social justice project 1996 und 2000 (ISJP 1996 und 2000) – Deutschland*, ZA4409 Datenfile Version 1.0.0. Köln: GESIS Datenarchiv. https://doi.org/10.4232/1.4409.
Wegener, B. (2015). *International social justice project 2006 (ISJP 2006) – Deutschland*, ZA5177 Datenfile Version 1.0.0. Köln: GESIS Datenarchiv. https://doi.org/10.4232/1.5177.
Wegener, B., & Liebig, S. (2000). Is the inner wall here to stay? Justice ideologies in unified Germany. *Social Justice Research*, *13*, 177–197.
Wegener, B., & Liebig, S. (2010). Gerechtigkeitsvorstellungen in Ost- und Westdeutschland im Wandel: Sozialisation, Interessen, Lebenslauf. In P. Krause & I. Ostner (Eds.), *Leben in Ost- und Westdeutschland: Eine sozialwissenschaftliche Bilanz der deutschen Einheit 1990–2010* (pp. 83–102). Campus: Frankfurt.
Wegener, B., & Mason, D. S. (2002). *International social justice project 1991 and 1996 (ISJP 1991 and 1996)*, ZA3522 Datenfile Version 1.0.0. Köln: GESIS Datenarchiv. https://doi.org/10.4232/1.3522.
Yaari, M. E., & Bar-Hillel, M. (1984). On dividing justly. *Social Choice and Welfare*, *1*(1), 1–24.

Chapter 5
Collective Decisions on Need-Based Distribution: A Political Science Perspective

Frank Nullmeier, Tanja Pritzlaff-Scheele, Kai-Uwe Schnapp, and Markus Tepe

Abstract In this chapter, we present the main areas of empirical research and theoretical thought in political science related to need-based distributive justice. From the perspective of positive political research, we discuss how need is conceptualized as a motive for political action in the theory of post-materialism, how different strands of political economy study processes of need-based redistribution in democratic states, and how studies on poverty reduction constitute the starting point for the use of the 'need'-terminology. Furthermore, a closer look at several fields of public policy shows how need functions as a central category in empirical decision-making processes. From the perspective of normative political theory, we show how need is conceptualized as a contested concept in political discourse, how it served as a core idea in justifications of the welfare state in the 1980s and early 1990s, and why the idea of "basic human needs" became a core maxim in international politics in the 1970's and was later replaced by the concept of capabilities. Finally, we demonstrate how the concept of need continues to play an important role in the literature on global justice.

F. Nullmeier (✉) · T. Pritzlaff-Scheele
SOCIUM & FOR 2104, University of Bremen, Bremen, Germany
e-mail: frank.nullmeier@uni-bremen.de

T. Pritzlaff-Scheele
e-mail: tanja.pritzlaff@uni-bremen.de

K.-U. Schnapp
Department of Social Sciences & FOR 2104, University of Hamburg, Hamburg, Germany
e-mail: kai-uwe.schnapp@wiso.uni-hamburg.de

M. Tepe
Institute of Social Sciences & FOR 2104, University of Oldenburg, Oldenburg, Germany
e-mail: markus.tepe@uni-oldenburg.de

S. Traub and B. Kittel (eds.), *Need-Based Distributive Justice*,
https://doi.org/10.1007/978-3-030-44121-0_5

5.1 Introduction

Concepts and theories of ‘need-based justice’ have not played a very prominent role in political science and political theory. From the beginning of the twentieth century until today, the semantic field of “need”, “needs”, ‘necessities”, ‘needy” and ”the needy” has been associated with poverty and the politics of poverty reduction (O’Connor 2001). In political science, “need” is considered as a specific category in a subfield of social policy. The general terminology of political science research is based on concepts like “power”, “interests”, and “institutions”. The category of need does not come into play at this level. Moreover, questions concerning the distribution of goods and resources are, first and foremost, questions about the design, institutionalization, and legitimization of collectively binding decisions. Political science is interested in institutions and procedures that offer channels for decision-making on questions of distribution and redistribution. The procedural and institutional focus of political science contrasts with the language of ‘need’ and ‘necessity’, which refers to settings that are not open to collective decisions.

In the context of a discussion on the nature of needs, Lawrence Hamilton suggests that there are two reasons why the concept of ‘need’ has been “out of vogue” for some time (Hamilton 2016, 137). The first reason, according to Hamilton, is that the concept of need is often associated with a line of thought that “falsely assumes the existence of a universal, unchanging list of basic human needs whose determination does not depend on or require the input or opinion of citizens” (Hamilton 2016, 143). While there are certainly some vital needs, like air and water, that are undisputed (Hamilton 2003, 29–30), a concept of needs as an unchanging list seems to be problematic. As Hamilton outlines, when needs are “unproblematically and unpolitically understood as ‘physical’ conditions for human functioning” (Hamilton 2003, 29) within basic needs approaches, the fact that most basic needs are situated on a continuum, depending on the way in which (healthy) living is defined, is neglected. Furthermore, when needs are granted above a level that is required in a biological sense, decisions about what vital or basic needs are—where to identify an acceptable floor to the standard of living—are ultimately political decisions. The second reason why political science has lost sight of the concept of need, according to Hamilton, is that a strong influence of utilitarianism has led to a misleading amalgamation of the concepts of need, individual preferences and interests. Contrary to these two lines of thought that seem to have limited the influence of need-based conceptions of distribution and distributive justice in political science, Hamilton himself argues for an understanding that highlights the importance of judgments, interactions and joint decision-making when it comes to human needs. As he outlines, “past and existing institutions and practices determine to an important degree the way we perceive our needs” (Hamilton 2016, 138).

As long as ‘needs’ are perceived as a domain that indicates a withdrawal of particular problems or options from the realm of political decision-making, political science will deny the analytic value of the category of ‘needs’. Conceptions of need that assume an intersubjective recognition of needs in a political process—based on scientific attempts to measure physical, cultural, social and economic necessities—

are able to establish a balance between objectification and the procedural focus of political science.

The chapter is organized as follows: The next three Sects. (5.2–5.4) are concerned with positive political research. In Sect. 5.2, we outline how the theory of post-materialism conceptualizes need as a motive for political action. Section 5.3 presents the different strands in political economy studying processes of need-based redistribution in democratic states. Poverty analysis and poverty reduction policies constitute the starting point for the use of the 'need' terminology. However, as Sect. 5.4 outlines, needs are researched in several fields of public policy. Sections 5.5 and 5.6 discuss contributions from normative political theory. Justifications of the welfare state are traditionally based on normative criteria, such as justice, equality and need. In Sect. 5.5, we provide an overview of the changing conceptualizations of needs in the welfare state literature. The rise and fall of the basic human needs approach in international politics, including its continuing influence in the literature on global justice, are discussed in Sect. 5.6. Finally, Sect. 5.7 presents the conclusion.

5.2 Positive Political Theory: Need as Motive and Political Change

Political science uses the concepts of interest and preference to designate the motives for political action. Recourses to needs as motives for action are very rare. The most extensive application of the concept of need as a motive within empirical political science can be found within the post-materialism debate. Ronald Inglehart (1977, 1990) has developed an interpretive scheme to characterize political change since the 1960s as moving from materialistic to post-materialistic attitudes. In this context, Inglehart refers to the psychological theory of Abraham Harold Maslow, especially to his 'hierarchy of needs' (Maslow 1970 [1954]; Inglehart 1977, 41; Inglehart 1990, 152–53). Inglehart employs Maslow's model of five levels of need, which was devised in 1943, in order to develop items for the measurement of value attitudes (reformulated in Inglehart and Abramson 1999).

According to Maslow, basic needs have to be fulfilled before higher needs take effect. The two lowest needs levels comprise physiological needs (food, water, warmth, shelter) and security needs (security, safety). Until these needs are satisfied, human beings are, first and foremost, driven by the motive to meet these basic needs. Psychological needs are located at the next two levels. Love needs are directed toward belongingness, love, and friendship, while esteem needs are directed toward prestige and feelings of accomplishment. It is not until the highest level of need is reached that self-expression takes effect as a motive for creative personal fulfillment and the development of the entire personal potential. Inglehart assigns the two lowest levels (physiological needs) to the area of materialist needs, while the other levels are attributed to the area of post-materialist needs (Inglehart 1977, 42; Inglehart 1990, 133–35). The reduced importance of the class conflict in party politics is explained by an increase of post-materialist attitudes. However, Inglehart does not take the political dynamics as an expression of an immediate need dynamism. He rather translates Maslow's hierarchy of needs into different types of values. Correspondingly, his investigations have been continued under the categories of 'values' and 'value change'. 'Needs' are not used as a genuine political science category, but are dropped immediately in favor of values that are measurable by traditional opinion and attitude research. To sum up, Inglehart introduces the concept of need only as a starting point for the discussion about value change. Therefore, his main category is 'value', not 'need'.

5.3 Positive Political Theory: The Political Economy of Need-Based Redistribution

The most extensive empirical research on the subject of needs deals with the question of how societies and polities determine redistribution. This research has developed at the intersection of economics and political science, and is now called 'political economy'. In this research field, however, 'need' does not come into play as a motive for action. Rather, the motivational basis identified in this line of research is self-interest, in the broader sense employed within the rational-choice tradition. 'Need' appears on the output page here. What degree of redistribution do citizens choose, and what role does the securing of their needs play? Scholars in the field of political economy tend to reason about politics as the process of individual preference aggregation with the goal of imposing collectively binding rules. With its focus on individuals' preferences and social interaction within the process of preference aggregation, political economy has a natural proximity to the experimental methodology as it enables researchers to manipulate the institutional context (e.g., the decision-making rule) and to observe individuals' choice behavior in real time (see Palfrey 2009 for a review). Within those politico-economic studies that explore collective decisions on inequality and redistribution (see Clark and D'Ambrosio 2015 for a review), the focus is on social justice in a broader sense, rather than on need-based justice. However, there are at least three strands of research that can be connected to need-based justice considerations and thereby offer leeway for further research in this direction:

1. Research on the choice of principles of justice in the tradition of Frohlich and Oppenheimer (Frohlich et al. 1987a, 1987b; Frohlich and Oppenheimer 1992, 1998, 1999).
2. Research on political decisions on redistributive justice that builds on the Meltzer–Richard model (Meltzer and Richard 1981).
3. Research on the relationship between procedural justice and the legitimacy of redistributive outcomes (Gilljam et al. 2010; Persson et al. 2013; Esaiasson et al. 2012).

The first strand of research addresses one of the fundamental theorems in positive political economy, namely the assumption of rational self-interested agents. In a world in which agent's choices are probabilistically linked to outcomes, rational agents are predicted to choose the action with the highest expected utility over other alternatives (see von Neumann-Morgenstern utility theorem, von Neumann and Morgenstern 1953). Laboratory experiments conducted by Frohlich and Oppenheimer (Frohlich et al. 1987a, 1987b; Frohlich and Oppenheimer 1990) provide valuable insight into whether maximizing expected utility also applies in the context of redistribution. In a series of papers, Frohlich and Oppenheimer (Frohlich et al. 1987a, 1987b) and others (e.g., Michelbach et al. 2003; Cabrales et al. 2012) utilize laboratory designs to test Rawls' (1971) theory of social justice. Subjects are confronted with different distributions of income and asked which they believe is better.

Specifically, Frohlich et al. (1987a) test whether, under the 'veil of ignorance', individuals reach a unanimous consensus on Rawls' (1971) difference principle of redistributive justice. According to this principle, a society is predicted to agree upon maximizing the welfare of the worst-off individual in society. In the experiment, groups of subjects choose between four different income distributions, where each distribution represents a certain distribution principle. Subjects choose between (1) maximizing the lowest income, (2) maximizing the average income, (3) maximizing the average income while guaranteeing a minimum income and (4) maximizing the average income with a maximum difference between highest and lowest income. Expected utility maximizers are expected to choose (2), while subjects following the Rawlsian principle of justice should choose (4). To simulate the 'veil of ignorance', experimental subjects must choose and agree upon a distribution before knowing their own position in the distribution. Their position in the finally implemented income distribution is determined by a lottery. Experimental results clearly show that the majority of groups are neither expected utility maximizers nor Rawlsians, but prefer to maximize the average income while guaranteeing a minimum income above Rawls' difference principle. These experimental results largely corroborate the Boulding (1962, 83) principle, which states that "Society lays a modest table at which all can sup and a high table at which the deserving can feast". A related interpretation of this principle can be found in Raphael (1980, 54), who states that justice requires "a basic minimum of equal satisfactions (...) Above that line, room is left for individuals to do as they think fit". Thus, even though need-based justice has not been at the center of these studies, experimental results indicate that need-based justice considerations set in when a certain standard of minimal social protection has not been met.

The second strand of literature exploring collective decisions on redistributive justice builds on the Meltzer–Richard model (Meltzer and Richard 1981), or a simplified version of it. An individual's attitude toward inequality is no longer characterized by a disinterested evaluation of alternative income distributions, but is guided by self-interest, with the additional assumption that individuals not only care about how much they receive, but also about how much they receive compared to others (Clark and D'Ambrosio 2015, 1149). The Meltzer–Richard model consists of two components: Majority voting and proportional taxation providing an equal lump-sum payment for each group member. It has become the workhorse model in the political economy of redistribution (see also Persson and Tabellini 2002). In the absence of any excess burden of taxation, its solution under the presumption of fully rational and self-interested individuals is straightforward: According to the median voter theorem (Downs 1957), the vote of the median voter is decisive. If the median voter's net income is below the average net income, he will vote for 100 percent redistribution. If the median voter's net income is above the average net income, he will vote for 0 percent redistribution. If the median voter's net income is equal to the average net income, he will decide randomly.

While macro-comparative research provides limited evidence in favor of the prediction derived from the Meltzer–Richard model (see Alesina and Giuliano 2009 for a review), laboratory results are rather supportive (see Kittel et al. 2015 for a review). Most of the existing laboratory applications of the Meltzer and Richard model by political scientists use a simplified version that does not take into account subjects' labor-leisure decisions, even though those in favor of redistribution must take into account that net payers of redistribution might adjust their labor supply in the next round. Agranov and Palfrey's (2015) experimental design explicitly focuses on subjects' labor-leisure decision in the Meltzer–Richard model. Altering the amount of wage inequality and the political process used to determine tax rates, they find that higher inequality leads to higher tax rates. Both the tax rates and labor supply functions are quantitatively close to the model.

Utilizing a simplified version of the Meltzer–Richard model, Esarey et al. (2012a) conduct an experiment in which subjects' net incomes are earned through a real-effort task. The experimental treatment alters the wage rate for tokens earned in this task. While the treatment has no effect on subjects' preferred tax rate, they also find that voting behavior is almost entirely in accordance with rational self-interest. Above-average earners vote for low tax rates and below-average earners vote for high tax rates. Subjects' self-reported preferences for fairness and equality (which are collected in a post-experimental survey), however, have no effect on subjects' voting behavior in this experiment. Even though it turns out that altering the wage rate has no impact on the individually preferred tax rate in this particular experimental design, this may still present a fruitful avenue for introducing need. If subjects hold need-based justice preferences, their vote choice should take into account the cause of income inequality. Hence, groups in which wage rates are distributed randomly should agree on higher taxation than groups in which the allocation of wage rates is in one way or another legitimated through individual effort.

Again, using a simplified version of the Meltzer-Richard model, the studies by Barber et al. (2013) and Esarey et al. (2012b) explore how risk exposure affects willingness to redistribute. Redistribution programs can be driven by insurance and income equalization concerns, while both adhere to different fairness principles. The experimental design by Esarey et al. (2012b) distinguishes two basic treatment conditions. First, earnings are redistributed according to the simplified Meltzer-Richard model and, second, a 20 percent (resp. 80 percent) chance is imposed that group members will experience a random loss (e.g., due to natural disaster, job loss, medical condition) that destroys 80 percent of their earnings. The experimental findings suggest that willingness to redistribute is generally higher with a higher risk of losing 80 percent of their earnings, and that a person's self-reported political ideology is associated with his or her willingness to reduce income inequality that is caused by luck. In a related laboratory experiment, Barber et al. (2013) explore how the risk of earning losses (operationalized in terms of unemployment) affects subjects' willingness to redistribute. They also find strong evidence that loss aversion increases the willingness to redistribute. This robust pattern points toward the debate on deservingness and redistribution, which also touches on concepts of need-based justice. It appears that some attributes of those in need (e.g., gender, age, ethnicity and, in particular, individual effort) matter for the willingness to redistribute. Thus, if, in the case of individual effort, poor income is the result of bad luck, society's willingness to redistribute is higher compared to a situation in which someone's poor income is the result of laziness (e.g., see Clark and D'Ambrosio 2015, 1166, for experimental results).

In addition, there is some laboratory evidence that willingness to redistribute is subject to framing. Utilizing a simplified version of the Meltzer–Richard model with numerical communication, Lorenz, Paetzel, and Tepe (2017) have designed a laboratory experiment to test whether it matters if voters are asked to decide on a tax rate or a minimum income, leaving the redistribution mechanism itself unchanged. Framing the vote about redistribution as a decision about minimal income increases the ideally preferred level of redistribution. This effect outlives the group's deliberation process and leads to the implementation of a higher level of redistribution. These results indicate that framing the decision on redistributive taxation in the direction of those in need alters the collectively agreed-upon level of redistribution.

The third strand of literature steps outside of the expected utility and rational-choice framework. Instead, it explores how aspects of procedural justice affect the legitimacy of redistributive outcomes (e.g., Gilljam et al. 2010; Persson et al. 2013; Esaiasson et al. 2012). Drawing on procedural justice theory (e.g., Lind and Tyler 1988; Tyler et al. 1997), Esaiasson et al. (2012) conduct an exploratory randomized field experiment with Swedish high school pupils to evaluate how fairness in the implementation of institutional arrangements affects the legitimacy of redistributive decisions. Each class is asked to allocate a fixed sum of money either to charity (group altruism) or to a festivity of their own choosing (group egoism). Each class is randomly assigned to one of four forms of individual preference aggregation mechanisms: (1) direct majoritarian voting, (2) election of three representatives, (3) expert decision-making, meaning that the decision is taken by the class teacher, and (4) participants choose their preferred decision-making arrangement (1, 2, or 3). After each class makes its decision, pupils are informed about the outcomes and asked to fill out a survey about their legitimacy beliefs associated with the decision procedure. Surprisingly, the experimental results indicate that subjects' legitimacy beliefs do not differ if the decision mechanism is imposed exogenously, indicating that consensual agreement on voting rules adds no legitimacy to distributive outcomes (Esaiasson et al. 2012, 797). Therefore, contrary to previous findings from experimental economics (Sutter et al. 2010), Esaiasson et al. (2012) find no support for the idea that participation in constitution-making generates stronger legitimacy beliefs. Confronted with these limited and mixed experimental results, there is certainly need for a more systematic exploration of the link between procedural justice and the legitimacy of redistributive outcomes in general and, more specifically, one might question whether the linkage is moderated by the purpose of the redistribution program, specifically income equalization or insurance. Regarding insurance, procedural fairness considerations might be guided by the need-based justice principle. In this case, the use of expert knowledge and expert-based decision-making becomes more likely, compared to standard democratic rules of preference aggregation.

While the experimental results on need-based distribution and need-based justice are still limited, the preceding sections also hint at a high research potential and a wide variety of applications when studying need-based distribution and decision procedures in the lab.

5.4 Positive Political Theory: Public Policy Between Substantive and Procedural Justice

A closer look at the literature on empirical decision-making processes shows that, contrary to the above-cited assumptions presented by Hamilton (2016), the concept of need is not necessarily associated with the existence of a universal, unchanging list of basic human needs that does not require the input or opinion of citizens. In fact, a large number and wide variety of societal and political actors is involved in decisions on a need-based provision of goods and services, and, moreover, constant revisions and changes of the previous decisions are being made. Needs are contested political constructions that have to be developed and affirmed in political discourses and institutional procedures. Modern societies do agree on levels of need-based provisions of goods and on the extent of redistribution by way of political decisions. Those processes may take into account the conceptual and ethical discourses of experts on need-based justice, but in the end, it is politics that determines what is to be done about needier members of society. In particular, national political institutions and national political practices determine what is considered as need in a given society and how to treat the needy. For political scientists, questions of need-based justice are closely related to questions of institutional arrangements, and the decision-making processes in those institutions. The question is how issues of need-based provisions of goods and services are processed in a polity, and what the procedural understanding of needs justification and needs fulfillment is. Specifically, which actors are participating in the respective decisions, and which institutional arenas and practices are used to specify levels of need-based provision (Geißel et al. 2015)?

From the perspective of democratic political processes, decisions on a need-based provision of goods and services have no particular status. Need-oriented decisions are dealt with in the established parliamentary processes of political decision-making. Hence, when discussing needs-based redistribution or political processes around need-based justice, we talk about established political decision-making and about the ensuing administrative processes. As a result, a specified political science literature on needs-based decisions has never emerged. However, need and need-based justice are a prominent issue in the broader field of social policy studies. Policy fields where explicit references to needs and the fulfillment of needs are prevalent include child care, elderly care, welfare and health care.

5.4.1 Individual and Aggregate Levels of Need

In many policy fields, reference to need is made on two levels: individual and aggregate levels of need. In the case of individual neediness, the political process is directed toward the identification and approval of what is necessary for individuals to live at a minimum level of subsistence in a decent way. Fundamental questions on the level of necessities shape these debates. In the case of an aggregate level of need, political decisions are directed toward the (financial, personnel, and infrastructural) resources that are necessary to fulfill the wants and needs of the citizens. In most of the literature, aggregate levels of need are referred to as the fulfillment of demands. The term demand does not allow for a differentiation between the aggregation of individual preferences and the aggregation of publicly recognized needs. The reference to needs highlights the moment of an intersubjective, collective process of need attribution. Aggregate levels of need-based provision (or demand planning) are relevant in administrative planning processes. In the fields of health and elderly care (Hasseler and Görres 2010), as well as child and youth social services (Fischer et al. 2013a, 2013b), expert and administrative debates concentrate both on issues of individual needs and their effects on the specification of aggregate need levels. In health care, the discussion about individual needs focuses mainly on how to meet individual needs in health care provision.

Therefore, the differentiation between individual and aggregate needs is an important analytical step, but only rarely made explicit in politics. For individual needs, the main questions include the following: Which needs can and should be recognized in political decisions? How does the recognition process work? At the aggregate level, the main questions are as follows: What is the total amount of resources required to meet the total of all individual needs? What institutional and organizational precautions are required to successfully deal with politically recognized needs?

Individual needs are clearly center stage when we talk about social policy and redistributive payments or services to alleviate poverty. The extant literature focuses on a number of need-related issues here: The measurement of individual needs and the individual fulfillment of needs as a political precondition for decisions on need-based redistribution (Cárthaigh 2014), the characteristics of dependent people that are decisive (or not) for the societal acceptance of their neediness or deservingness (e.g., Park 2014; Bashevkin 2000; Harell et al. 2016), and the public discourse on individual needs. Beechey (2016) demonstrates how individual affectedness, emotional arguments and the respective framing of neediness or deservingness define political decision-making about needs and needs-based redistribution, even in the parliamentary arena.

The discussion about aggregate levels of need provision becomes more vibrant in health policy. Technically, health care systems are able to cure more and more diseases or at least improve on the conditions under which a sick person has to live. Due to the fact that resources for the health sector are ultimately limited, health policy cannot actually do everything for everyone (Herlitz and Horan 2016; Landwehr 2006, 2013, 2015; Landwehr and Böhm 2011).

At the aggregate level, the discussion in health care turns toward a variety of different issues: How does the system of financing health care affect the density of doctors in different areas and thus the ability of the system to meet individual health care needs as a function of location? Is healthcare planning suited to ameliorating the effects of doctors self-selecting into different locations and, if so, how does it accomplish that (Ozegowski and Sundmacher 2013)? What are legitimate principles for healthcare planning, and who decides which principles are legitimate (Stollmann 2015)? Discussions on this issue, however, can be found mainly in the law and ethics literature, since normative questions on the legitimacy of healthcare rationing dominate the debate.

Numerous publications in social policy, elderly care, and youth care are related to needs, but focus on the aggregate level from an administrative and planning perspective only. For example, they ask what organizational structures and aggregate resources are required for the satisfaction of individual needs. In this literature, the individual level of need is rarely discussed explicitly, but rather taken for granted. These discussions are rather technocratic, since need levels often seem to be understood as being "just there", that is, as fixed by some transcendent entity. There is, in fact, an implicit awareness that levels are decided upon by some agency (politicians, administrators, experts), but in many instances, discussions do not focus on that aspect. Neither the actors nor the norms and rules guiding decisions on needs levels are much reflected upon in the literature.

5.4.2 Measurement and Objectivation

The origins of measurement and objectivation of human needs lie in the field of poverty research. Starting with Benjamin Seebohm Rowntree's (1901) path-breaking studies on poverty in the English town of York, the tensions between the measurement of physical necessities and necessary expenditures, the expert evaluation of social and moral necessities, and the intersubjective political decision on the public recognition of needs shape the debate on poverty and social assistance. In a more recent attempt to develop a need-based operationalization of poverty, Cárthaigh states that "(. . .) claims about poverty will only be intelligible when the end-states for which the 'poor' lack the necessary conditions are clearly understood" (Cárthaigh 2014, 470). With this as a starting point, he defines need as a necessary condition to an end-state which is ascribed objectively to a person who is the subject of this need (Cárthaigh 2014, 460–461). Poverty is defined as an individual status in which some or all of the needs related to "normal" participation in society and everyday life are not fulfilled. This leads to an understanding of objectivation as a recognition of a set of activities that are normally undertaken by a member of a given society.

Objectivation of health needs takes a different approach. In an attempt to make health needs intelligible, Herlitz and Horan (2016) focus on the relative health improvement of a person with respect to the status quo of her health. They ask a set of guiding questions: (1) Who will have the highest end-state with respect to health after treatment? (2) Who is furthest away from the perfect end-state before treatment? (3) Who will have improved the most after treatment? These questions are supposed to solve the meta-problem of an order of provision of health treatments, under the condition that not everyone can be treated, at least not at the same time. Herlitz and Horan develop a formula based on the concepts of severity of health condition (question 2 above) and health improvement through treatment (question 3 above). Health needs of a specific person are then operationalized as the difference between the current and attainable health (health improvement) of that person, weighted by the difference between the current and perfect health (severity of health condition) of that person, and the sum of the same differences for all persons in a given society (Herlitz and Horan 2016, 100). In its structure, Herlitz' and Horan's proposal is an intersubjectively understandable way of determining individual needs.

With respect to poverty, for example, Cárthaigh's "normal" participation could serve as an equivalent for the standard against which all improvements have to be measured. Individual need would then have an absolute standard, below which neediness would be recognized as such. In addition, neediness would become comparable between individuals at different levels of need. However, even with such a magic formula, societies still need to decide upon its application.

Even the most advanced forms of measurement of needs require a set of rules that define who is responsible for the measurement of needs, which methodical instruments for the measurement of needs are to be used, which bodies or institutional entities are responsible for the recognition of the measured level of needs, whether there is some room for discretion within these bodies and entities, and how these rules can be changed in the future. The discourse on measurement and recognition tends to neglect the procedural questions. Conversely, the literature on specific procedures for questions of need-based provision of goods and services neglects the requirement to measure needs and to decide on needs as a specific object of decision-making.

5.4.3 Procedures

Decisions on need-based provision of goods and services might have a very different outcome in case the disposable resources of a society are higher than the total sum of individual needs—if compared to a case of undersupply. The procedures selected to legitimate decisions on need-based distributions may be different in the two cases. More attention could be given to procedures in the case of undersupply. Empirical research has to study whether, in this case, highly regulated procedures of expert decisions and/or participatory arrangements are selected or not. Normative questions concerning the selection of legitimate procedures might also arise.

In a series of articles, Landwehr (2006, 2012, 2013, 2015) turns to procedural questions regarding the recognition of healthcare needs. She takes for granted that rationing in health care is inevitable (Landwehr 2006, 84). In the assumed scenario of undersupply, it is clear that societies need to strictly decide who gets what, when, and how from the healthcare system. Landwehr asserts that "the question of how decisions are to be made, and thus the question of procedural justice in allocation, has begun to replace questions of substantial distributive justice" (Landwehr 2013, 297), and she refers to this development as the "procedural turn of the debate". She states that "after the procedural turn, considerations of justice are no longer addressed at the distributive results themselves but rather at the way in which they are produced, thus applying criteria of procedural rather than substantial justice" (Landwehr 2013, 302). If the key question is "What do societies do with needs?", and the focus is on the necessity of making decisions about needs, Landwehr's answer is that this kind of problem is largely solved by developing cascades of procedures, rather than substantive decisions. That might imply that primary decision-making bodies, like parliaments, do not take on the direct substantive question of needs. They tend to delegate decisions to specific bodies, which decide on the substantive issues (Landwehr and Böhm 2011). However, "(...) designing political institutions to produce decisions that accord with specific conceptions of justice is problematic in modern, pluralistic societies in which decisions can derive legitimacy only from impartial majority decisions" (Landwehr 2006, 306). Procedures or chains of procedures that specialize in making decisions on need-based provision of goods and services, and ensure that need-based justice will inform the legislation, do not exist in Western democracies. The empirical part of Landwehr's work shows a variety of institutional solutions in different policies and countries for questions of need-based provision, but no general or best-practice solution.

Therefore, from a normative perspective, it is important to look for principles according to which decision-making mechanisms for these cases can be constructed. Landwehr mentions three such criteria: (1) independence and delegation, (2) inclusiveness (ranging from expert only to involving regular citizens) and (3) publicity and transparency (Landwehr and Böhm 2011). She compares several empirical examples of decision-making structures in health care rationing, searching especially for evidence of the above-mentioned principles. Her findings range from closed and independent bureaucratic expert bodies as exemplified by the 'Gemeinsamer Bundesausschuss" in Germany, to a combination of parliamentary and expert bodies in Sweden, widely inclusive and highly pluralistic bodies like the National Institute of Clinical Excellence (NICE) in the UK, and, finally, open citizen involvement in the Oregon Health Plan with its consensus conferences (Landwehr 2006).

At least for the area of health care, it is apparent that, apart from classical bureaucratic and parliamentary decision-making, expert committees as well as citizen fora play an increasingly important role in deciding upon needs and their recognition. With respect to expert involvement, some argue that the outsourcing of decisions to expert bodies diminishes the role of classical government bureaucracies as providers of problem definitions and advice. This development could hamper decision-making that is independent of particularistic interest (May et al. 2016). Therefore, while expert fora can foster policy learning and imitation through the knowledge that they make available (Shipan and Volden 2014), they need to be balanced by other actors in the decision-making process in order to prevent them from making decisions that are divorced from citizens' demands (Van Damme et al. 2011). In addition, it is important that citizens are not side-lined by expert fora, and that sufficient room for open and public deliberation is available (Straßheim 2015). This seems to be even more imperative, since decisions on need are strongly value-based—and the more value-based the decisions, the stronger the request for citizen involvement (Bruni et al. 2008). Empirically, there is an increasing role for the public in all kinds of political decisions, with various modes of public consultation, such as deliberative modes, becoming more commonplace (Landwehr 2015). While different mechanisms of citizen consultation are in use (Bruni et al. 2008), the public usually plays a purely advisory role, while binding political decisions are still made in the classical institutions or in new expert committees. This may constitute a problem in its own right (Daudelin et al. 2011), since at some point, the citizens involved may doubt the significance and impact of their role in the participatory process.

The specificity of decisions on needs seems to vanish in the literature on procedural justice. The challenge for future research on this topic might be the clarification of the interplay between substantial questions of measurement of needs, and the procedural dimension of decisions for a need-based provision of goods and services.

5.5 Normative Political Theory: Need-Based Social Policy

5.5.1 Critical Theory: On the Road to a Constructivist View on Needs

In the 1980s, need-based justice was a central topic in the debates about the crisis of the welfare state. Increasing criticism of the welfare state led to an intense debate within normative political theory and social policy research. Criticisms of the normative foundations of the welfare state were not limited to the political right. From the perspective of Critical Theory, the welfare state had become a bureaucratic institution, which was increasingly detached from the needs of its citizens. In The Theory of Communicative Action (Habermas 1987 [1981]), Jürgen Habermas criticizes the way in which tendencies of juridification within the welfare state have led to the individualization of life-risks—risks that have been transformed into "individual legal entitlements under precisely specified general legal conditions" (Habermas 1987, 362). In the context of this discussion, he hints at the eventual non-transferability of needs into valid claims in a legal sense: "Compensation is made in the event of a valid claim to benefit. The juridification of social situation-definitions means introducing into matters of economic and social distribution an if-then structure of conditional law that is 'foreign' to social relations, to social causes, dependencies and needs. This structure does not, however, allow for appropriate, and especially not for preventive, reactions to the causes of the situations requiring compensation" (Habermas 1987, 362). Habermas demands a recovery of needs not only within the legal system and in expert committees, but also within public discourse.

His view contributed to an international debate about need interpretation and the justification of need within the critical strand of normative political theory. In "Struggle over Needs", Nancy Fraser takes up Habermas' above-cited characterization of the effects of welfare state bureaucracies on needs from a feminist perspective. She hints at the effects of decontextualization and recontextualization that administrative "expert needs discourse" (Fraser 1989, 174) has on politicized needs: "These discourses consist in a series of rewriting operations, procedures for translating politicized needs into administrable needs. Typically, the politicized need is redefined as the correlate of a bureaucratically administrable satisfaction, a 'social service'" (Fraser 1989, 174). Fraser identifies debates on people's needs as an important part of recent political discourses. Therefore, Fraser shifts the focus of her discussion "from needs to discourses about needs"—and "from the distribution of need satisfaction to 'the politics of need interpretation'" (Fraser 1989, 162). For Fraser, needs are not simply given, they are politically constructed and defined in public debates. It is crucial to take a closer look at the respective agents who interpret needs, and to stay alert to the question of whether or not the public discourse is open for divergent interpretations of needs and allows for a fair discussion. Discourse about needs can be unfair in cases in which "groups with unequal discursive (and nondiscursive) resources compete to establish as hegemonic their respective interpretations of legitimate social needs" (Fraser 1989, 166).

To answer the question of whether one can "distinguish better from worse interpretations of people's needs" (Fraser 1989, 181), Fraser offers two kinds of considerations: procedural and consequentialist. The procedural considerations are summed up as follows: "All other things being equal, the best need interpretations are those reached by means of communicative processes that most closely approximate ideals of democracy, equality, and fairness." Consequentialist considerations, on the other hand, "dictate that, all other things being equal, the best need interpretations are those that do not disadvantage some groups of people vis-à-vis others" (Fraser 1989, 181). For Fraser, the balancing of procedural and consequentialist considerations might be summed up as a balancing of democracy and equality. Ultimately, she expresses the hope that "justified needs claims" may serve as "the bases for new social rights" (Fraser 1989, 183). Discursive resources in this sense are also discussed by Joel Anderson, who highlights the crucial importance of "need-interpretive competence" (Anderson 2001, 214) in the context of Habermas' discourse ethics (see also Noonan 2006, 177–178 and Habermas 1993, 90–91).

Fraser shifts the debate on the welfare state to the procedural dimension of fair public discourses. Her work exemplifies the rising new approach in theories of democracy, namely, deliberative democracy. Her argumentation supersedes the substantial question of which level of needs should be recognized in the legislative process by focusing instead on the quality of public debate. With Nancy Fraser's 1989 work, a constructivist perspective on the need debate has arisen. Basic needs are constructions that must be asserted in the political process. Therefore, need interpretations are a kind of weapon in political discourse. Instead of implying "inherent needs" as universal, objectively attributable human demands, Nancy Fraser's contribution to the politics of need interpretation uses a line of thought that aims at "interpreted needs" (Dean 2002, 25–28). But the shift towards a constructivist perspective on needs and a procedural perspective on debates on the interpretation of needs restricts the normative potential of Critical Theory. It allows for a critical reconstruction of political processes and discourses from a power-critical perspective, or an instrumental use of categories of need in the political struggle. However, Fraser's intervention has not led to new conceptual sources for the defense of the welfare state.

5.5.2 Reasons for the Welfare State

A different way of thinking has developed mostly in the UK in reaction to the neoliberal attack on the welfare state by Margaret Thatcher and the growing relevance of theories of justice in political philosophy. This strand of research has sought new justifications for the welfare state. Instead of accentuating the procedural questions of a fair discourse on need interpretation, the authors in this debate present substantial arguments for the existence and quality of the welfare state. In the mid-1970s, monographs from philosophy, such as Social Philosophy (Feinberg 1973), Social Justice (Miller 1976), and Reason and Morality (Gewirth 1978), not to mention A Theory of Justice (Rawls 1971), signaled a growing interest in questions of social and political philosophy with clear reference to the current questions of the future of the welfare state. Need was included in these writings as a category that regards and supports the model case of the British Welfare state as it was created after World War II. When Margaret Thatcher took office in 1979, disputes about the welfare state intensified, and need became a key category in discussions that involved political science, political philosophy and social policy research. As a follow-up to "Political Philosophy and Social Welfare. Essays on the Normative Basis of Welfare Provisions" by Raymond Plant, Harry Lesser and Peter Taylor-Gooby (2009 [1980]), the academic debate on need-based justice increasingly expanded not only within, but also outside of, the UK (Weale 1978, 1983, 2013; Dean 2002, 2008, 2010, 2013). At the same time, the task of developing a philosophy of needs (Wiggins 1987; Braybrooke 1987; Thomson 1987) was taken up by normative political theory and welfare state analysis.

A first line of argumentation highlights the importance of basic needs in the sense of basic rights. In his book "Basic Rights: Subsistence, Affluence, and U.S. Foreign Policy", Henry Shue (1996 [1980]) argues for a set of moral rights that cut across the distinction between liberal, democratic, and social rights. According to Shue, basic rights are the necessary foundation for the ability to exercise any other right. Shue outlines this fundamental importance of basic rights in the following way: "Basic rights, then, are everyone's minimum reasonable demands upon the rest of humanity" (Shue 1996 [1980]), 19). They serve "to give the powerless a veto over some of the forces that would otherwise harm them the most" (Shue 1996 [1980], 18). Need-based approaches to social and economic rights "assume that all people have valid social and economic needs that should not be dismissed" (Osiatynski 2007, 63). Henry Shue employs the semantics of rights to demonstrate the priority of some physical and economic rights over liberal and political rights. Shue postulates a right to physical security that serves to fulfill essential needs of material subsistence. However, he does not infer a complete set of economic rights from the right to physical security. Basic needs and the right to physical security relate to standard threats of the powerless. The extent of potential harm defines the scope of "inherent necessities" (Shue 1996 [1980], 26) and the range of social and economic rights.

The most far-reaching attempt to develop a justification of a universal set of basic human needs has been undertaken by Len Doyal and Ian Gough (1984, 1991). They show that all political theories do at least implicitly refer to conceptions of need. This counts as a strong indication that it should be possible to work out a "concept of objective and universal human needs" (Doyal and Gough 1991, 45). Personal autonomy and physical survival are identified as "the preconditions for any individual action in any culture. (…) they constitute the most basic human needs—those which must be satisfied to some degree before actors can effectively participate in their form of life to achieve any other valued goals" (Doyal and Gough 1991, 54). The authors offer methods to measure the fulfillment of basic needs. Doyal and Gough use these methods for a second purpose: They want to determine an "optimal" degree of need fulfillment in addition to "the minimal levels of basic need-satisfaction" (Doyal and Gough 1991, 73). Thus, the two authors develop an extensive version of a strong, universal and specifiable need concept. Shue's basic rights denote a real bottom line, which should not be missed in any case. Doyal's and Gough's basic needs offer an increasingly optimal realization of needs.

In response to these attempts to develop a basic needs approach for the justification of the welfare state, Robert E. Goodin established an opposing stance in his monographs "Protecting the Vulnerable. A Reanalysis of Our Social Responsibilities" (1985) and 'Reasons for Welfare. The Political Theory of the Welfare State' (1988). In a first step, he determines that the traditional justification of mature welfare states using the values of equality, community and needs is a failed strategy of the Old Left. Attempts to base the welfare state on needs gives needs a higher status than wants and preferences. Whatever has been designated as a need gains a higher degree of legitimacy in comparison to wants, and therefore a greater chance of fulfillment in the sense of a "principle of precedence". As a result of the decline of leftist argumentative resources to defend the social security system, the neoliberal attack on the welfare state succeeded in the late 1970s and early 1980s. Goodin aims to present a new justification of the welfare state, a justification that concentrates on reasons for a minimal welfare state primarily, but should be open for a more expansive welfare state (Goodin 1988, 19). With arguments adapted from the philosophers Joel Feinberg (1973) and Harry Frankfurt (1984), Goodin tries to disprove all statements that highlight the priority of needs over wants and regard state intervention as compelling if needs are not met by the market.

The starting point for the questioning of needs as the argumentative foundation of social policy can be found in the writings of Harry Frankfurt (and Brian Barry, who already uses this formulation, see Barry 1965, 47–49). Frankfurt argues that something is not simply necessary, but necessary for something: "We need *X* for *Y*" (Frankfurt 1984). He calls those type of needs, in which *Y* is only wanted (i.e., a desire), "volitional needs". The decisive cases are "non-volitional needs", in which the *Y* itself appears as a need, not as a want or desire. Goodin rejects the strong version of a need-based justification of the welfare state for a surprising reason: "To say that the objectively needed should take precedence over the subjectively desired is to say that the objectively good should take precedence over the subjectively good" (Goodin 1988, 31). According to Goodin, this would lead to a much wider conception of state intervention that would even justify a "command economy" (Goodin 1988, 31). Securing the supremacy of needs over wants makes an argument for socialism, which provides a general precedence for the state's supply of goods. Goodin, however, is looking only for arguments that justify a minimal welfare state and limited intervention into the market: "The welfare state (…) is a system of public interventions" (Goodin 1988, 32). Goodin does not reject the idea that relevant needs might be non-volitional needs. He infers from the far-reaching consequences of such an argumentation that needs should not be understood as non-volitional needs.

Goodin's own reasoning is based on the terms "vulnerability", "dependency", and "exploitation". In "Protecting the Vulnerable" from 1985, Goodin defines vulnerability as the situation that *A* is dependent on *B* and can be harmed by *B* (Goodin 1985, 112; see also Brock 1998, 5). In "Reasons for Welfare" from 1988, the category "dependency" replaces vulnerability and is strongly linked to "exploitation" (Goodin 1988, 174; critical: Weale 2013, 93–94). In Goodin's approach, the welfare state should not have the duty to resolve dependencies. Dependencies that might be exploited constitute obligations for state intervention (Goodin 1988, 177). However, a Marxist concept of "exploitation" would lead to great difficulties for that justification of the welfare state. To capture the situation of those who have not entered the labor market, and thus cannot be exploited by definition, but are 'needy" precisely because of the fact that they play no part in the labor market and lack all means of subsistence, a Marxist conception of "exploitation" cannot be useful (see Weale 2013, 93–94). Accordingly, Goodin develops a very broad concept of exploitation, in the sense of taking unfair advantage of a person and his or her situation (Goodin 1988, 124–129). Although one of the goals of Goodin's construction is to counteract Charles Murray's (1984) highly effective criticism of the welfare state by use of the term "welfare dependency", his own construction of dependency and exploitation does not offer a clear-cut alternative conception. Goodin's justification of the welfare state is also directed only at a particular group of the population, the vulnerable or the needy as linguistic successors of the "deserving poor". They are only a part of the total population, a part that should be protected by Goodin's minimal welfare state. The category need is refused due to its tendency to justify a universal welfare state.

The late 1980s marked the climax of the academic and political debate on a need-based justification of the welfare state. With Doyal's and Gough's theory (1991), a phase of intense political and philosophical debates on a needs-based social policy ended. In the meantime, a need-based justification of social policy had lost ground in theoretical debates, as well as in practical politics. Occasional attempts to reestablish needs as an argumentative resource are still made. In 2012, the philosopher Dale Dorsey presented a proposal for a welfarist version of a "basic minimum", which uses the term need as an anchor term. Former conceptions of an unconditional basic income, however, explicitly deny any link to basic needs, for example, Philippe van Parijs: "The 'basic' of basic income is only meant to convey the image of a basis to which all other incomes can be added. Basic income is therefore not definitionally tied to some notion of 'basic needs'" (Van Parijs 1995, 30).

The concept of needs has also been discussed in the context of a defense of the welfare state as part of the nation-state when faced with the issue of (illegal) immigration (Macedo 2011; Bauböck 2011). Starting from the assumption that in the case of the U.S., immigration and immigration policy have had a negative effect on distributive justice, Macedo argues that citizens of a society have "special obligations to one another with respect to distributive justice" (Macedo 2011, 302) and infers that a "political community's special and urgent obligations to its least well-off members may take priority over the claims of some even poorer people abroad" (Macedo 2011, 302). Although there are "urgent reasons to assist those who are in need (in absolute terms), including very poor persons abroad" (Macedo 2011, 317), and although the U.S. has to "fulfill its duties to aid the world's poorest" (Macedo 2011, 321), Macedo advocates a more restrictive immigration policy. Migration issues tend to bring propositions to the floor, which markedly differentiate between the urgency or the level of basic human needs of natives and migrants, refugees and asylum seekers.

5.6 Normative Political Theory: Basic Human Needs in International Politics

5.6.1 Basic Human Needs as a Developmental Strategy

In politics, the practical uptake of the basic needs strategy led to a whole decade of developmental policy based on the idea of basic human needs (Vetterlein 2015). In 1976, the International Labour Organization organized the "World Conference on Employment, Income Distribution and Social Progress and the International Division of Labour", also known as "World Employment Conference", and published the Director-General's Report to the Conference, entitled "Employment, Growth and Basic Needs: A One-world Problem" (ILO 1976). Again, Maslow's hierarchy of needs served as the theoretical background. The idea behind the basic needs approach can be summed up as follows: While the economically advanced countries have already reached the higher levels of human needs, the developing countries should at least be put in a position to meet the needs of the entire population regarding basic levels of food, housing, clothing, education, and public transportation.

One of the core ideas of the basic needs strategy is the departure from orientations toward economic growth in developmental policy (Stewart 1985a, 1985b). A minimum of food, nutrition, shelter, and health is to be provided to citizens of each developing country, regardless of the funding directed towards economic growth and productivity. The basic needs strategy aims at "meeting specified needs of the poorest people, not primarily in order to raise productivity", but "as an end in itself" (Streeten and Burki 1978, 413). Since the main problems for basic needs strategies are, according to its proponents, "not conceptual, but operational", i.e., problems of "access and delivery" (Streeten and Burki 1978, 414), basic needs strategies not only aim at the provision of goods and services through markets, but also at the provision of "certain public services like education, sanitation, health and water" (Streeten and Burki 1978, 414).

Approaches that aim at the provision of goods on the basis of different levels of human needs have been criticized due to the fact that "the normative specification that lower needs must be satisfied before attention is given to higher needs could be used to justify deliberate inattention to non-material needs and for preserving an unacceptable status quo" (Fisher 1990, 92; see also Galtung 1980). This criticism includes concerns that structures that had been installed to satisfy only material needs "may later stand in the way of satisfaction of non-material needs" (Galtung 1990, 311). Following his critique of existing basic need approaches, Galtung himself develops a more open typology of basic human needs as a "working hypothesis" (Galtung 1990, 309) that avoids "any built-in hierarchization of needs" (Galtung 1990, 312). A debate has ensued between need theorists who focus on human development, on the one hand, and conflict theorists as well as practitioners, on the other hand, who identify frustrated human needs as an explanation for human conflict (Burton 1990; Avruch and Mitchell 2013).

5.6.2 From Needs to Capabilities

The period of the basic needs strategy of developmental policy ended at the beginning of the 1990s. In the first World Development Report from 1990, Amartya Sen, in his position as a member of the advisory group of the UNDP, changed the justification of developmental policy from needs to capabilities, as explained in the chapter on the goal and measurement of human development and the construction of the Human Development Index (HDI): "The basic needs approach usually concentrates on the bundle of goods and services that deprived population groups need: food, shelter, clothing, healthcare and water. It focuses on the provision of these goods and services rather than on the issue of human choices. Human development, by contrast, brings together the production and distribution of commodities and the expansion and use of human capabilities. It also focuses on choices—on what people should have, be and do to be able to ensure their own livelihood. Human development is, moreover, concerned not only with basic needs satisfaction but also with human development as a participatory and dynamic process" (HDR 1990, 11). This position is repeated in the most recent report: "Human development is development of the people through building human capabilities, for the people by improving their lives and by the people through active participation in the processes that shape their lives. It is broader than other approaches, such as the human resource approach, the basic needs approach and the human welfare approach" (HDR 2015, 2). In these reports, the language of needs is still used in many places. The broader theoretical approach has not completely replaced the description of certain claims as needs.

Amartya Sen's work has made a decisive contribution to the replacement of a basic human needs conception in the debates on human development in the Global South and on global justice. The capability approach, supported by him and, in a slightly varying form, by Martha Nussbaum, has established a different viewpoint and a different terminology that seems superior to the basic human needs approach. A detailed explanation for the rejection of the need approach despite its expressly acknowledged importance for shifting the international development policy away from a pure growth policy is found in Sen's Tanner-Lecture, which was published in 1987 under the title "The Standard of Living":

> The strategic relevance of basic needs is not a controversial matter. What is open to debate and disputation is the foundation of this concern. Are basic needs important because and only because their fulfilment contributes to utility? If not, why are they important? Closely related to this question of justification is the issue of the form in which basic needs have to be seen. Are they best seen in terms of commodities that people may be reasonably expected to possess (typically the chosen form in the basic needs literature)? This would relate nicely to some extended sense of opulence and to a justification in terms of the value of popular opulence. (…) Why should we be concerned—not just strategically but fundamentally—with opulence, rather than with what people succeed in doing or being? And if it is accepted that the concern is basically with the kind of lives people do lead or can lead, then this must suggest that the 'basic needs' should be formulated in line with functionings and capabilities. (…) If the objects of value are functionings and capabilities, then the so-called 'basic' needs in the form of commodity requirements are instrumentally (rather than intrinsically) important. The main issue is the goodness of the life that one can lead (Sen 1987, 25).

The role of needs as commodity requirements, and therefore only as a means, is Sen's central point of attack (see also Sen 1992, 109). Needs have no value; they are a transitory or intermediate stage in the discussion about what constitutes the quality of human life (Nussbaum and Sen 1993; Sen 1993). Sen cannot accept arguments that are only directed to "necessary goods" (Brock 1998). Further criticism can be found in "The idea of justice" from 2009. The need terminology leads to the attribution of a passive, suffering character to human beings: "(…) we are not only 'patients' whose needs deserve consideration, but also 'agents' whose freedom to decide what to value and how to pursue what we value can extend far beyond our own interests and needs. The significance of our lives cannot be put into the little box of our own living standards, or our need fulfillment. The manifest needs of the patient, important as they are, cannot eclipse the momentous relevance of the agent's reasoned values" (Sen 2009, 252). To speak of needs is implicitly an act of passivating the human image. The "patient" person must be "cured" of his or her "suffering", the needs that oppress him or her must be fulfilled (for a critical discussion of Sen, see Crocker 2008, 129–140).

The continuation of a need-based approach under a different terminological roof also applies to Martha Nussbaum's variant of the capability approach. Her starting point is Aristotle's conception of the state as a citizenship, which regulates that every citizen is supplied with the essentials of life. Therefore, Nussbaum brings the need approach closer to the ancient tradition of the "good life". The necessary requirements for a good life form the bridge that leads to a non-minimalistic view of needs. Accordingly, Nussbaum's concept of capabilities preserves the essentials of a basic need approach. Her list of capabilities, which is derived from the constitutive conditions of humanity (Nussbaum 2006, 76–78), corresponds in many respects to the list of needs in the philosophy of needs (Braybrooke 1987, see also Doyle and Gough 1991). She characterizes the relationship between need and capabilities as well as her own approach to Sen's as follows: "My capabilities approach supports Sen's proposal, using Sen's arguments and some additional arguments. Sen bases the case for capabilities on individuals' varying needs for resources, and also on their varying abilities to convert resources into functionings. Variations in need, he insists, are pervasive features of human life: children need more protein (an expensive nutrient) than adults, for example. (…) So the question of variation cannot be postponed; it is omnipresent" (Nussbaum 2006, 164–165). In fact, there is a high variance in the levels of necessary goods. However, the task of bridging the invariance of basic needs and the variance of necessary requirements to fulfill the needs in a concrete historical and territorial context has already been done by Doyal and Gough, as they have distinguished between "basic needs" and "basic needs satisfiers", or "intermediate needs", in response to Sen's critique (Doyal and Gough 1991, 155–159; see also Dean 2002, 28).

5.6.3 Theories of Need-Based Global Justice

A theory of need-based global justice can currently be found in the field of political philosophy. One author who succeeds in bringing together the normative concepts of developmental policy, the philosophy of needs, and the normative justification of the welfare state is the New Zealander Gillian Brock (1998, 2009). She combines the approaches of Doyal and Gough, Sen and Nussbaum as well as Braybrooke in a way that offers a new and fresh approach to global justice. In the debates on normative conceptions of global distributive justice, she delivers a consistent way of reinstalling the concept of need as a central category of justice in her book, "Global Justice. A Cosmopolitan Account". She attacks the dominant rights-based approaches in the global justice debate. Thinking in categories of needs instead of rights is superior because each catalog of human rights cannot be constructed without reference to basic human needs. She argues "that we must know what our basic needs are before we can sensibly define the entitlements that will be protected by human rights. In order to draw up a list of our human rights we must have a sense of our basic needs (…). A needs-based account is thus more fundamental than a human rights account" (Brock 2009, 72). Additional pragmatic reasons support the priority of a need-based conception. It is easier to speak globally in categories of needs, because the rights-based discourse is viewed with suspicion, or is even rejected, in many regions of the world as an expression of European-American thinking (Brock 2009, 71). In the theoretical debates on international politics and global justice, the categories of need and need-based justice are ever-present, and part of an ongoing discussion.

5.7 Conclusion

While there are certain areas within positive political research and normative political theory in which the concepts of "need" and "need-based distribution" play a role, overall, a certain degree of restraint, caution and reluctance dominates the debates in political science about the concept of need.

As a core concept for the driving forces of political action, "need" only appears briefly in theories of post-material change, but is soon supplanted by "value" and "interest". As a concept in normative political theory, "need" is strongly contested because it seems to refer to pre-political, "natural" facts. Therefore, many scholars in normative political theory emphasize the political process of decision-making on need-based distribution and the collective discourse about the recognition of needs. From this perspective, needs are distribution criteria that are determined and decided upon politically. If needs have to be politically recognized, the political processes in which this recognition takes place are fundamental. Hence, some authors push the idea of need-based justice aside and highlight questions of procedural justice.

However, it is problematic for normative political theory to follow this displacement of the idea of need-based justice by questions of procedural justice, especially in debates about social policy issues at the national or international level. Even established democratic procedures do not yet guarantee that the needy receive sufficient benefits. Therefore, the concept of "basic needs" has been introduced as a normative reference point in debates on a social minimum for all people around the world. Some political scientists have contributed to the establishment of a theory of human needs while others express strong criticism of this approach. Some political scientists prefer Amartya Sen's capability theory to the concept of need while others focus on 'dependency' and other concepts instead. As a consequence, a broadly acknowledged theory of need-based justice has not been established in these debates between supporters and opponents of the basic needs approach in normative political theory.

In contrast, positive political research has focused on the societal use of need as a criterion for distribution decisions. Ever since the experimental research of Frohlich and Oppenheimer, the "mixed" nature of distribution decisions has become more and more apparent. Support for basic needs is a constant component in distribution decisions, but need is not the single guiding principle in those decisions.

As a result, further research in positive political research should aim for a framework of typical mixtures and combinations between different justice principles (need, equality, desert/equity), while normative political theory should elaborate on an account that systematically demonstrates the superiority of those multi-criterion solutions (which include need-based justice) over simple references to single principles of justice.

Acknowledgments This chapter has been written as part of DFG Research Group 2104 "Needs-based Justice and Distribution Procedures", Projects B2 "Needs-based Justice, Uncertainty and Expertise" (Tepe, reference TE 1022/2 – 1), C1 "Limits of Proceduralism? Experimental Studies on the Stability of Procedures of Need Determination " (Nullmeier, reference NU 108/4 – 1; and Pritzlaff-Scheele, reference PR 1551/1 – 1) and D1 "Fairness, Needs, and Incentives of Voting Procedures" (Schnapp, Schn 1282/4-1). This funding is gratefully acknowledged.

References

Agranov, M., & Palfrey, T. R. (2015). Equilibrium tax rates and income redistribution: A laboratory study. *Journal of Public Economics*, *130*, 45–58.

Alesina, A.F., & Giuliano, P. (2009). *Preferences for Redistribution*, NBER Working Paper 14825.

Anderson, J. (2001). Competent need-interpretation and discourse ethics. In W. Rehg., & J. Bohman (Eds.), *Pluralism and the pragmatic turn. The transformation of critical theory. Essays in honor of Thomas McCarthy* (pp. 193–224). Cambridge: MIT Press.

Avruch, K., & Mitchell, C. (Eds.). (2013). *Conflict resolution and human needs: Linking theory and practice*. London: Routledge.

Barber, B. R., Beramendi, P., & Wibbels, E. (2013). The behavioral foundations of social politics: Evidence from surveys and a laboratory democracy. *Comparative Political Studies*, *46*(10), 1155–1189.

Barry, B. (1965). *Political argument*. London: Routledge and Kegan Paul.

Bashevkin, S. (2000). Rethinking retrenchment: North American Social policy during the early Clinton and Chrétien years. *Canadian Journal of Political Science*, *33*(1), 7–36.

Bauböck, R. (2011). Citizenship and free movement. In R. M. Smith (Ed.), *Citizenship, borders, and human needs* (pp. 343–376). Philadeplphia: University of Pennsylvania Press.

Beechey, S. N. (2016). *Social security and the politics of deservingness*. New York: Palgrave Macmillan.

Boulding, K. E. (1962). Social justice in social dynamics. In R. Brandt (Ed.), *Social justice* (pp. 73–92). Englewood Cliffs: Prentice Hall.

Braybrooke, D. (1987). *Meeting needs*. Princeton: Princeton University Press.

Brock, G. (Ed.). (1998). *Necessary goods. Our responsibilities to meet others' needs*. Oxford: Rowman and Littlefield.

Brock, G. (2009). *Global justice. A cosmopolitan account*. Oxford: Oxford University Press.

Bruni, R. A., Laupacis, A., & Martin, D. K. (2008). Public engagement in setting priorities in health care. *Canadian Medical Association Journal*, *179*(1), 15–18.

Burton, J. (Ed.). (1990). *Conflict human needs theory*. New York: St. Martin's Press.

Cabrales, A., Nagel, R., & Mora, J. R. (2012). It is Hobbes, not Rousseau: An experiment on voting and redistribution. *Experimental Economics*, *15*(2), 278–308.

Cárthaigh, S. M. (2014). Need and poverty. *Policy and Politics*, *42*, 459–473.

Clark, A. E., & D'Ambrosio, C. (2015). Attitudes to income inequality: Experimental and survey evidence. In A. Atkinson., & F. Bourguignon (Eds.), *Handbook of income distribution* (pp. 1147–1208). Amsterdam: Elsevier.

Crocker, D.A. (2008) *Ethics of global development. Agency, capability, and deliberative democracy*. Cambridge: Cambridge University Press.
Daudelin, G., Lehoux, P., Abelson, J., & Denis, J. L. (2011). The integration of citizens into a science/policy network in genetics: Governance arrangements and asymmetry in expertise. *Health Expectations*, *14*(3), 261–271.
Dean, H. (2002). *Welfare rights and social policy*. Harlow: Pearson Education.
Dean, H. (2008). Social policy and human rights: Re-thinking the engagement. *Social Policy and Society*, *7*(1), 1–12.
Dean, H. (2010). *Understanding human need*. Bristol: The Policy Press.
Dean, H. (2013). The translation of needs into rights: Reconceptualising social citizenship as global phenomenon. *International Journal of Social Welfare*, *22*(1), 32–49.
Dorsey, D. (2012). *The basic minimum. A welfarist approach*. Cambridge: Cambridge University Press.
Downs, A. (1957). *An economic theory of democracy*. New York: Harper and Row.
Doyal, L., & Gough, I. (1984). A theory of human need. *Critical Social Policy*, *4*(10), 6–38.
Doyal, L., & Gough, I. (1991). *A theory of human need*. Basingstoke: Macmillan.
Esaiasson, P., Gilljam, M., & Persson, M. (2012). Which decision-making arrangements generate the strongest legitimacy beliefs? Evidence from a randomised field experiment. *European Journal of Political Research*, *51*(6), 785–808.
Esarey, J., Salmon, T., & Barrilleaux, C. (2012a). Social insurance and income redistribution in a laboratory experiment. *Political Research Quarterly*, *65*(3), 685–698.
Esarey, J., Salmon, T., & Barrilleaux, C. (2012b). What motivates political preferences? Self-interest, ideology, and fairness in a laboratory democracy. *Economic Inquiry*, *50*(3), 604–624.
Feinberg, J. (1973). *Social philosophy*. Englewood Cliffs: Prentice-Hall.
Fischer, J., Huth, C., & Römer, R. (2013a). *Bedarfsgerechte Bildungs- und Sozialsteuerung in der Stadt Gera*. Familie und Gesundheit, Erfurt: Studie im Auftrag des Thüringer Ministeriums für Soziales.
Fischer, J., Huth, C., & Römer, R. (2013b). *Bedarfsgerechte Bildungs- und Sozialsteuerung in der Stadt Weimar*. Familie und Gesundheit, Erfurt: Studie im Auftrag des Thüringer Ministeriums für Soziales.
Fisher, R.J. (1990). Needs theory, social identity and an eclectic model of conflict. In J. Burton (Ed.), *Conflict. Human needs theory* (89–112). New York: St. Martin's Press.
Frankfurt, H. (1984). Necessity and desire. *Philosophy and Phenomenologial Research*, *45*(1), 1–13.
Fraser, N. (1989). Struggle over needs: Outline of a socialist-feminist critical theory of late capitalist political culture. In N. Fraser (Ed.), *Unruly practices. power, discourse, and gender in contemporary social theory* (161–187). Minneapolis: University of Minnesota Press.
Frohlich, N., & Oppenheimer, J. A. (1990). Choosing justice in experimental democracies with production. *American Political Science Review*, *84*(2), 461–477.
Frohlich, N., & Oppenheimer, J. A. (1992). *Choosing justice: An experimental approach to ethical theory*. Berkely: California University Press.
Frohlich, N., & Oppenheimer, J. A. (1998). Some consequences of e-mail vs. Face-to-face communication in experiment. *Journal of Economic Behavior and Organization*, *35*(3), 389–403.
Frohlich, N., & Oppenheimer, J. A. (1999). Values, policies, and citizen competence: An experimental perspective. In S. L. Elkin & K. E. Soltan (Eds.), *Citizen competence and democratic institutions* (pp. 161–187). University Park. PA: Pennsylvania State University Press.
Frohlich, N., Oppenheimer, J. A., & Eavey, C. L. (1987a). Laboratory results on Rawls's distributive justice. *British Journal of Political Science*, *17*(1), 1–21.
Frohlich, N., Oppenheimer, J. A., & Eavey, C. L. (1987b). Choices of principles of distributive justice in experimental groups. *American Journal of Political Science*, *31*(3), 606–636.
Galtung, J. (1980). The basic needs approach. In K. Lederer, J. Galtung, & D. Antal (eds.), *Human needs. A contribution to the ongoing debate* (55–125). Cambridge: Oelschlager, Gunn and Hain.

Galtung, J. (1990). International development in human perspective. In J. Burton (Ed.), *Conflict. Human needs theory* (301–335). New York: St. Martin's Press.
Geißel, B., Neunecker, M., & Kolleck, A. (2015). Dialogorientierte Beteiligungsverfahren: Wirkungsvolle oder sinnlose Innovation? *Das Beispiel Bürgerhaushalte. Zeitschrift für Parlamentsfragen, 46*(1), 151–165.
Gewirth, A. (1978). *Reason and morality*. Chicago: University of Chicago Press.
Gilljam, M., Esaiasson, P., & Lindholm, T. (2010). The voice of the pupils: An experimental comparison of decisions made by elected pupil councils, pupils in referenda, and teaching staff. *Educational Assessment, Evaluation and Accountability, 22*(1), 73–88.
Goodin, R. E. (1985). *Protecting the vulnerable. A reanalysis of our social responsibilities*. Chicago: University of Chicago Press.
Goodin, R. E. (1988). *Reasons for welfare. The political theory of the welfare state*. Princton: Princeton University Press.
Habermas, J. (1987 [1981]). *The theory of communicative action, lifeworld and system. A critique of functionalist reason* (Vol. 2), Boston: Beacon Press.
Habermas, J. (1993) Remarks on discourse ethics. In J. Habermas (Ed.), *Justification and application. Remarks on discourse ethics* (19–111). Cambridge: MIT Press.
Hamilton, L. (2003). *The political philosophy of needs*. Cambridge: Cambridge University Press.
Hamilton, L. (2016). Justice and real politics. Freedom, needs and representation. In C. Boisen, & M.C. Murray (Eds.), *Distributive justice debates in political and social thought. Perspectives on finding a fair share* (128–147). New York: Routledge.
Harell, A., Soroka, S., & Iyengar, S. (2016). Race, prejudice and attitudes toward redistribution: A comparative experimental approach. *European Journal of Political Research, 55*(4), 723–744.
Hasseler, M., & Görres, S. (2010). *Was Pflegebedürftige wirklich brauchen ...Zukünftige Herausforderungen an eine bedarfsgerechte ambulante und stationäre pflegerische Versorgung*, Hannover: Schlütersche Verlagsgesellschaft.
HDR (1990): *Human Development Report 1990*, http://hdr.undp.org/en/global-reports.
HDR (2015): *Human Development Report 2015*. http://hdr.undp.org/en/global-reports.
Herlitz, A., & Horan, D. (2016). Measuring needs for priority setting in healthcare planning and policy. *Social Science and Medicine, 157*, 96–102.
ILO. (1976). *Employment, growth and basic needs: A one world problem*. Geneva: ILO.
Inglehart, R. (1977). *The silent revolution. Changing values and political styles among western publics*. Princeton: Princeton University Press.
Inglehart, R. (1990). *Culture shift in advanced industrial society*. Princeton: Princeton University Press.
Inglehart, R., & Abramson, P. R. (1999). Measuring postmaterialism. *American Political Science Review, 93*(3), 665–677.
Joseph, B. H. R. (1986). *The discovery of need, 1880–1914: A case study of the development of an idea in social welfare thought*. New York: Columbia University School of Social Work.
Kittel, B., Paetzel, F., & Traub, S. (2015). Competition, income distribution and the middle class: an experimental study. *Journal of Applied Mathematics*, 303912, 15. https://doi.org/10.1155/2015/303912.
Landwehr, C. (2006). Kann über die Verteilung von Gesundheitsgütern demokratisch entschieden werden? *Forschungsjournal Neue Soziale Bewegungen, 19*(4), 84–97.
Landwehr, C. (2012). Demokratisches Institutionendesign in der Priorisierung und Rationierung von Gesundheitsleistungen. *Zeitschrift für Evidenz, Fortbildung und Qualität im Gesundheitswesen, 106*(6), 407–411.
Landwehr, C. (2013). Procedural justice and democratic institutional design in health-care priority-setting. *Contemporary Political Theory, 12*(4), 296–317.
Landwehr, C. (2015). Democratic meta-deliberation: Towards reflective institutional design. *Political Studies, 63*(S1), 38–54.
Landwehr, C., & Böhm, K. (2011). Delegation and institutional design in health care rationing. *Governance, 24*(4), 665–688.

Lind, E. A., & Tyler, T. R. (1988). *The social psychology of procedural justice*. New York: Plenum.
Lorenz, J., Paetzel, F., & Tepe, M. (2017). Just don't call it tax! framing in an experiment on voting and redistribution. *Journal of Experimental Political Science* (forthcoming).
Macedo, S. (2011). When and why should liberal democracies restrict immigration? In R. M. Smith (Ed.), *Citizenship, borders, and human needs* (pp. 301–323). Philadelphia: University of Pennsylvania Press.
Maslow, A. H. (1970)[1954]). Motivation and personality (2nd ed.). New York: Harper and Row.
May, P. J., Koski, C., & Stramp, N. (2016). Issue expertise in policymaking. *Journal of Public Policy*, *36*, 195–218.
Meltzer, A. H., & Richard, S. F. (1981). A rational theory of the size of government. *Journal of Political Economy*, *89*(5), 914–927.
Michelbach, P. A., Scott, J. T., Matland, R. E., & Bornstein, B. H. (2003). Doing Rawls justice: An experimental study on distribution norms. *American Journal of Political Science*, *47*(3), 523–539.
Miller, D. (1976). *Social justice*. Oxford: Clarendon Press.
Murray, C. (1984). *Losing ground: American Social Policy 1950–1980*. New York: Basic Books.
Noonan, J. (2006). *Democratic Society and human needs: towards a renewed critique of liberal capitalism*. Montreal: McGill-Queen's University Press.
Nussbaum, M. C. (2006). *Frontiers of justice. Disability, nationality, species membership*. Cambridge: Belknap Press, Harvard University Press.
Nussbaum, M. C., & Sen, A. K. (Eds.). (1993). *The quality of life*. Oxford: Clarendon Press.
O'Connor, A. (2001). *Poverty knowledge. Social science, social policy, and the poor in Twentieth-Century U.S. History*. Princeton: Princeton University Press.
Osiatynski, W. (2007). Needs-based approach to social and economic rights. In S. Hertel., & L. Minkler (Eds.), *Economic rights. conceptual, measurement, and policy issues* (56–75). Cambridge: Cambridge University Press.
Ozegowski, S., & Sundmacher, L. (2013). Bedarfsplanung - quo vadis? *G&S Gesundheits- und Sozialpolitik*, *67*(6), 60–67.
Palfrey, T. R. (2009). Laboratory experiments in political economy. *Annual Review of Political Science*, *12*, 379–388.
Park, S. (2014). The politics of redistribution in local governments. The effect of gender representation on welfare spending in California counties. *Journal of Public Policy*, *34*(2), 269–301.
Persson, M., Esaiasson, P., & Gilljam, M. (2013). The effects of direct voting and deliberation on legitimacy beliefs: An experimental study of small group decision-making. *European Political Science Review*, *5*(1), 381–399.
Persson, T., & Tabellini, G. (2002). *Political economics explaining economic policy*. Cambridge: MIT Polity Press.
Plant, R., Lesser, H., & Taylor-Gooby, P. (Eds.). (2009 [1980]). *Political philosophy and social welfare. essays on the normative basis of welfare provisions* (reprint). New York: Routledge (1980, London: Routledge and Kegan Paul).
Raphael, D. D. (1980). *Justice and liberty*. London: Athlone Press.
Rawls, J. (1971). *A theory of justice*. Cambridge: Belknap Press of Harvard University Press.
Rowntree, B. S. (1901). *Poverty: A study of town life*. London: Macmillan.
Sen, A. K. (1987). *The standard of living*. Cambridge: Cambridge University Press.
Sen, A. K. (1992). *Inequality reexamined*. Oxford: Oxford University Press.
Sen, A. K. (1993). Capability and well-being. In M. C. Nussbaum & A. K. Sen (Eds.), *The quality of life* (pp. 30–53). Oxford: Clarendon Press.
Sen, A. K. (2009). *The idea of justice*. New York: Penguin.
Shipan, C.R., & Volden, C. (2014). When the smoke clears. expertise, learning and policy diffusion. *Journal of Public Policy*, *34*(3), 357–387.
Shue, H. (1996 [1980]): *Basic rights. Subsistence, affluence, and U.S. foreign policy* (2nd ed.,). Princeton University Press.
Stewart, F. (1985a). *Planning to meet basic needs*. London: Macmillan.
Stewart, F. (1985b). *Basic needs in developing countries*. Johns Hopkins University Press.

Stollmann, F. (2015). Bedarfsanalyse bei Krankenhausplanung - Durchschnittswerte zur Krankenhaushäufigkeit. *Medizinrecht*, *33*(4), 290–293.
Straßheim, H. (2015). Politics and policy expertise. In F. Fischer, D. Torgerson, M. Orsini, & A. Durnova (Eds.), *Handbook of critical policy studies* (pp. 319–430). Cheltenham: Edward Elgar.
Streeten, P., & Burki, S. J. (1978). Basic needs: Some issues. *World Development*, *6*(3), 411–421.
Sutter, M., Haigner, S., & Kocher, M. (2010). Choosing the Carrot or the Stick? Endogenous institutional choice in social dilemma situations. *Review of Economic Studies*, *77*(4), 1540–1566.
Thomson, G. (1987). *Needs*. London: Routledge und Kegan Paul.
Tyler, T. R., Boeckmann, R. J., Smith, H. J., & Huo, Y. J. (1997). *Social justice in a diverse society*. Boulder: Westview Press.
Van Damme, J., M. Brans., & E. Fobé (2011). Balancing expertise, societal input and political control in the production of policy advice. a comparative study of education councils in Europe. *Halduskultuur—Administrative Culture*, *12*(2), 126–145.
Van Parijs, P. (1995). *Real freedom for all. What (if anything) can justify capitalism?*. Oxford: Clarendon Press.
Vetterlein, A. (2015). The discursive power of international organisations. social policy language and concepts in the world bank and the international monetary fund. In D. Béland., & K. Petersen (Eds.), *Analysing social policy concepts and language. comparative and transnational perspectives* (101–125). Bristol: Policy Press.
von Neumann, J., & Morgenstern, O. (1953). *Theory of games and economic behavior*. Princeton: Princeton University Press.
Weale, A. (1978). *Equality and social policy*. London: Routledge and Kegan Paul.
Weale, A. (1983). *Political theory and social policy*. Basingstoke: Macmillan.
Weale, A. (2013). *Democratic justice and the social contract*. Oxford University Press.
Wiggins, D. (1987). *Needs, values, truth. Essays in the philosophy of value*. Oxford: Basil Blackwell.

Chapter 6
Need-Based Justice and Distribution Procedures: The Perspective of Economics

Andreas Nicklisch and Fabian Paetzel

Abstract In this chapter, we present both macro-empirical and micro-experimental evidence of how subjects redistribute resources. We identify a moderate level of redistribution both in macro-empirical and experimental work. We present evidence that moderate levels of redistribution are due to the preferences of individuals rather than other possible explanations, such as the interests of elites or institutions. Particularly, we find that moderate redistribution, which transfers resources based on the fairness principle of need-based justice is generally accepted and brings along productivity-enhancing effects instead of efficiency losses.

6.1 Introduction

From each according to his ability, to each according to his need...
A phrase popularized by Karl Marx in his 1875 Critique of the Gotha Program.

There is a fundamental imbalance embedded in many modern states: a substantial inequality of incomes coexists with a demand for equal political rights. The poor majority of citizens accepts a considerably unfavorable inequality of wealth despite having the voting power to eliminate that inequality by means of redistribution (see Corneo and Gruener 2000).

One reason for abstaining from a rigorous form of redistribution is that tax collection and money transfers do not come at a zero cost. There are obvious costs of

A. Nicklisch (✉)
Center for Economic Policy Research & FOR 2104, Fachhochschule Graubünden, Chur, Switzerland
e-mail: andreas.nicklisch@fhgr.ch

F. Paetzel
Department of Economics & FOR 2104, Helmut-Schmidt-University, Hamburg, Germany
e-mail: fpaetzel@hsu-hh.de

S. Traub and B. Kittel (eds.), *Need-Based Distributive Justice*,
https://doi.org/10.1007/978-3-030-44121-0_6

redistribution: tax declarations have to be administered, money has to be transferred between bank accounts, and so on. However, economists are far more concerned with the hidden costs of redistribution: taking away income and providing funds affects incentives to work. In other words, the same person receiving governmental transfers provides a different production effort than when paying taxes than if she neither receives transfers nor pays taxes. Therefore, the size of redistribution affects the total welfare within societies.

There is a large body of economic research dealing with biased incentives and the resulting welfare consequences. In a nutshell, distorted incentives predominantly amplify a loss in welfare. However, in the last 20 years, economists have uncovered yet another important facet of the problem, which influences the costs of redistribution and may even turn them into benefits: redistribution may support people's fairness sentiments. In other words, people are willing to pay for a "fair" distribution of wealth within a society. A moderate, more even distribution of incomes may stimulate production, both by taxpayers and transfer receivers.

Thus, it is crucial to think about the wise fairness principle that guides and organizes our redistribution activities. Traditionally, the literature conceptualizes three distinct fairness principles (Miller 1999): equity (or accountability), equality, and need. All three are usually deemed essential fairness principles. As pointed out elsewhere, the context crucially influences which fairness principle is activated and applied (Konow 2001, 2009).

Surprisingly, the major focus of contemporary research on social justice and social contracts is aimed at understanding equality and equity preferences, and how both the principles affect the behavior (see the recently published survey of the relevant literature by Konow and Schwettmann 2016).

Although one may argue that equality and equity are of great importance, it seems that actual redistribution follows largely need-based considerations: governmental transfers satisfy individual needs that recipients are unable to finance themselves; subsidies are implemented to avoid suffering, and institutional settings such as minimum income, basic income or breadline income (margin of subsistence) reflect considerations of need-based justice in a social contract rather than trying to equalize the net wealth within societies.

An empirical example is the "Gallup Poll Social Series: Economy and Personal Finance".[1] In this questionnaire, participant are asked, "What is the smallest amount of money a family of four needs to make each year to get by in your community?" On average, participants state that $58.000 would be enough to "just get by". In contrast, the federal poverty threshold for a family of four is under $24.000. This example points to two important things. First, subjects do not solely focus on surviving but on "getting by in their community". Secondly, stated demands differ from what is universally accepted as a need.

Need-based justice is focused on social needs. These needs are stated individually as demands for specific goods or services. The electorate has to agree on the needs that they want to accept. Once, the need is accepted, society has to fulfill these needs.

[1]http://www.gallup.com/poll/162587/americans-say-family-four-needs-nearly-60k.aspx.

It is an open question that needs to get accepted and to what extent the process of acceptance depends on, for instance, information and beliefs. The concept of need-based justice is very flexible: if commonly accepted as a social need, need-based redistribution is able to take into account various reasons that subjects may feel deprived relative to others in the society (Runciman 1966). In contrast, the fairness principle of equality would "automatically" yield redistribution, which (at least to some extent) equalizes inequalities.

We consider the discussion of redistribution as incomplete without reference to need-based reasoning. Nevertheless, compared to other principles, little is known about need-based justice and its distributive consequences in economics. This chapter tries to close this gap by discussing the interplay between redistribution and need-based justice in greater detail. First, we introduce the orthodox perspective on taxation and redistribution (Sect. 6.2). In Sect. 6.3, we introduce the fairness views of equality and equity. Section 6.4 then focuses in detail on need-based justice. Section 6.5 provides a general discussion about the interplay between need-based redistribution and welfare within societies, and why this fairness principle is especially important for understanding how voters determine the social contract. Section 6.6 concludes and highlights the importance of improving scientific understandings of need-based redistribution in economics.

6.2 The Cost of Redistribution, Part 1

There are good reasons to collect taxes: a society pools individual risks such that societal goals (e.g., fighting poverty, running a nationwide health-care system, enabling universal participation in socioeconomic life) are financed by means of taxation (cf. Lampert and Althammer 2001). In other words, efficiency concerns justify social security insurance. Society finances this insurance by necessary violations of individual property rights (Barr 1998; Barr and Diamond 2008, 2010).

The rather surprising (for non-economists) question is why we observe so little taxation. The income distribution of almost all societies is skewed to the right. That is, there is a majority in society that earns significantly less than a minority of people. At its extreme, the few possess almost the entire wealth of a nation while all others own almost nothing. In democratic states, it follows from the right skewness of both the income and the wealth distribution that those who benefit from redistribution constitute the majority, and—according to the median voter theorem—determine the size of taxation (see e.g., Meltzer and Richard 1981; Acemoglu and Robinson 2000, while this view is criticized by Korpi 1983; Huber and Stephens 2012). According to this perspective, the welfare state is a mechanism that empowers the poor.

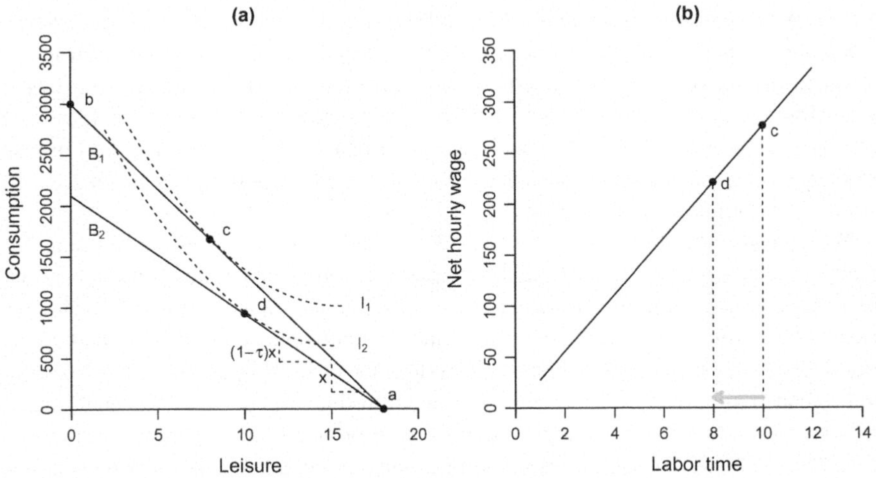

Fig. 6.1 Taxation biases the optimal time allocation in favor of leisure

6.2.1 A Standard View on Taxation

The reason we observe predominantly moderate levels of redistribution is that even the majority of society has to balance the benefits of receiving transfers with the disincentives for labor provision. That is, excessive redistribution is likely to generate socially inefficient outcomes because it undermines the willingness of those who are more able to expend effort (Alesina and Perotti 1996; Persson and Tabellini 1994).

Figure 6.1 sketches the traditional labor-leisure-time reasoning of workers: in panel (a) of the figure, we measure on the horizontal axis the time spent on leisure activities, and on the vertical axis the economic outcome of time spent on labor. Let us begin in a world without taxes. On the vertical axis, we measure the consumption expenditure the worker can afford from her labor income. As a consequence, there is a feasible set within the diagram from which the worker can pick her most favorable leisure-consumption mix. That is, the worker may choose any combination of time for leisure and for work below the time constraint B_1. If she chooses a in the lower corner of the set, she spends all the time at her disposal (say 18 out of 24 h per day) on leisure activities, but has no labor income and cannot consume anything. At the other extreme (b), she spends all her time working, yielding maximum consumption but no free time.

Each point within the set of time allocation corresponds to a certain utility for the worker. There are certain points she likes more and there are points she likes less (implying more utility resulting from the choice of the former points than from the choice of the latter points). Points she is indifferent to in terms of resulting utility lies on an "indifference" curve (the dotted curves I_1 and I_2), while all points on I_1 are more preferable than all points on I_2: for every point on I_2 there is a corresponding point north-east on I_1 implying more consumption and more leisure. In other words, moving north-east to higher indifference curves increase the worker's utility.

Obviously, the worker optimizes her labor-leisure mix by picking the point on her highest indifference curve, which is still within the feasible set of leisure-consumption combinations (say, this is point c). Notice that in this simplified model, the slope of the budget constraint B_1 equals the hourly wage of the worker: spending one hour less on leisure increases the consumption by x (the wage the worker earns in this hour).

How does taxation change the choice of the labor-leisure mix? Let us assume that the worker has to pay a fraction of τ from her hourly wage to the state. Her net hourly wage becomes $(1 - \tau)x$. Importantly, leisure time is not taxed, meaning her time constraint changes and becomes B_2. Again, she chooses the point associated with the highest indifference curve, which is still inside her new time constraint B_2 (say this is point d). Obviously, taxation decreases the net salary of workers and biases the optimal labor-leisure-time choice in favor of leisure time—since leisure is not taxed—meaning that the worker spends less time working (panel (b) of Fig. 6.1).

6.2.2 *Taxation and the Struggle for Redistribution*

Based on the standard approach of taxation, society has to consider the work disincentive for the rich when the social contract is set. Despite the biasing effect of taxation, even the traditional paradigm admits that there are strategic reasons to pay taxes. For example, we mentioned the insurance character of governmental transfers earlier in this chapter. Mirrlees (1971) highlights that, from a welfare-maximizing point of view, the level of redistribution should be at a level at which the poor do not suffer and both the poor and the rich have an incentive to spend effort. Mirrlees also motivates the insurance aspect with fairness considerations.

Another reason is that transfers decrease the likelihood of radical forms of power and income transition or revolutions within societies (Barro 2000; Forbes 2000). That is, moderate redistribution stabilizes democracy at the price of biasing the labor-leisure-time mix. Another branch of the literature stresses that redistribution reduces the disincentives for the poor to take risks that are too high (e.g., Aghion and Bolton 1997). Redistribution increases the endowments of the poor. The poor reduce the demand for loans and invest more efficiently, which means that they take fewer risks. Thus, efficiency in the economy is improved.

Lorenz et al. (2013) points to the so-called portfolio effect through redistribution. Assuming that individual human capital follows a risky multiplicative stochastic process, the authors show that, even if redistribution comes with costs and the stochastic process leads to decreasing human capital, redistribution leads to the growth of aggregated human capital. By exclusively focusing on the portfolio rebalancing effect, they propose a new approach about the link between inequality, redistributive taxation, and wealth. They have shown that taxation and redistribution can be a crucial ingredient in ensuring the survival and development of a society.

The politico-economic literature stresses that either an institutional or a structural condition is sufficient to protect a society against excesses from both sides. On the one hand, institutional rules of collective decision-making giving veto power to all stakeholders (Buchanan and Tullock 1962; Miller and Vanberg 2013) enforce a consensual decision and, thereby, make the distributive struggle an issue of explicit negotiation. On the other hand, the existence of a neutral but opportunistic middle class serves as a buffer between the upper and the lower classes because they fear expropriation from both sides and will thus side with the weaker group in case of conflict (Scharpf 1987; Easterly 2001; Glaeser et al. 2003; Kittel et al. 2015). Moreover, not being the main target of redistribution, members of the middle class will let their decisions be guided more by moral values such as justice norms than the other two socioeconomic groups (Arts and Gelissen 2001; d'Anjou et al. 1995; Jaeger 2006).

Besides the above mentioned protection through institutional hurdles or the existence of a neutral middle class, another stream in the literature stresses different explanations for why the poor median voter does not necessarily follow the median voter's prediction. The "prospects of upward mobility" (POUM) hypothesis brings forward the argument that some voters who have an income below the mean expect that their future income will be above the mean (Benabou and Ok 2001). Therefore, they prospectively vote against high levels of redistribution. Roemer (1998) and Lee and Roemer (2006) show that voting on redistribution is also affected by religion and race. The more fragmented the population is with regard to both dimensions, the lower is the willingness to redistribute. Alesina and Angeletos (2005) and Fong (2001) show that if the poor believe that the rich are rich because they invested greater efforts and have greater abilities, the pressure for redistribution is low.

Yet, in recent years, public awareness of an increasingly lopsided distribution of income and wealth in Western countries has strongly increased (Piketty 2014). Most OECD countries have witnessed growing inequality over the past 20 years (OECD 2008). In particular, the gap between the bottom and the top deciles of the household income distribution has risen dramatically. The decile ratio currently amounts to about 1:15 in the US and 1:9 in the OECD-34, and even in a Nordic welfare state like Sweden, it is close to 1:6. In recent years, the growth of inequality seems to be slowing down in some countries (see OECD 2011).

Observers note the formation, as well as deliberate establishment, of a winner-takes-all society in which the middle class is gradually being eroded (Frank and Cook 1995; Frank 2007; Hacker and Pierson 2010). A few superstars, which may or may not be the most able practitioners in a particular area, receive all the profit while the efforts of others are in vain (e.g., Rosen 1981; DiPrete and Eirich 2006; Franck and Nüsch 2012). This development may result in increasing societal division, distributive struggle, and violent conflict (e.g., Stiglitz 2012). On the other hand, the fall of communist regimes in the late 1980s and early 1990s has demonstrated the crippling effects of excessive egalitarianism on economic efficiency and growth (Fukuyama 2006; Alesina and Angeletos 2005). So, do we observe a change from redistribution and mild equality to radical equity? We argue that this and similar questions cannot be answered without the consideration of need-based justice. Before we introduce need-based justice, we present the most prominently mentioned concepts of justice, namely equality and equity.

6.3 Varieties of Fairness: Two Rivaling Sisters

There are two leading views on fairness in economics, equality and equity. We characterize them as two sisters from the same family of fairness sentiments. They do not get along very well with each other. However, once separated from one another, they miss each other terribly.

On the one hand, one may argue that the increasing dispersion of incomes and the division of classes lead to inherently unfair—*unequal*—distributions of wealth within societies. But this is just one side of the coin. On the other hand, there is the notion of equity: those who earn the highest wages have, in fact, deserved it. One may say that equity reflects the fairness of *achievements*. In the following, we elaborate on both notions of fairness.

6.3.1 Equality

Equality is probably one of the oldest and most common paradigms for human coexistence. The New Testament quotes Jesus' second Great Commandment as "Thou shalt love thy neighbor as thyself" (Mark 12: 31), while, for example, there is one Hanukiya (the Hanuka lamp) for each family member at the Jewish holiday of Hanuka.

Despite its omnipresence, it has taken economists a very long time to accept that people have a desire for equality. That is, for a long time there was no general agreement that inequality decreases the utility of people. In 1982, Werner Güth and his coauthors published their article on the 'ultimatum game' and provided evidence that people are fair-minded. In this game, two anonymous players bargain in a very stylized form over some money. More precisely, one of the two persons, called the "proposer", is endowed with E monetary units. The proposer has to offer her counterpart, the "responder", a fraction x of E. The responder may accept x, in which case the responder earns x and the proposer $E - x$, or rejects it, in which case both earn nothing.

When testing the game with students and other participants from various socioeconomic and ethnic backgrounds, Güth and many other researchers observed two stylized facts: (i) the modal and median offers are 40–50% of E, and (ii) the few offers at or below 20% are frequently rejected (see the survey by Gueth and Kocher 2014). Is this surprising for non-economists? Certainly, not. But for economists, it is a big deal to admit that people's behavior departs from the standard assumption of money maximization. Since accepting even the smallest offer possible yields a higher payoff than rejecting it, rejections violate narrow self-interest. The anticipation of the non-rejection of any $x > 0$ leads any money-maximizing proposer to offer the smallest (non-zero) amount. In turn, anticipating that small, unfair offers are to be rejected leads to an increase of offers to the level that we observe in experiments.

Thus, equality of outcomes matters for people. However, what drives this behavior? Is it fairness towards others or anticipation of others' preferences for fairness? If the latter, then the preferences for fairness may simply be a "mis-anticipation" of others' preferences. To clarify this point, researchers have explored the "dictator game" (Kahneman et al. 1986). In this setup, proposers (now called "dictators") make offers, but responders have no choice regarding their response and have to accept whatever the dictator offers. Narrow money maximization suggests that the offer will be zero. Forsythe et al. (1994), however, find mean offers of roughly 20%, which is significantly less than in the ultimatum game, but also significantly greater than zero. Thus, there is evidence that altruism partly impacts our choices. Particularly, the general tendency to choose equal splits when negotiating has been attributed to a preference for equality.

Consequently, economic theory has developed preference models that nest both pure self-interest and inequality aversion. Most prominently, Fehr and Schmidt (1999) as well as Bolton and Ockenfels (2000), and many others, formalize utility functions implementing disutility for unequal allocations of outcomes, while nesting perfectly selfish preferences for certain parameter constellations. For instance, Fehr and Schmidt introduce an individual taste parameter that amplifies the disutility per unit of unequally divided money (economists refer to this as the marginal disutility) in the following way[2]:

$$u_i = m_i - \alpha_i \max(0, m_y - m_i) + \beta_i \max(0, m_i - m_y), \tag{6.1}$$

where m_i (u_i) denotes my money (utility), m_y the money of the opponent with whom I am interacting, and α_i (β_i) my marginal disutility from inequality, which disadvantages (advantages) me. In other words, α_i and β_i are my individual tastes for envy and shame. If m_y is larger than m_i, every money unit y's payment is exceeding i harms i utility by α_i (a similar rational applies when m_i exceeds m_y). Bolton and Ockenfels (2000) provide an alternative to the Fehr-Schmidt utility function. Instead of introducing individual weights for inequality they claim that it is the relative payoff standing that drives fairness considerations.

Despite its simplicity and its ability to accommodate an enormous number of empirical observations in which behavior departs from the pure money maximization prediction, there have been serious doubts over the years about whether equality subsumes *completely and correctly* the fairness sentiment driving peoples' choices. The criticism follows two directions: one deals with the consistency and persistence of fairness across choices, another with the dominance of the equality principle over alternative ones. Blanco et al. (2011) assess individual fairness sentiments in a modified dictator game utilizing a within-subjects design. Based on the estimated

[2]Notice that we show here a simplified version of Fehr and Schmidt's utility function restricted to the two-person case only. For the complete framework, we refer to their article (1999).

strength of individual fairness concerns they predict behavior in a sequential prisoners' dilemma game. Actual decisions, though, show that there is little consistency between predictions and behavior.

Along this line of argument, Hoffman et al. (1996) show that minor modifications in terms of wording or the level of anonymity cause substantial changes in the dictator's giving. Likewise, systematic changes in the set of alternatives the dictator can choose from (e.g., if the experimenter allows the dictator also to take from the receiver) lead to dramatic changes in the share of dictators who give positive amounts (e.g., Cappelen et al. 2013; List 2007; Bolton et al. 1998).[3]

Finally, a stream of the literature reinterprets the individual sentiments in favor of equality differently. Andreoni and Bernheim (2009) argue that people like to be perceived by others as fair or at least non-selfish rather than inherently preferring to behave fairly. This claim is supported by Bartling and Fischbacher (2011). In their experiment, dictators can choose the money allocation themselves or delegate this decision to a third party. Most dictators delegate the decision, clearly avoiding selfish choices, which they, however, expect the third party to choose for them. In a related experiment, Dana et al. (2007) allow dictators to camouflage selfish choices at the cost of the receiver. Results show significantly less giving if dictators can disguise their intentions.

Summarizing the arguments against the fairness principle of equality, it seems that equality is an important sentiment for human behavior, but it may not influence decisions as robustly and persistently as economists believed at first glance. Konow (2001, 2003) concludes that the social context induces fairness motives, particularly equality, and that the frequent choice of equal splits in the laboratory may be an experimental artifact. Experiments eliminate a lot of everyday contexts, which may draw subjects away from equal splits.

The second line of criticism questions whether equality is the exclusive motive for fair behavior, even if we stay in a reduced framework that fosters the salience of equal distributions. To test the predominance of equality over other fairness sentiments, Falk et al. (2003) develop the following design: they analyze the likelihood of an identical offer of $m_y = 8$, $m_i = 2$ being rejected in the ultimatum game with only two alternative offers. The rate of rejections more than triples if the alternative not chosen is more equal ($m_y = 5$, $m_i = 5$), than when it is more unequal ($m_y = 10$, $m_i = 0$) compared to the proposed one.

This finding is a direct contradiction of the social preference system like in equation (1): since my monetary utility (2) and the distance between payoffs (6) is identical, there cannot be differences in the utility of accepting the offer. Thus, there should be no systematic difference in rejection rates for identical offers. Related to this issue is the observation by Blount (1995). She reports on experimental ultimatum games in which offers are randomly chosen by a computer on behalf of a human receiver. In this setting, offers are rejected significantly less often than when offers are actually chosen by human receivers themselves.

---

[3] A comprehensive survey of the dictator game literature is provided by Engel (2011).

Again, those systematic differences do not surprise non-economists: the rejection rates are influenced by the circumstances under which the offers are chosen. In the Falk et al. experiment, it is the unchosen alternative that matters; in the Blount experiment, it is the proposer's responsibility for the suggested outcome. Thus, it seems that people's fairness sentiments reflect not only the outcome of a procedure, but also the process that leads to the outcome. In other words, we interpret choice, derive intention, and try to reciprocate by matching the intention accordingly. If somebody treats us kindly by proposing a nice offer, we respond kindly by accepting the offer; if however, somebody treats us unkindly by proposing a mean offer, we respond unkindly by rejecting the offer.

Although the general idea of reciprocity—"do ut des"—is very straight forward and easy to understand, there is still an ongoing debate among economists on how to formalize kindness in a very general way (see for this discussion, e.g., Sobel 2005; Nowak and Sigmund 2005). Charness and Rabin (2002) utilize a simple indicator function to account for reciprocity. If person y behaves nicely towards person i, the indicator value is in i's utility function is equal to one, and person i's utility increases also in the size of person y's payoff (who treated person i nicely). Despite this formal problem, it is generally accepted that a concept of fairness that refers exclusively to the outcome of a distribution process—for instance, equality—does not capture our notion of fairness completely. Rather, the distribution process in itself matters for our judgment, and there is a large heterogeneity regarding the weight people put on each of those motives (see, e.g., Nicklisch and Wolff 2012).

6.3.2 *Equity*

From the fact that people's fairness sentiments relate to the procedure that brings about the outcomes, it follows that if a process does not favor one particular person, provides equal chances for everybody, and does not permit "bypassing of" the chance equality, one can call such a process fair. This holds even if the process yields unequal outcomes. Specifically, if we consider it fair when a process provides equal chances for everybody, and allows any individual to increase the chance of a favorable outcome for herself by means of individual effort and individual talent, we apply an equity principle. In other words, an equity process renders outcomes proportionally to the input people deliver.

Following this rationale, one can say that the resources people provide during the production (e.g., working time) represent their claims to whatever is divided afterward (e.g., the production surplus).[4] People acquire entitlements to some fraction of the pie. In turn, it is fair that those who do not acquire entitlements, receive nothing or dramatically less than the others.

Equity motives play an important role in social perceptions regarding the fairness of relative positions in income and wealth. These motives depend on the extent

[4] Moulin (2002) gives an overview of the literature of surplus sharing.

to which individuals are perceived as accountable for differences in economic performance (see Konow 2000; Fong 2001). The notion of "equity theory" was first advocated by Adams (1965) and Homans (1974) in psychology and sociology. In economics, the notion of equity is also called the theory of entitlements (Croson and Konow 2009; Gill and Stone 2010; Krawczyk 2010; Cappelen et al. 2013; Gill and Stone 2015; Mollerstrom et al. 2015).

There is evidence pointing to the existence of a preference for proportional distributions, particularly when individual claims exceed the available pie.[5] Gächter and Riedl (2006) introduce a real effort experiment in which participants bargain over money previously "produced" in a quiz task. In a second treatment condition, participants are asked to choose hypothetically the fairest allocation facing the same distribution problems. Proportionality is the most preferred rule in the latter treatment condition, while a mixture of equity and equality determines allocations in the former treatment condition.

Bosmans and Schokkaert (2009) analyze how participants hypothetically divide surplus in the context of firm earnings and pension payments. With varying individual claims and surplus sizes, a majority of participants prefer the proportionality rule across different tasks in which subjects earn their claims. Finally, Herrero et al. (2010) confirm Gächter and Riedl's earlier finding: across different claims, contexts, and surpluses, hypothetical choices predominantly follow proportionality. However, subjects in the paid experiment choose a mixture of different rules depending on the game. Thus, it seems that equity is an important component of fair division of resources, but people apply this principle less rigorously when it affects their own outcomes.

One reason for the restricted implementation of equity in experimental studies—and even more so in real scenarios—is the issue of deserts. Quite often, it is unclear which attribute must be assigned to which proportionality to yield a fair outcome. Inequalities based on attributes that fall into the responsibility of individual persons are commonly assumed to be justified, whereas attributes that cannot be influenced by individual persons do not justify unequal outcomes (Konow 1996). For instance, a very common assessment of behavior is that people are responsible for their effort but not for their luck. Successful people often downplay the role of luck as a reason for success—a phenomenon known as "illusion of control" (Langer 1975). Consequently, people should be held accountable for the effort they choose to exercise, and agents should be rewarded for their effort, but not for their luck. Cappelen and Tungodden (2009) call this the principle of responsibility. However, it is less clear, and more challenging to define, if one should be held responsible for talent, initial endowment of knowledge, wealth, etc. Defining deserts is a challenging issue (for an extensive discussion, see Fleurbaey 2008).

Of course, in the context of laboratory experiments, we can manipulate entitlements, and, therefore, the acceptance of inequality. In dictator game experiments by Cherry et al. (2002), dictators 'earn' their endowments in a quiz task. Depending on

[5]Note that there is a rich literature on bankruptcy and repayment rules dealing with solutions for this type of problem (e.g., Chun 1999; Thomson 2003).

variations on the level of endowment and anonymity, the vast majority (70–97%) of dictators give nothing at all, while 15–19% of the dictators do so when endowments are granted for free. The authors conclude that "when assets are legitimized with effort and strategic concerns are controlled with isolation, altruism was the exception and self-interest was the rule" (Cherry et al. 2002, 1221). However, deserts are fragile, and so are the result of this experiment: in Cherry et al.'s design, receivers could not participate in the quiz task. In a modified version of the game, Mittone and Ploner (2012) allow both dictators and receivers to participate in the task. As a result, only 21–48% of dictators transfer nothing to recipients. In other words, keeping everything or almost everything is justified when dictators exclusively provide the effort to 'generate' the incomes.

Studying the role of performance differences in a cognitive-effort task on the so-called 'in-group bias', Paetzel and Sausgruber (2018) argue that high-performing groups should exhibit a greater tendency to favor the in-group over the out-group if individuals recognize entitlements in line with the equity principle and performance differs across groups. They provide experimental evidence in support of their argument. 'In-group bias' is strong in groups consisting of high-performing members, and it is weak in low-performing groups. This holds although high-performing subjects exhibit no and low-performing subjects exhibit a strong 'in-group bias' in a minimal group setting.

At the end of the day, equity as much as equality seems to be an important ingredient for human fairness. In their seminal paper, Cappelen et al. (2007) document a large variety of fairness sentiments. In particular, they introduce two-dimensional heterogeneity among participants. In their one-shot dictator game with production, people are put into pairs and must invest from homogeneous endowments. Subjects are paired with different counterparts possessing different investment levels and either different or equal return rates from their investments. Finally, all subjects have to decide on how to split the sum of returns from both investments. Actual payoffs are based on one randomly chosen matching and one randomly chosen dictator. Results show subjects can mostly be classified into three categories: 44% are egalitarians and prefer equal total payoffs for both players, 18% are libertarians promoting extreme equity and leaving payoffs unchanged, and 38% are liberal egalitarians partially accepting inequalities. The latter group does not compensate for payoff differences resulting from different investments when splitting up the money, but compensate differences due to different return rates. Results from Konow (2009) seem to support the overall picture: stakeholders (i.e., people actually deciding upon their own money) redistribute payoffs according to an attenuated form of proportionality, while, interestingly, spectators (i.e., people deciding upon others' payoffs) redistribute in a strictly proportional way.

Some scholars claim that the unstable and impartial implementation of proportionality can be explained by the influence of pure self-interest. Konow (2000) concludes that more than 60% of decisions in his experiments can be interpreted as some self-serving understanding of competing distribution rules. Unfair behavior may be masked as being fair. Other scholars have questioned whether participants are actually responsible for production differences, since money is still distributed by the experimenter exogenously in these experiments. That is, people do not generate values when solving quizzes, counting letters, or adding numbers. Thus, it is unclear to what extent subjects consider their activities as being productive, and, consequently, to what extent they distribute payoffs proportionally with respect to those rather meaningless activities (Konow and Schwettmann 2016).

6.3.3 *Efficiency: Advantage Equity*

Regardless of its vague notion of desert and responsibility, economists favor equity for a different reason: proportional distribution of payoffs according to effort yields the incentive to deliver effort. Specifically, if the amount people receive in terms of governmental transfers is proportional to their tax burden (i.e., they receive a fraction ρ of τx), then proportionality decreases the bias of taxation in favor of leisure to $(1-\rho)\tau x$, as introduced in Sect. 6.2. In other words, unlike equality, equity enhances the implementation of efficient labor-leisure-time choice.

There are two reasons why enhancing efficiency is actually good news for all members of a society. First, the redistribution process that decreases the bias in favor of leisure, in turn, increases the amount of resources that can be distributed among members of the society. That is, if people have an incentive to provide effort, more is produced, and each member receives higher transfers from the state. Conversely, redistribution that increases equality reduces incentives to deliver effort, since, regardless of individual contribution, each member of the state receives the same outcome. Less is produced and the entire society is poorer. For that reason, equity-based distribution is, at least to some extent, in the interest of all members of a society.[6]

The second reason is that people seem to have a preference for efficiency in the sense of surplus maximization. That is, people are willing to forgo their own payoffs or larger equality of payoffs for the sake of a higher sum of payoffs for all involved parties. In their seminal papers, Charness and Rabin (2002) and Engelmann and Strobel (2004) test the limits of the efficiency-selfishness and the efficiency-equality trade-offs using experiments with multiple distribution decisions.

Engelmann and Strobel employ three-person dictator games where—always keeping the payoff for the decision maker constant—options include either minimizing the distance between individual payoffs (option 1), changing others' payoffs such that one's own payoff represents the average (option 2), or choosing an allocation for the other two subjects that maximizes the total sum (option 3). Note that option 1 is the most preferable considering the utility function presented in equation (6.1). That is, option 1 maximizes Fehr and Schmidt-type utility, while option 2 yields the higher utility under Bolton and Ockenfels-type utility. Finally, option 3 maximizes efficiency even though this allocation creates greater inequality than the other options.

---

[6]There is an extensive literature on how taxation can be optimal given the different disincentives stemming from taxation. For an overview of optimal taxation, see Auerbach (1985) and Mankiw et al. (2009).

The results show that the majority of people predominantly choose option 3 across a number of different payoff constellations. Likewise, Charness and Rabin find in similar distribution tasks that many people opt for the alternatives that maximize the sum of payoffs. Consequently, they propose a utility function that adds, beside individual income maximization, concern for the least well-off member in the group and concern for the sum of payoffs:

$$u_i = (1 - \lambda)m_i + \lambda[\delta \min(m_i, m_{y1}, \ldots, m_{yN}) + (1 - \delta)(m_i + m_{y1} + \ldots + m_{yN})], \tag{6.2}$$

where m_{yk} denotes the money of group member k, and λ (δ) being my taste parameter for other-regarding preferences (concern for the wellbeing of the least well-off person in the group). Charness and Rabin (2002) consider a convex combination between a subject's own monetary payoff and a social welfare function, which can be seen as a Rawlsian and a utilitarian social welfare function.

However, some papers cast doubts on the generalization of this result. While Engelmann and Strobel use mainly economics students as subjects, Fehr and Schmidt (2006) report on results for similar experiments with samples of students from other fields of study and nonacademic employees. Finally, Pelligra and Stanca (2013) run their experiments with a representative pool of subjects. Both latter studies find substantially lower concerns for efficiency and stronger concerns for equality, with only a minority of people preferring efficiency over the other fairness motives. As shown in Andreoni and Miller (2002), when there is a trade-off between fairness concerns and narrow self-interest, efficiency has minor priority: in their experiments, only one-fifth of participants prefer efficiency over self-interest and equality.

6.4 The Forgotten Brother: Need-Based Justice

As mentioned earlier, redistribution based on equity leads to higher efficiency and increases economic surplus in comparison to redistribution based on equality. Therefore, states with the equity based redistribution system are ceteris paribus richer than states with equality-based redistribution systems. More and more states are adapting their social systems, such that equity suppresses equality: for example, Krieger and Traub (2013) show that pension systems in many OECD countries converge on a more 'Bismarckian' system with less intragenerational redistribution.

So, is the transition from an equality-based system towards equity-based system the reason for growing inequality in the OECD countries? The OECD itself names developments in labor earnings and labor markets as the main reasons for increasing inequality (OECD 2011).[7]

[7]The OECD (2011) lists the following determinants as driving forces for increasing inequality: globalization brought by rapid economic integration; skill-biased technological changes; institutional and regulatory reforms; changes in employment patterns; changes in family formation and household structures; and changes in tax and benefit systems.

Another important part of the answer relates to a forgotten brother of equality and equity, need-based justice. That is, need-based justice recognizes that people are heterogeneous with respect to their needs and adjust redistribution accordingly. Instead of focusing on the distribution of income within society (i.e., equality), or on the supply of resources within society (i.e., equity), need-based redistribution focuses on socially accepted needs.

Despite the dominance of the two sisters, equality and equity, in the economic literature, even economists confess that need-based justice crucially influences our fairness perception (e.g., Baxter and Moosa 1996).

These needs are stated individually as demands for specific goods or services. The electorate has to agree on the needs that they are willing to accept. Only if a specific need is accepted society will fulfill that need. As a consequence, need-based justice is a principle for redistribution that helps particularly weak and poor segments of the population.

However, the process of accepting a stated need or demand as a socially accepted need is an understudied issue and requires more research. We surmise that the process of recognition depends, among others, on information and beliefs. Konow (2001) shows that specific information about a subject can completely change evaluations of what is fair and unfair. A hard-working person is deserving, but her benefiting from redistribution would be unfair if at the same time a substantial part of the population is below an 'appropriate' minimum income.

Redistribution based on need-based justice secures that the needy do not suffer, but at the same time guarantees that incentives to invest efforts are high. The resultant societal level of redistribution is moderate. We argue that the concept of a welfare state that encourages people to invest effort and be more responsible for their own social security (Pierson 1995; Dingeldey 2007) is in line with need-based justice.

Beyond its complexity and ambiguity, need-based justice has an enormous empirical relevance in today's social welfare states. In fact, substantial elements of the redistribution system in the majority of all OECD countries redistribute based on need-based justice. For instance, governmental support for health insurances refinances the special needs of those who are in desperate need of medical treatment. Likewise, child allowance helps families and their special needs at the cost of the entire society.

In almost all OECD countries, the level of social assistance is calculated as a sum of the cost that allows a social life comparable to the life of the lowest quintile of the income distribution. Gough et al. (1997) find that social benefits in all OECD countries are at least partly, but most often entirely, means-tested. Hereby, the level of benefits differs substantially between countries. Some countries are only concerned about providing a 'minimum' while others, like Austria, Germany or Luxembourg, emphasize that benefits should allow a 'decent life with human dignity' (which allows people to take part in social life). Apportioning social benefits according to means-testing reflects the recognition of individual-specific needs. We interpret a means-testing benefit system as a system based on the fairness principle of social needs.

In turn, redistribution based on need-based justice may be orthogonal to our feelings about equality. Sometimes, it may even increase the level of inequality when the neediness category does not correspond with lower income classes: older people are not necessarily poor, but they have their special needs. Therefore, growing income inequality in the OECD countries results not only from the stronger influence of equity on redistribution, but also as a result of the recognition of special needs for an increasing number of groups in the population.

6.4.1 Evidence About Need-Based Justice

Frohlich et al. (1987) and Frohlich and Oppenheimer (1990) are the first to study a richer set of redistribution principles in an experimental setting. They vary the underlying redistribution procedure to elicit subject's preferences about the fairness principle (e.g., equal distribution, redistribution according to needs). In some treatments, subjects get to discuss their preferred redistribution principle. Frohlich and Oppenheimer, therefore, analyze public spending and not public revenue. The most preferred principle implements a minimum income for the worst-off members in society, whereas money redistribution beyond the minimum income follows proportionality. Moreover, results show that active participation in implementing the redistribution principle (i.e., its endogenous determination) leads to lower inefficiencies in production.

Gerber et al. (2013) extend Frohlich and Oppenheimer's work in several aspects. They analyze both theoretical and experimental voting by feet by allowing subjects to switch between societies. Subjects join societies implementing the redistribution principles that are individually preferred by all members of that society.[8] In addition, they vary the 'thickness' of the veil of ignorance behind which people vote on their type of redistribution. That is, people either do not know, partly know, or fully know their productivity when choosing their redistribution principle. The authors find redistribution to be lower than predicted when behind the full veil of ignorance, and redistribution to be higher than predicted when the veil of ignorance is partly lifted. However, the most interesting finding is that regimes with different redistribution principles emerge and exist side by side.

Barberá et al. (2015) study the core of a coalition formation game, where players first form coalitions before having to vote on a distribution principle. These can be either meritocratic (no redistribution) or egalitarian. Hence, unlike in Gerber at al. and Frohlich and Oppenheimer's work, the players do not select themselves into a priori given distribution rules but choose the distribution principle ex post, after coalitions have been formed and the productivities of all coalition members are known. Moreover, players do not invest in this model. That is, the effect of different distribution principles on players' investment incentives and economic efficiency is

[8]The very basic idea of voting by joining into the preferred society can be traced back to Tiebout (1956).

not considered. Nonetheless, findings are similar: different distribution principles coexist, and stable coalition structures may include non-segregated groups.

Cabrales et al. (2012) conduct an experiment with costly production, followed by majority voting on egalitarian redistribution. They find that redistribution in conjunction with high effort is not sustainable because the rich are never willing to reward the poor even if the poor have put in high effort in the production phase.

A different branch of the literature analyzes the question of the preferred extent of redistribution. In their seminal article, Meltzer and Richard (1981) analyze the emergence of tax rates, and consequently the size of redistribution in a political system with voting. Particularly, they focus on the production inefficiencies caused by redistribution (along the line of arguments presented in Sect. 6.2 of this chapter). Meltzer and Richards show that, for simple majority voting and the resulting pivotal position of the median voter, the size of redistribution and the inefficiencies due to redistribution decrease as the productivity of the median voter increases. The larger the median voter's productivity relative to the average of society, the smaller the redistribution and inefficiencies.

Following this tradition, Konrad and Morath (2010) analyze a simplified version of the Meltzer-Richard model. They study how prospects of income mobility may affect preferences for redistributing taxes in an individual decision-making experiment without strategic interaction between subjects. Each human subject is paired with two computers that choose actions to maximize their own earnings. It is important to stress that human subjects are aware of the computers' strategies. In a treatment without mobility, observed tax rates are in line with theoretically predicted ones, while past or future changes in the income hierarchy affect the choice of the tax rate in the current period.

Agranov and Palfrey (2015) also report results regarding equilibrium tax rates, inequality, and income redistribution from laboratory experiments on the Meltzer-Richard model. The authors vary the amount of wage inequality and the political process used to determine tax rates. Unlike most papers in the literature, which fix the amount of resources to be distributed exogenously, the authors allow for an endogenous production of the pie and a complete reallocation of resources (not just the surplus). Their results indicate that higher inequality leads to higher tax rates. The tax rates and labor supply functions are both quantitatively close to the theory. The result is robust to the political institution (direct and representative democracy). The authors do not find evidence that inequity aversion might have an effect on behavior.

Finally, work by Kittel et al. (2015) introduces an interesting variant of the redistribution experiment on surplus sharing. Their game involves a communication phase before voting on the tax, and they vary both the initial distribution of endowments and the institutional background in terms of the quorum. The experiment consists of two consecutive stages: a multiple-prize rank-order contest, which involves a simple cognitive ability task, and a surplus sharing stage. In the second stage where subjects vote on redistribution, the authors find that subjects most often equalize payoffs. This finding confirms their initial hypothesis that the existence of a middle class is as effective as institutional hurdles in limiting the power of the less able in order to protect the more able players from being exploited.

Regarding the quorum variation, the unanimity rule as the institutional hurdle spurs production, and as such minimizes external costs due to the inclusion of all members of society. It also allows every member to uphold the decision until the outcome meets particular interests. However, majoritarian voting with a middle class involves fewer bargaining impasses than granting veto rights to the more able players and is, therefore, more efficient.

In other words, there are two ways to counterbalance the abuse of redistribution: institutional hurdles and the presence of a middle class. The existence of a middle class quasi-automatically corrects for both excessive inequality and equality without generating the hold-up effect of a sufficiently high quorum. The position-based interests of the middle class limit the costs burdened upon the minority because its members will shift sides as soon as demands on the minority become exploitative.

A new field of research analyzes how equivalence framing has an effect on the level of redistribution. Utilizing a simplified version of the Meltzer-Richard model, Lorenz et al. (2017) show that if subjects have to set the level of redistribution by agreeing on a redistributive tax rate, the individually preferred and finally implemented level of redistribution is about 50% lower than in cases where subjects have to agree on a minimal income level, holding everything else constant.

Paetzel et al. (2018) find that increasing the transparency of the redistributive consequences by providing a simple calculation tool that informs subjects about the ex post distribution for each tax rate or minimum income, diminishes the above mentioned framing-effect. Transparency has an asymmetric effect on both the individually preferred and finally implemented level of redistribution. In the minimal income framing, a high degree of transparency decreases both the preferred and implemented level of redistribution. In the tax frame, transparency has a contrary effect on redistribution. Here, higher transparency increases the level of redistribution. When subjects are fully aware of the redistributive consequences, they decide on average on the same level of redistribution.

Traub et al. (2009) conclude that most of their subjects preferred a distribution that is equitable enough not to be protested but still allows some to outperform others. Overall, the literature shows a preference for a moderate, two-part redistribution scheme: the first part of the redistribution scheme, that is, its lower section guarantees a minimum income for the poor members of the society. We interpret this as a desire for need-based justice regarding the basic provision of income for all members of society. The second part, its upper section, proportionally redistributes incomes beyond the basic needs. This yields a combination of needs-based justice and equity.

6.4.2 *What is Neediness?*

Of course, a crucial question for need-based justice is what the determinants of the justified need are. To improve our understanding of how need-based justice defines redistribution, we have to understand how a society or a group jointly agrees upon the level of subsistence. Of course, the prospect of what such a level of subsistence should look like differs significantly and might be very subjective. Even the actual levels of social assistance differ to a large extent between countries (compare, e.g., Gough et al. 1997).

The threshold for social assistance does not appear from nowhere. For example, suppose all subjects state a demand for food. If someone states that he demands twice as much food as another, his demand will likely be rejected and result in no satisfaction of that individual need. If the same person provides information that he has the hardest job in the country, his demand is more likely to be accepted and result in the satisfaction of the need. The context (i.e., the additional information provided) has an effect on the acceptance of individual needs and, therefore, on the level of redistribution. Although it is long known that needs are taken into account in allocation decisions (Lamm and Schwinger 1980), economists have little to say regarding the issue beyond this point.

One of the few exceptions are studies on the desert. Gaertner and Schokkaert (2012) distinguishes between allocations of granted resources and allocations of resources that are created collectively. In the first case, the fairness principles of equality and need are predominant. In the latter case, when resources are created by individual contributions or efforts, entitlements play an important role.

Balafoutas et al. (2013) conduct an experiment with heterogenous initial endowments and majority voting, varying the entitlement of endowments, which are either earned or randomly assigned. They find that the player with the highest and the lowest endowments are mainly driven by material self-interest. Low-endowment players, however, signal their willingness to cooperate by increasing their contributions if the redistribution rate is determined by the majority of the votes.

Mollerstrom et al. (2015) differentiate in an experiment between uncontrollable and controllable (insurable) bad luck. They show experimentally that many spectators condition the compensation for bad outcomes caused by uncontrollable bad luck on the subject's previous insurance decision, even though this choice is irrelevant. Durante et al. (2014) investigate how preferences for redistribution vary with social preferences, risk aversion, self-interest and the source of pre-tax inequality. The main finding is that subjects' preferences for redistribution decreases substantially when the initial distribution of endowments is determined based on the task performance rather than randomly. Durante et al. (2014) use experiments with large groups and compare subjects' demand for redistribution when they are directly affected or when they are unaffected third parties. Between treatment conditions, the authors vary the deadweight loss associated with redistribution (taxation costs). The majority of subjects prefer less inequality when they are third parties, and are sensitive to changes in the cost of taxation.

Along the same line of research, Esarey et al. (2012) analyze under which circumstances subjects with various ideological convictions are willing to redistribute. They show that conservatives have a strict preference for a society with low taxes and almost no redistribution. Subjects with liberal attitudes are willing to redistribute only if redistribution helps the poor, whose poverty is due to bad luck. Thus, liberal subjects favor a combination of redistribution based on equity and on need-based justice. However, differences in individual productivity or performance are hardly the only reasons for redistribution, either for conservatives or liberals.

We would like to stress that this literature is far from matured. Particularly, we do not know how people solve potential conflicts between 'dimensions' of neediness, for example, how much to allocate to someone who is deserving due to high effort when, at the same time, a substantial part of the population is below an 'appropriate' minimum income. Although the research agenda is far from new, some basic issues like framing, individual dispositions or the interactions between different context variables remain unexplored. A lot of work lies ahead of the academic community to improve the knowledge on different facets of fairness.

6.5 The Cost of Redistribution, Part 2

Let us return to the earlier discussion on the (indirect) cost of redistribution, this time assuming minimum income levels. That is, people have a basic minimum consumption level that they cannot undercut. Theory predicts a censored distribution of the labor-leisure time-mix. Specifically, some individuals may have strong preferences for leisure. If their most preferred mix of working and leisure yields less than a minimum income, in the absence of redistribution and taxation, they would have to increase their labor time and choose a labor time corresponding to the minimum income level. On the other hand, in the presence of taxation and redistribution, people may rely on the transfer and may allocate less or no time to labor. We describe the rationale in greater detail below.

6.5.1 *Choice Restrictions and Need-Based Redistribution*

Suppose workers pick their most preferred labor-leisure mix under the restriction that income must exceed C_0 (say, 500 Euros). Further, we assume that there is initially no taxation and no redistribution. The individual worker chooses in this scenario the leisure-consumption combination associated with the highest indifference curve within the feasible set of alternatives. Notice that leisure-consumption combinations yielding a consumption of less than C_0 are not feasible. There are two possibilities: (1) The indifference curves of the worker are 'sufficiently' flat (so that she values ceteris paribus consumption a lot, but leisure little). Then she will choose point c on her budget constraint B_1—which is the same point as in the scenario without minimum income. That is to say, her consumption is so high that the minimum income does not influence her decision about the optimal leisure-work-time-mix (panel (a) of Fig. 6.2). (2) the indifference curves of the worker are 'sufficiently' steep (so that she values, ceteris paribus, consumption little but leisure a lot). Then she will choose the point y (panel (b) of Fig. 6.2). In point y, the worker spends only a few hours working.

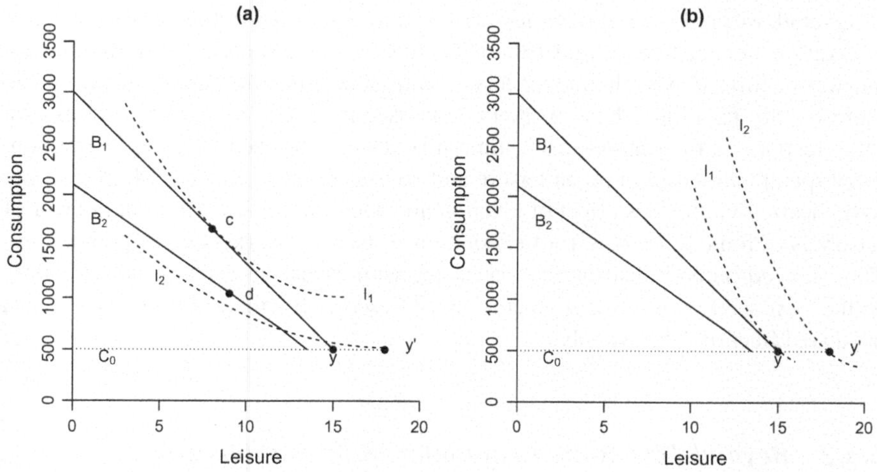

Fig. 6.2 Need-based redistribution leads to a bifurcation regarding the time allocation between leisure and labor

Now let us assume that there is taxation and redistribution based on need-based justice. That is, workers whose income (and consequently their consumption) fall short of C_0, receive the difference of their labor income and C_0 as a transfer from the state. If a worker has no labor income, her transfer equals C_0. In turn, workers whose net income exceed C_0 pay a fraction of τ from their labor income as tax in order to finance transfers to needy members of the society.

What happens to the total labor supply? For this, we have to consider the indifference curve I_2 through the point y' with leisure $= 18$ and consumption $= C_0$ (in our specific example $= 500$). Again, there are two possibilities: (1) I_2 is 'sufficiently' flat and I_2 intersects the budget constraint after tax B_2. Then there are points on B_2 which lie beyond I_2 (i.e., lie on higher indifference curves). Thus, the worker will choose point d which is on her budget constraint B_2. This is the most preferable point in her set of alternatives (i.e., lies on the highest indifference curve intersecting her budget constraint), and leads to less leisure than 18 and more consumption than 500 (panel (a) of Fig. 6.2). (2) I_2 is 'sufficiently' steep and I_2 does not intersect the budget constraint after tax B_2. Then there is no point on B_2 that is more attractive than y' (i.e., lies on higher indifference curves).[9] Thus the worker will choose point y', which is the most preferable point in her set of alternatives (i.e., lies on the highest indifference curve). This leads to the leisure of 18 and consumption of 500 financed by redistribution (panel (b) of Fig. 6.2).

[9]Finally, it could be the case that I_2 only marginally intersects B_2 (i.e., only in the point d). Then the worker is indifferent between y' and d, and we do not know which of the two points is chosen by the worker. It is, however, very unlikely that the budget constraint and the indifference curve intersect exactly in one point.

Overall, we predict a bifurcation regarding the response of workers to the existence of taxation and need-based redistribution. Those workers valuing consumption a lot and leisure little, choose their labor-leisure-time-mix in the same biased way as when there is only taxation. Those workers emphasizing leisure a lot and consumption little, respond in their labor-leisure-time-mix strongly to need-based redistribution. They spend their entire time on leisure and no time on working. Therefore, one can hypothesize that the bias effect of taxation and need-based redistribution in favor of leisure is extreme (if there is a sufficient number of latter workers in the population). That is, need-based redistribution may come with excessive costs of redistribution. In the next section, we assess whether need-based redistribution necessarily has a negative effect on labor supply.

6.5.2 *Beyond Text-Book Economics: Substitution- and Income Effect*

Is need-based redistribution devastating for the efficiency of the leisure-labor-time-mix? Unfortunately, research on this issue is still scarce. What we know is that redistribution, in general, is less efficiency decreasing than predicted: Grosser and Reuben (2013) conduct a two-stage experiment in which participants first earn their income by trading assets in a double auction. The authors use the final allocation of assets in the market to measure (allocation) efficiency. That is, efficiency measures whether those participants with the highest valuations own assets at the end of the trade. In the second stage, participants agree on how they want to redistribute part of their earnings by applying majority voting.

Since taxes are non-distortionary and the median voter has a low income, the theoretical equilibrium tax rate is 100%. As this tax rate equalizes earnings after the trade, participants have little incentive to increase their surplus during the auction stage. Results show tax rates close to what is predicted. If endowments are equalized, the final asset allocation is less efficient, however, not as inefficient as theoretically predicted. Redistribution impedes efficiency, but less than predicted.

Kessler and Norton (2016) compare the framing effect of a wage cut in comparison to an income tax of the same size in a real effort experiment. They show that the wage cut leads to a significantly lower average decline in productivity than the corresponding income tax, regardless of the use of the tax. Notice, however, that in this setting, no minimum income requirement exists, and individual needs play a rather minor role.

Sharif (2000) as well as Nakamura and Murayama (2010) analyze the labor supply for wage variations, distinguishing between the supply behavior of the working poor and that of the non-poor. That is, they compare the labor supply curve of people in very low-income categories at or near the minimum standard of subsistence requirements for those in higher income classes. They show that reservation wages of the working poor and of the non-poor are likely to be fundamentally different leading to an inverted S-shape labor supply curve of both groups of workers.

Chugunova et al. (2017) take on the idea of subsistence requirements and present-to the best of our knowledge-currently the only experiment specifically analyzing the effect of taxation when workers have a minimum income requirement. In their real effort experiment, participants face several stages with a piece-rate payment for numeric tasks. In their baseline treatment, participants have to earn a certain total amount in a stage to be allowed to work in the next stage. In the redistribution treatment, participants have to pay a piece-rate tax of 30% per solved task. The tax return is in some treatment conditions used to support other, systematically disadvantaged participants in this experiment, or in other treatment conditions destroyed altogether. The results of Chugunova et al. show that the productivity of taxed workers increases steeply. In other words, there is hardly any evidence in favor of a negative effect of taxation on productivity. Rather it seems that workers try to compensate for the income loss due to taxation and react to the neediness of disadvantaged members of society by increasing the effort.

To understand this puzzle, let us have a look at the opposite case, i.e., wage increases. Several empirical studies analyze the effect of per-mile wage increases for cab drivers (e.g., Camerer et al. 1997; Farber 2005, 2008). Of course, based on the theoretical considerations in Sect. 1.2, we could claim that a wage increase raises the price of leisure. Therefore, workers 'demand' more work and less leisure time. However, Camerer et al. find that the daily wage elasticity of labor supply of New York City cab drivers is substantially negative. This means that a wage increase leads to less labor time.

This result is less surprising if we acknowledge that there is not only the substitution effect of a wage variation (i.e., leisure becomes more expensive, so workers demand less), but also an income effect. If the worker has a target income, she needs less time in order to reach this income. Therefore, she demands less labor time. Indeed, Farber (2008) provides evidence suggesting that cab drivers are target earners and hold reference-dependent preferences.[10]

In the same vein, Fehr and Goette (2007) do a controlled field experiment with bicycle messengers in Zurich. They pay them for a certain time interval a wage premium of 25% per ride and compare the number of rides and shifts that they take under the new payment scheme to their previous behavior. Fehr and Goette provide evidence for both the substitution effect and the income effect: on the one hand, bicycle messengers take more shifts, implying that they substitute leisure time for labor time, and on the other hand, they take on less rides per shift, implying that they work less hard as the income target is reached nonetheless.

It seems that the effect of wage increases is at best ambiguous. Both the substitution effect and the income effect are at work. If the substitution effect dominates the income effect, the total effect may be positive, but this is far from clear. Likewise, the results on the effect of income taxation when workers have a minimum income

[10]Altman (2001) discusses a richer model of labor supply for target real income and target non-market time in further detail.

requirement suggest target incomes, as workers try to compensate for the income effect of taxation. Overall, it seems the effect of moderate taxation and need-based redistribution does not have to be necessarily negative in terms of productivity. Yet, the results are, to the best of our knowledge, inconclusive.

6.6 Conclusion

This chapter adds to the long list of economic papers dealing with biased incentives caused by redistribution and resulting welfare consequences. We discuss the indirect costs of redistribution. We focus on the effects of redistribution following the principle of need-based justice (i.e., whether people have basic needs and whether redistribution is used to satisfy those needs). This is a rather new perspective for the taxation literature.

We disentangle need-based justice from the two other major principles of justice, equality and equity, which are discussed far more often in the economic literature. Evidently, equity has systematic advantages in terms of increasing efficiency when compared to equality. Redistribution based on equity provides incentives for effort provision, while redistribution based on equality impedes incentives for effort provision.

In contrast, taxation according to need-based justice generates no such strong effects. This finding is particularly surprising as a large percentage of real-world redistribution seemingly follows this fairness principle. Therefore, debates about redistribution based on need-based justice appear very important for a greater part of the population.

The limited evidence we present here provides a rather optimistic view regarding the consequences of need-based redistribution. Overall, need-based justice is a generally accepted principle of redistribution. Also, there is little proof that (moderate) income taxation has a negative effect on the labor supply of workers who have specific needs. On the contrary, it seems that workers try to compensate for the decrease in income due to taxation. One way to explain this finding is that target income fosters a strong income effect.

Of course, research on this topic is far from complete and more discussion is required. For example, the experimental studies we cite leave out the important question of how societies agree upon justified needs. Yet, the effect of need-based redistribution may be more negative if needs are less objective and salient. Another example is the effect of receiving transfers. That is, the primary focus in the economic analysis of redistribution is on the people who pay the taxes. However, the benefits created for recipients of need-based redistribution are also important. As these questions are vital and have far-reaching consequences for the long-term success of our socioeconomic systems and our societies, we invite further research on this long unattended issue.

Acknowledgments This chapter has been written as part of DFG Research Group 2104 "Need-based Justice and Distributive Procedures", Project D1 "Justice, Need and Incentives in Voting Procedures" (Nicklisch, reference Ni 1610/1-1). This funding is gratefully acknowledged. We thank all members of FOR 2104 for making such a project possible.

References

Acemoglu, D., & Robinson, J. A. (2000). Why did the west extend the franchise? Democracy, inequality, and growth in historical perspective. *The Quarterly Journal of Economics*, *115*(4), 1167–1199.

Adams, J. S. (1965). Inequity in social exchange. *Advances in Experimental Social Psychology*, *2*, 267–299.

Aghion, P., & Bolton, P. (1997). A theory of trickle-down growth and development. *The Review of Economic Studies*, *64*(2), 151–172.

Agranov, M., & Palfrey, T. R. (2015). Equilibrium tax rates and income redistribution: A laboratory study. *Journal of Public Economics*, *130*, 45–58.

Alesina, A., & Perotti, R. (1996). Income distribution, political instability, and investment. *European Economic Review*, *40*(6), 1203–1228.

Alesina, A., & Angeletos, G. M. (2005). Fairness and redistribution. *American Economic Review*, *95*(4), 960–980.

Altman, M. (2001). A behavioral model of labor supply: Casting some light into the black box of income-leisure choice. *Journal of Socio-Economics*, *30*(3), 199–219.

Andreoni, J., & Bernheim, B. D. (2009). Social image and the 50–50 norm: A theoretical and experimental analysis of audience effects. *Econometrica*, *77*(5), 1607–1636.

Andreoni, J., & Miller, J. (2002). Giving according to GARP: An experimental test of the consistency of preferences for altruism. *Econometrica*, *70*(2), 737–753.

Arts, W., & Gelissen, J. (2001). Welfare states, solidarity and justice principles: Does the type really matter? *Acta Sociologica*, *44*(4), 283–299.

Auerbach, A. J. (1985). The theory of excess burden and optimal taxation. In A. Auerbach & M. Feldstein (Eds.), *Handbook of public economics* (Vol. 1, pp. 61–127). Amsterdam: North-Holland.

Balafoutas, L., Kocher, M. G., Putterman, L., & Sutter, M. (2013). Equality, equity and incentives: An experiment. *European Economic Review*, *60*, 32–51.

Barberá, S., Bevia, C., & Ponsati, C. (2015). Meritocracy, egalitarianism and the stability of majoritarian organizations. *Games and Economic Behavior*, *91*, 237–257.

Barr, N. A. (1998). *The economics of the welfare state*. Stanford: Stanford University Press.

Barr, N., & Diamond, P. (2008). *Reforming pensions: Principles and policy choices*. Oxford: Oxford University Press.

Barr, N., & Diamond, P. (2010). Reforming pensions: Lessons from economic theory and some policy directions. *Economia*, *11*(1), 1–14.

Barro, R. J. (2000). Inequality and growth in a panel of countries. *Journal of Economic Growth*, *5*(1), 5–32.

Bartling, B., & Fischbacher, U. (2011). Shifting the blame: On delegation and responsibility. *The Review of Economic Studies*, *79*(1), 67–87.

Baxter, J. L., & Moosa, I. A. (1996). The consumption function: A basic needs hypothesis. *Journal of Economic Behavior and Organization*, *31*(1), 85–100.

Benabou, R., & Ok, E. A. (2001). Social mobility and the demand for redistribution: The POUM hypothesis. *The Quarterly Journal of Economics*, *116*(2), 447–487.

Blanco, M., Engelmann, D., & Normann, H. T. (2011). A within-subject analysis of other-regarding preferences. *Games and Economic Behavior*, *72*(2), 321–338.

Blount, S. (1995). When social outcomes aren't fair: The effect of causal attributions on preferences. *Organizational Behavior and Human Decision Processes*, *63*(2), 131–144.
Bolton, G. E., Katok, E., & Zwick, R. (1998). Dictator game giving: Rules of fairness versus acts of kindness. *International Journal of Game Theory*, *27*(2), 269–299.
Bolton, G. E., & Ockenfels, A. (2000). ERC: A theory of equity, reciprocity, and competition. *American Economic Review*, *90*(1), 166–193.
Bosmans, K., & Schokkaert, E. (2009). Equality preference in the claims problem: A questionnaire study of cuts in earnings and pensions. *Social Choice and Welfare*, *33*(4), 533–557.
Buchanan, J. M., & Tullock, G. (1962). *The calculus of consent: Logical foundations of constitutional democracy*. Ann Arbor: Ann Arbor Paperbacks.
Cabrales, A., Nagel, R., & Rodríguez Mora, J. V. (2012). It is Hobbes, not Rousseau: An experiment on voting and redistribution. *Experimental Economics*, *15*(2), 278–308.
Camerer, C., Babcock, L., Loewenstein, G., & Thaler, R. (1997). Labor supply of New York City cabdrivers: One day at a time. *Quarterly Journal of Economics*, *112*(2), 407–441.
Cappelen, A. W., Hole, A. D., Sørensen, E. Ø., & Tungodden, B. (2007). The pluralism of fairness ideals: An experimental approach. *American Economic Review*, *97*(3), 818–827.
Cappelen, A. W., Konow, J., Sørensen, E. Ø., & Tungodden, B. (2013). Just luck: An experimental study of risk-taking and fairness. *American Economic Review*, *103*(4), 1398–1413.
Cappelen, A. W., & Tungodden, B. (2009). Rewarding effort. *Economic Theory*, *39*(3), 425–441.
Charness, G., & Rabin, M. (2002). Understanding social preferences with simple tests. *Quarterly Journal of Economics*, *117*(3), 817–869.
Cherry, T. L., Frykblom, P., & Shogren, J. F. (2002). Hardnose the dictator. *American Economic Review*, *92*(4), 1218–1221.
Chugunova, M., Nicklisch, A., & Schnapp, K.-U. (2017). Redistribution and production with the subsistence income constraint: A real effort experiment. FOR 2104 Discussion Paper 2017–18.
Chun, Y. (1999). Equivalence of axioms for bankruptcy problems. *International Journal of Game Theory*, *28*(4), 511–520.
Corneo, G., & Gruener, H. P. (2000). Social limits to redistribution. *American Economic Review*, *90*(5), 1491–1507.
Croson, R., & Konow, J. (2009). Social preferences and moral biases. *Journal of Economic Behavior and Organization*, *69*(3), 201–212.
Dana, J., Weber, R. A., & Kuang, J. X. (2007). Exploiting moral wiggle room: Experiments demonstrating an illusory preference for fairness. *Economic Theory*, *33*(1), 67–80.
d'Anjou, L., Steijn, A., & van Aarsen, D. (1995). Social position, ideology, and distributive justice. *Social Justice Research*, *8*(4), 351–384.
Dingeldey, I. (2007). Between workfare and enablement-The different paths to transformation of the welfare state: A comparative analysis of activating labour market policies. *European Journal of Political Research*, *46*(6), 823–851.
DiPrete, T. A., & Eirich, G. M. (2006). Cumulative advantage as a mechanism for inequality: A review of theoretical and empirical developments. *Annual Review of Sociology*, *32*, 271–297.
Durante, R., Putterman, L., & Weele, J. (2014). Preferences for redistribution and perception of fairness: An experimental study. *Journal of the European Economic Association*, *12*(4), 1059–1086.
Easterly, W. (2001). The middle class consensus and economic development. *Journal of Economic Growth*, *6*(4), 317–335.
Engel, C. (2011). Dictator games: A meta study. *Experimental Economics*, *14*(4), 583–610.
Engelmann, D., & Strobel, M. (2004). Inequality aversion, efficiency, and maximin preferences in simple distribution experiments. *American Economic Review*, *94*(4), 857–869.
Esarey, J., Salmon, T., & Barrilleaux, C. (2012). Social insurance and income redistribution in a laboratory experiment. *Political Research Quarterly*, *65*(3), 685–698.
Falk, A., Fehr, E., & Fischbacher, U. (2003). On the nature of fair behavior. *Economic Inquiry*, *41*(1), 20–26.

Farber, H. S. (2005). Is tomorrow another day? The labor supply of New York City cabdrivers. *Journal of Political Economy, 113*(1), 46–82.
Farber, H. S. (2008). Reference-dependent preferences and labor supply: The case of New York City taxi drivers". *American Economic Review, 98*(3), 1069–1082.
Fehr, E., & Goette, L. (2007). Do workers work more if wages are high? Evidence from a randomized field experiment. *American Economic Review, 97*(1), 298–317.
Fehr, E., & Schmidt, K. M. (1999). A theory of fairness, competition, and cooperation. *Quarterly Journal of Economics, 114*(3), 817–868.
Fehr, E., & Schmidt, K. M. (2006). The economics of fairness, reciprocity and altruism–Experimental evidence and new theories. In S.-C. Kolm (Ed.), *Handbook of the economics of giving, altruism and reciprocity* (Vol. 1, pp. 615–691). Amsterdam: North Holland.
Fleurbaey, M. (2008). *Fairness, responsibility, and welfare*. Oxford: Oxford University Press.
Fong, C. (2001). Social preferences, self-interest, and the demand for redistribution. *Journal of Public Economics, 82*(2), 225–246.
Forbes, K. J. (2000). A reassessment of the relationship between inequality and growth. *American Economic Review*, 869–887.
Forsythe, R., Horowitz, J. L., Savin, N. E., & Sefton, M. (1994). Fairness in simple bargaining experiments. *Games and Economic Behavior, 6*(3), 347–369.
Franck, E., & Nüsch, S. (2012). Talent and/or popularity: What does it take to be a superstar? *Economic Inquiry, 50*(1), 202–216.
Frank, R. H. (2007). *Falling behind: How income inequality harms the middle class*. Berkely: University of California Press.
Frank, R. H., & Cook, P. J. (1995). *The winner-take-all society*. New York: Free Press.
Frohlich, N., Oppenheimer, J. A., & Eavey, C. L. (1987). Choices of principles of distributive justice in experimental groups. *American Journal of Political Science, 31*(3), 606–636.
Frohlich, N., & Oppenheimer, J. A. (1990). Choosing justice in experimental democracies with production. *American Political Science Review, 84*(2), 461–477.
Fukuyama, F. (2006). *The end of history and the last man*. New York: Simon and Schuster.
Gächter, S., & Riedl, A. (2006). Dividing justly in bargaining problems with claims. *Social Choice and Welfare, 27*(3), 571–594.
Gaertner, W., & Schokkaert, E. (2012). *Empirical social choice: Questionnaire-experimental studies on distributive justice*. Cambridge: Cambridge University Press.
Gerber, A., Nicklisch, A., & Voigt, S. (2013). *Strategic choices for redistribution and the veil of ignorance: Theory and experimental evidence*. Wiso Working Paper Series 2013/5, Hamburg.
Gill, D., & Stone, R. (2010). Fairness and desert in tournaments. *Games and Economic Behavior, 69*(2), 346–364.
Gill, D., & Stone, R. (2015). Desert and inequity aversion in teams. *Journal of Public Economics, 123*, 42–54.
Glaeser, E., Scheinkman, J., & Shleifer, A. (2003). The injustice of inequality. *Journal of Monetary Economics, 50*(1), 199–222.
Gough, I., Bradshaw, J., Ditch, J., Eardley, T., & Whiteford, P. (1997). Social assistance in OECD countries. *Journal of European Social Policy, 7*(1), 17–43.
Grosser, J., & Reuben, E. (2013). Redistribution and market efficiency: An experimental study. *Journal of Public Economics, 101*, 39–52.
Gueth, W., & Kocher, M. G. (2014). More than thirty years of ultimatum bargaining experiments: Motives, variations, and a survey of the recent literature. *Journal of Economic Behavior and Organization, 108*, 396–409.
Hacker, J. S., & Pierson, P. (2010). *Winner-take-all politics: How Washington made the Rich Richer–and turned its back on the middle class*. New York: Simon and Schuster.
Herrero, C., Moreno-Ternero, J. D., & Ponti, G. (2010). On the adjudication of conflicting claims: An experimental study. *Social Choice and Welfare, 34*(1), 145–179.
Hoffman, E., McCabe, K., & Smith, V. L. (1996). Social distance and other-regarding behavior in dictator games. *American Economic Review, 86*(3), 653–660.

Homans, G. C. (1974). *Social behavior: Its elementary forms*. New York: Harcourt Brace Jovanovich.
Huber, E., & Stephens, J. D. (2012). *Democracy and the left: Social policy and inequality in Latin America*. Chicago: University of Chicago Press.
Jaeger, M. M. (2006). What makes people support public responsibility for welfare provision: Self-interest or political ideology? A longitudinal approach. *Acta Sociologica, 49*(3), 321–338.
Kahneman, D., Knetsch, J. L., & Thaler, R. H. (1986). Fairness and the assumptions of economics. *Journal of Business, 59*(4), 285–300.
Kessler, J. B., & Norton, M. I. (2016). Tax aversion in labor supply. *Journal of Economic Behavior and Organization, 124*, 15–28.
Kittel, B., Paetzel, F., & Traub, S. (2015). Competition, income distribution, and the middle class: An experimental study. *Journal of Applied Mathematics*, Article ID 303912.
Konow, J. (1996). A positive theory of economic fairness. *Journal of Economic Behavior and Organization, 31*(1), 13–35.
Konow, J. (2000). Fair shares: Accountability and cognitive dissonance in allocation decisions. *American Economic Review, 90*(4), 1072–1091.
Konow, J. (2001). Fair and square: The four sides of distributive justice. *Journal of Economic Behavior and Organization, 46*(2), 137–164.
Konow, J. (2003). Which is the fairest one of all? A positive analysis of justice theories. *Journal of Economic Literature, 41*(4), 1188–1239.
Konow, J. (2009). Is fairness in the eye of the beholder? An impartial spectator analysis of justice. *Social Choice and Welfare, 33*(1), 101–127.
Konow, J., & Schwettmann, L. (2016). The economics of justice. In C. Sabbagh & M. Schmitt (Eds.), *Handbook of social justice theory and research* (pp. 83–106). Heidelberg: Springer.
Konrad, K. A., & Morath, F. (2010). *Social mobility and redistributive taxation*. Max Planck Institute for Tax Law and Public Finance Working Paper No. 2011–02.
Korpi, W. (1983). *The Democratic Class Struggle*. London: Routledge.
Krawczyk, M. (2010). A glimpse through the veil of ignorance: Equality of opportunity and support for redistribution. *Journal of Public Economics, 94*(1), 131–141.
Krieger, T., & Traub, S. (2013). The bismarckian factor: A Measure of intra-generational redistribution in international pension systems. *DICE Report, 11*(1), 64–66.
Lamm, H., & Schwinger, T. (1980). Norms concerning distributive justice: Are needs taken into consideration in allocation decisions? *Social Psychology Quarterly, 43*(4), 425–429.
Lampert, H., & Althammer, P. D. J. (2001). Sozialhilfe. In *Lehrbuch der Sozialpolitik* (pp 307–319). Heidelberg: Springer.
Langer, E. J. (1975). The illusion of control. *Journal of Personality and Social Psychology, 32*(2), 311–328.
Lee, W., & Roemer, J. E. (2006). Racism and redistribution in the United States: A solution to the problem of American exceptionalism. *Journal of Public Economics, 90*(6), 1027–1052.
List, J. A. (2007). On the interpretation of giving in dictator games. *Journal of Political Economy, 115*(3), 482–493.
Lorenz, J., Paetzel, F., & Schweitzer, F. (2013). Redistribution spurs growth by using a portfolio effect on risky human capital. *PloS ONE, 8*(2), e54904.
Lorenz, J., Paetzel, F., & Tepe, M. S. (2017). Just don't call it a tax! Framing in an experiment on voting and redistribution (forthcoming). *Journal of Experimental Political Science*.
Mankiw, N. G., Weinzierl, M., & Yagan, D. (2009). Optimal taxation in theory and practice. *The Journal of Economic Perspectives, 23*(4), 147–174.
Meltzer, A. H., & Richard, S. F. (1981). A rational theory of the size of government. *Journal of Political Economy, 89*(5), 914–927.
Miller, D. (1999). *Principles of Social Justice*. Cambridge: Harvard University Press.
Miller, L., & Vanberg, C. (2013). Decision costs in legislative bargaining: An experimental analysis. *Public Choice, 155*(3–4), 373–394.

Mirrlees, J. A. (1971). An exploration in the theory of optimum income taxation. *Review of Economic Studies*, *38*(2), 175–208.
Mittone, L., & Ploner, M. (2012). Asset legitimacy and distributive justice in the dictator game: An experimental analysis. *Journal of Behavioral Decision Making*, *25*(2), 135–142.
Mollerstrom, J., Reme, B. A., & Sørensen, E. Ø. (2015). Luck, choice and responsibility–An experimental study of fairness views. *Journal of Public Economics*, *131*, 33–40.
Moulin, H. (2002). Axiomatic cost and surplus sharing. In K. J. Arrow, A. K. Sen, & K. Suzumura (Eds.), *Handbook of social choice and welfare* (Vol. 1, pp. 289–357). Amsterdam: North Holland.
Nakamura, T., & Murayama, Y. (2010). A complete characterization of the inverted S-shaped labor supply curve. *Metroeconomica*, *61*(4), 665–675.
Nicklisch, A., & Wolff, I. (2012). On the nature of reciprocity: Evidence from the ultimatum reciprocity measure. *Journal of Economic Behavior and Organization*, *84*(3), 892–905.
Nowak, M. A., & Sigmund, K. (2005). Evolution of indirect reciprocity. *Nature*, *437*, 1291–1298.
OECD. (2008). *Growing unequal?: Income distribution and poverty in OECD countries*. Paris: OECD publishing.
OECD. (2011). *An overview of growing income inequalities in OECD countries: Main findings. Divided we stand: Why inequality keeps rising*. Paris: OECD publishing.
Paetzel, F., Lorenz, J., & Tepe, M. S. (2018). Transparency diminishes framing-effects in voting on redistribution: Some experimental evidence. *European Journal of Political Economy*,. https://doi.org/10.1016/j.ejpoleco.2017.12.002.
Paetzel, F., & Sausgruber, R. (2018). Cognitive ability and in-group bias: An experimental study. *Journal of Public Economics*. https://doi.org/10.1016/j.jpubeco.2018.04.006.
Pelligra, V., & Stanca, L. (2013). To give or not to give? Equity, efficiency and altruistic behavior in an artefactual field experiment. *The Journal of Socio-Economics*, *46*, 1–9.
Persson, T., & Tabellini, G. (1994). Is inequality harmful for growth? *American Economic Review*, *84*(3), 600–621.
Pierson, P. (1995). *Dismantling the welfare state?: Reagan, thatcher and the politics of retrenchment*. Cambridge: Cambridge University Press.
Piketty, T. (2014). *Capital in the 21st century*. Cambridge: Harvard University Press.
Roemer, J. E. (1998). Why the poor do not expropriate the rich: An old argument in new garb. *Journal of Public Economics*, *70*(3), 399–424.
Rosen, S. (1981). The economics of superstars. *American Economic Review*, *71*(5), 845–858.
Runciman, W. G. (1966). *Relative deprivation and social justice: Study attitudes social inequality in 20th century England*. London: Routledge Kegan Paul.
Scharpf, F. W. (1987). A game-theoretical interpretation of inflation and unemployment in Western Europe. *Journal of Public Policy*, *7*(3), 227–257.
Sharif, M. (2000). Inverted 'S'–The complete neoclassical labour-supply function. *International Labour Review*, *139*(4), 409–435.
Sobel, J. (2005). Interdependent Preferences and Reciprocity. *Journal of Economic Literature*, *43*(2), 392–436.
Stiglitz, J. E. (2012). *The price of inequality: How today's divided society endangers our future*. New York: WW Norton and Company.
Thomson, W. (2003). Axiomatic and game-theoretic analysis of bankruptcy and taxation problems: A survey. *Mathematical Social Sciences*, *45*(3), 249–297.
Tiebout, C. M. (1956). A pure theory of local expenditures. *Journal of Political Economy*, *64*(5), 416–424.
Traub, S., Seidl, C., & Schmidt, U. (2009). An experimental study on individual choice, social welfare, and social preferences. *European Economic Review*, *53*(4), 385–400.

Chapter 7
Towards a Theory of Need-Based Justice

Frank Nullmeier

Abstract In the previous chapters, we summarized the academic debates and findings on need-based justice in five scientific disciplines: philosophy, psychology, economics, sociology, and political science. The objectives of this concluding chapter are to confront the results and theoretical approaches of the individual disciplines with each other and to draw some preliminary conclusions for the design of an interdisciplinary theory of need-based justice. In each of the following ten sections, we present a thesis on the further development of a theory of need-based justice and subsequently, explain it in more detail. In the previous chapters, we summarized the academic debates and findings on need-based justice in five scientific disciplines: philosophy, psychology, economics, sociology, and political science. The objectives of this concluding chapter are to confront the results and theoretical approaches of the individual disciplines with each other and to draw some preliminary conclusions for the design of an interdisciplinary theory of need-based justice. In each of the following ten sections, we present a thesis on the further development of a theory of need-based justice and subsequently, explain it in more detail.

7.1 The Concept of Need

> The core element of the concept of need is the notion of something that is necessary, compelling, imperative, indispensable, essentially required—something that goes beyond mere desires or preferences and takes precedence over desires.

Need is different from desire, interest, or preference. A merely subjective definition of need as a desire makes the concept of need obsolete. Need aims at a necessary and compelling determination of personal demands beyond subjective feelings and desires. Need divides the totality of all demands, desires, and concerns into those which are mere wishes and those which are considered as necessary, and therefore, claim priority (Miller 1999; Braybrooke 1987; Hamilton 2003). How the line between

F. Nullmeier (✉)
SOCIUM & FOR 2104, University of Bremen, Bremen, Germany
e-mail: frank.nullmeier@uni-bremen.de

S. Traub and B. Kittel (eds.), *Need-Based Distributive Justice*,
https://doi.org/10.1007/978-3-030-44121-0_7

these two groups of demands should be drawn and what counts as necessary forms the central parts of a theory of need-based justice.

The differentiation between needs and mere desires can be scientifically objectified by means of a list or a hierarchy of needs or it can be entrusted to social and political processes of recognition. The basic requirement for a theory of need-based justice is a method that allows for this demarcation—as always modifiable and revisable—of mere desires from needs. Without such a line, the logical possibility of a theory of need-based justice is no longer given.

Therefore, to define and justify need as necessary is a central subject of theory building. However, a theoretical approach that allows for an indisputable and invariable scientific basis for the definition of needs has not been developed so far. Considerable conceptual efforts have been made, especially in philosophy. Distinctions between instrumental and fundamental needs, between volitional and non-volitional necessities, and between comparative and non-comparative approaches contribute to the task of detaching need from purely subjective aspirations such as preferences and desires (Chap. 2).

From an interdisciplinary perspective, it makes sense to suppose that needs are best understood as a socially constructed necessity resulting from social and political processes in which we bind ourselves by giving a special value to some desires or demands that we justify as necessary especially because of the occurrence of significant harm in cases of rejecting it as necessary (Fraser 1989; Hamilton 2003, see Chap. 5). The supposition that needs are socially constructed and could be defined by using the terminology of necessities and harm should be placed at the *core of the concept of need*. This *socially and politically self-constructed necessity* might use empirical findings on social situations, physiological processes and psychological dynamics as clues in order to assert and defend this attribution of being necessary, but these linkages can only count as specific methods in a complex process of the construction of needs.

An elaborated theory of need-based justice will have to answer a variety of terminological questions, as well as the conceptual ones, especially because of the different understandings and translations of need in scientifically central languages. For example, in German, there is the distinction between “Bedürfnisse” and “Bedarf”, which has no complement in English. Minor confusions might also spring from the combination of the two ways in which the concept of need is used. On the one hand, need is what is necessary (need_1). On the other hand, need can also mean what is lacking in order to achieve what is necessary (need_2). Need_2 denotes the gap between the required resources to satisfy the needs and the present resources, while need_1 does not establish any relation between available resources and what is necessary. Need_1 defines the level of the necessary and need_2 aims at the means for the fulfillment of need_1. In the following, need will always be understood as need_1. Need_2 will be referred to as *need gap*.

Terminological clarifications of this kind must accompany the development of a theory of need-based justice as part of a theory of distributive justice. However, the essence of a theory of need-based justice is to demonstrate how the socially and politically produced necessity of certain wishes and concerns is safeguarded (positive theory) or should be safeguarded (normative theory) as an effective demarcation line to mere desires.

7.2 Positive and Normative Theory of Need-Based Justice

A theory of need-based justice should be based on the promotion of both normative and empirical research.

Normative research on needs and need-based justice investigates justifiable arguments in favor of need as a criterion (or "currency", see Chap. 2) for decisions on distributions. Empirical research analyzes people's everyday judgments on just distributions and the understandings of justice that are inherent in the structure of social interactions and institutions. In psychology, economics, sociology and political science, empirical social justice research has developed rapidly in the last decades (for synopses see Sabbagh and Schmitt Sabbaghetal 2016; Konow and Schwettmann 2016; Liebig and Sauer 2016). Since John Rawls's *A Theory of Justice* (1971), normative theories have multiplied in philosophy, economics, and political science. Some normative theories of social justice (Walzer 1983; Miller 1999) have tried to incorporate the results of empirical research on justice. The recent tendency to move away from a Rawlsian "ideal theory" of justice and instead develop a more "realistic" theory strengthens the call for the incorporation of empirical results in normative theories or even an integration of normative and empirical research. Nevertheless, normative considerations should not be absorbed by the re-narration of empirical results and instrumentalized for the affirmation of the given as a normative ideal.

Progress in the field of need-based justice can only fruitfully take place in the mode of an *empirically enlightened normative theory* and a *normatively informed positive theory*. Despite the promise of mutual enrichment, however, such approaches might justify normative statements that contradict empirical findings. Normative and positive theory often do not coincide even if one supports an integration of empirical and normative research on social justice. Yet normative and empirical research will face common challenges in the form of terminological and analytical questions. The following thus addresses normative and positive theory jointly rather than separately.

7.3 Pluralistic and Monistic Theories of Distributive Justice

Pluralistic theories of social justice can be distinguished from monistic theories. Need-based justice is listed in all pluralistic theories of justice as one of three, four or five central criteria of social justice.

In the field of social justice, *monistic* theories deduce all essential statements on preferential distributive orders from only one (but potentially complex) criterion of justice. Utilitarian and egalitarian theories of justice are examples of monistic theories of justice. John Rawls' egalitarian theory of justice (1971, 1993, 1999, 2001) conceives a monistic framework with an internally complex structure based on two principles of justice, the second principle again comprising two rules. However, apart from equality, no other criterion is inserted into Rawls's theory as a supporting element in the architecture of his theory: In particular, need, equity, desert, merit, and performance do not play any significant role in the formulation of the Rawlsian principles of justice.

In psychology, *Equity Theory* (Adams 1965) has long been a widely recognized positive monistic theory of justice. This theory claims to explain all everyday judgments and justice-based decisions by equity as a single, but broadly defined criterion of justice. Adele Diederich outlines in Chap. 3 that monistic theories might be capable of reintegrating different criteria of justice into a monistic approach. The conception of equity, as a continuation of Aristotle's proportional justice, works with inputs and outputs and measures equity according to its proportionality. The decisive question is what can count as input. With an extension of the term input, a reintegration of various criteria might be manageable. Under the name of *Contribution Theory*, which is also used for the equity approach, the term input covers all forms of one's own contribution. Diederich argues that need might also be understood as part of the input, as a negative input. Therefore, one can include requirements on the input side in equity equations. An explicit attempt to reintegrate the need into Equity Theory has not been undertaken yet.

Examples of *pluralistic* theories of justice in the realm of political philosophy include Michael Walzer's *Spheres of Justice* (1983), David Miller's *Principles of Social Justice* (1999) and Amartya Sen's itThe Idea of Justice (2009). Melvin J. Lerner (1974) and Morton Deutsch (1975) have established pluralistic frameworks for the empirical study of justice in psychology that have increasingly replaced Equity Theory. In economics, the works of James Konow (2001, 2003, Konow and Schwettmann 2016) shows that the manifold findings of experimental research on social justice only support a pluralistic theory. In sociology, Stephan Liebig and Carsten Sauer (2016) have presented a theory of distributive decisions and judgments based on four criteria (see Table 7.1). In all these very different theories, need appears as one out of three, four or five criteria of justice. Put differently, a pluralistic theory is inconceivable without the inclusion of need as a criterion of justice—at least for the social sciences.

This might be doubtful in the case of Amartya Sen's theory. He rejects the concept of need within the framework of his "capability approach" and uses solely the terms functionings and capabilities. But in his well-known and programmatic example of three children and a flute (2009, 12–15) he mentions need as one of three basic criteria of justice (Sen 1987). The following table will give an overview of pluralistic theories of justice and the criteria they list as central principles of distributive judgments.

While need or basic needs appear in each pluralistic theory listed above, the terminology and meanings in the context of desert are quite different. Equality is surprisingly absent in some theories. As far as these conceptions reach a certain level of elaboration, three to five criteria are mentioned, among which need seems to play an undisputed role.

Table 7.1 Criteria for distribution in pluralistic theories of social justice

Pluralistic	Criteria for distribution			
Theories of social justice	Need related	Desert related	Equality related	Other criteria of social justice
Lerner (1974)	Need	Equity	Parity	Law
Deutsch (1975)	Need	Equity, Contribution	Equality	—
Walzer (1983)	Need	Desert	—	Free Exchange
Miller (1999)	Need	Desert (Merit)	Equality	—
Sen (2009)[a]	Need	Desert (Work)	—	Desert/Utility (Skill)
Konow (2001, 2003)	Basic needs	Efficiency	—	Accountability
Konow and Schwettmann (2016)	Basic needs	Efficiency	Equality	Responsibility, Proportionality
Liebig and Sauer(2016)	Need	Equity	Equality	Entitlement

Table notes. Source: Compilation by the author. [a]"Three children and a flute"

A pluralistic theory raises the question of how the above mentioned criteria should be related to each other. Which criterion can claim normative validity in which distributive decisions and when should combinations of two or more criteria be required? A model of different "spheres", as Walzer has presented (1983), assigns to each delimited societal area one specific criterion as the guiding principle of justice. The persuasive power of this model is grounded on the assumption that clear divisions between societal spheres are given or can be drawn. Social differentiation must translate into application fields for different justice criteria. The applicability of a criterion is limited to specific areas while combinations of principles as basic arrangements within societal areas are not envisaged. Therefore, Walzer's theory is perhaps the most consistent conception of a *separation model* of a pluralistic theory of justice.

Pluralistic theories of justice that provide for a combination of the three to five criteria of justice are also conceivable (e.g., Deutsch 1975). It is the objective of the following sections to advance this type of theory, which can be called a *combination model*. It seems much more in line with the findings from empirical work than the separation model. The key challenge for this type of theory is meaningfully integrating the different criteria of justice without transforming the theory into a monistic framework.

7.4 Different Versions of a Pluralistic Theory of Need-Based Justice

> Need is one of several criteria for determining a just order. Need-based justice can only be developed meaningfully as an element of a pluralistic theory of justice. The task of a theory of need-based justice is to determine when which combinations of criteria of just distribution occur empirically and when which combinations are required normatively.

Assuming only three criteria of justice, need, desert/merit, and equality (most notably Miller 1999), there can logically be combinations of equality and need, need and desert, desert and equality, and a mixture of all three principles. If further distinctions should be made between leading and subordinate criteria, mathematically six combinations of two and additionally six combinations of three criteria are possible. Whether a total of four or twelve options must be expected depends on the answer to the question whether it is possible to establish an order of priority of one justice criterion over another or not. While John Rawls' (1971, 1999) priority rules for his two principles of justice as different versions of the criterion of equality provide precise ideas on the relationship between the principles, these are rules for a theory conceived as a non-pluralistic theory of justice. In a pluralistic theory, less clearly structured relationships between the criteria of justice are conceivable. Even equations or connections that represent combinations without internal ordering can be expected. Then the number of combinations would even increase.

Let us first discuss the basic case of a non-ordered combination. A pluralistic theory of justice that does not follow the separation model is most appropriate for situations in which all three criteria are normatively involved in all questions of distribution, and when it can be empirically demonstrated that all three criteria are applied by individuals when evaluating everyday situations. This is to be named as a *weak pluralistic theory*. In contrast, a *strong pluralistic theory* assumes that only combinations of two of the three criteria are normatively relevant and can prove that exactly these combinations are empirically occurring. If it is not possible to identify *types* of situations for which specific combinations are relevant, then we conclude with a *contextualist theory of justice*.

Konow's theory, which in some of its variants acknowledges more than three justice criteria, is close to a contextualist theory with the idea of context-specific weightings between the basic justice criteria. However, Konow seems to be searching for patterns of these weightings and could, therefore, point in the direction of a strong pluralistic theory. Konow and Schwettmann (2016, 99) favor a context-related weighting between a fixed set of five justice criteria and lean towards a specific version of strong pluralistic theory:

> We conclude that justice is context-dependent, i.e., based on shared principles that are sensitive to the context, rather than context-specific, i.e., heterogeneous across different contexts. That is, there is an individual and even cultural variation in the interpretation of or weight placed on different fairness concepts and these respond to the context of the evaluator and the evaluated, but fairness values are shared in common. In addition, the results of surveys and economics experiments strongly support the claim that people value multiple principles, with robust evidence of responsibility, proportionality, efficiency, basic needs, and equality.

A *weak* pluralistic theory might be refuted from a normative perspective if it can be shown through argumentation that only one of the three criteria is relevant for specific types of situations, and from an empirical perspective if in experimental situations only one criterion is applied unambiguously. For example, need might be the only legitimate criterion in a situation where a relatively small number of persons are facing an existentially threatening situation and this can be remedied by a small redistribution of resources from a great many people. In this situation, multicriteriality is empirically not present and argumentatively not required. Therefore, *a weak pluralistic theory cannot be defended.*

If a specific amount for distribution or redistribution has already been fixed, existentially threatening situations of all those affected can be remedied with this, and there is still enough left for payments to additional persons, then we can expect combinations of need and at least one further criterion of justice. The combination of need and equality with strong redistributive effects contrasts with the combination of need and desert that allows for the desert principle to be applied above the need threshold. Both cases support a *strong* pluralistic theory. The inclusion of equality and desert in the combination of criteria, however, does not follow directly from the situation outlined above, but is dependent on further situational characteristics. If the responsibility for the occurrence of need gaps is attributed (at least in part) to the needy, the initial distribution is perceived as performance/desert-dependent and the provision of resources clearly depends on the participants' own contributions. This favors the combination of need and desert principles. If, on the other hand, the need gap is regarded as the result of circumstances that cannot be attributed to the needy, the initial distribution is not considered as performance-related and the resources for (re)distribution does not come from the participants' own contributions, then a combination of need and equality is more likely (e.g. Pritzlaff-Scheele and Zauchner 2017).

Some characteristics of the situation, such as how a distributive situation is assessed and perceived, are decisive in determining which combination of criteria of justice is chosen and which can appear normatively justifiable. But as the list of these factors expands, the argumentation goes towards a contextualist approach. Only an exhaustive list of factors or types of situations can save a strong pluralistic theory from transforming into contextualism where each situation may lead to the application of a different set of criteria of justice. The more the perception of distributive situations is determined by small differences, the more research is forced to take the road of a contextualist approach and the more difficult it becomes to develop meaningful typologies and theories. In view of the refutability of a weak theory of need-based justice and the ambivalent tendency towards contextualism, it seems most reasonable to continue working on a *strong* pluralistic theory.

7.5 Need-Based Justice and Procedural Justice

> There can be no theory of need-based justice without reference to a process by which needs are determined as socially or politically recognized. Recognition of needs, however, requires specific procedures in which what is recognized as need is also argumentatively identified as what is necessary.

What constitutes a need is determined by a process of social and political recognition (Fraser 1989; Hamilton 2003, see Chap. 5). How does this process of recognition take place? We have to differentiate between the social and the political recognition of needs. *Social* recognition of a desire, a demand, an interest, or a concern as a need is a societal communicative process recognizing that this demand can take precedence over other demands because it is necessary or compelling. Social recognition takes place in diverse processes, in interactions between persons or groups of persons as well as in the various social organizations or on the level of social-media exchange or public discourses. However, social recognition as a whole is not a *procedure* in the strong sense of the concept defined as (legally) ordered temporal sequences (Nullmeier 2018b). Although procedures may be used in individual social organizations to present desires as legitimate needs, social recognition is not absorbed in the use of these intra-organizational procedures. Social recognition of needs is a broad process at all levels, much more "anarchic", never leading to a result or even an interim conclusion, but always dependent on renewal and repetition. The challenges for the social sciences as an observer with the task to measure the social recognition of a need are, therefore, significant. Just as with the measurement of societal norm acceptance and the legitimation of political institutions, reference to surveys is not sufficient. Studies of public discourses, everyday interactions, and social practices within institutions and organizations are also required.

Such requirements increase when it comes to assessing the *quality* of the recognition process. An evaluation of the respective process of social recognition as appropriate, fair, just or not is highly complex given the diversity and plurality of relevant social processes of recognition. Neither the theories of fairness oriented towards market processes (for example Nozick 1974) nor those that construct abstract types of procedural justice (pure, perfect, imperfect; Rawls 1971) are suitable for setting standards for the assessment of the quality of *social* recognition processes.

The situation is much clearer if one looks at the terrain of *political* recognition of needs. Democracies are systems of institutions that know specific procedures for the recognition of desires or demands as needs: legislative procedures. Needs are politically recognized if they have been translated into the form of an applicable law, statutory ordinance or constitutional amendment. Whether a need can be considered as politically recognized can thus be seen from the perspective of positive law and the jurisprudence that accompanies it. Power, lobbying and micro-political strategies shape the outcome of legislation but, as far as the rule of law is respected, this usually takes place within the framework of a given legal procedure.

Therefore, political recognition can be examined as a procedural process embedded in the broader processes of social recognition. In political procedures, social recognition is translated into political recognition, and attempts to recognize a demand as need in the political realm might result in social recognition that is either more advanced than or skeptical towards the political attribution of need. Social and political recognition may diverge or largely coincide in this respect. Since it is much easier for the social sciences to empirically identify that a need is *politically* recognized, the reference to political recognition is a practical research tool but must not lead to an underestimation of the role of social recognition.

It is also much easier to assess whether the process of political recognition is appropriate, fair or equitable than it is to do the same with social recognition. Since political recognition is procedural, the criteria of procedural fairness can be used as a benchmark for assessing the process of political recognition. This puts *procedures* at the center of a theory of need-based justice. Only legitimate procedures can legitimize the political recognition of needs. If procedures are lacking legitimacy, the recognition of needs can be considered as arbitrary, power-determined, imposed or accidental. It is, therefore, crucial which procedures can be regarded as legitimate in order to recognize needs.

An assessment of the procedure of political recognition cannot rely solely on the established criteria of procedural justice, since this would mean that procedures regarded as just in theories of procedural justice are automatically also considered as suitable for determining legitimate processes of the political recognition of needs. Although need-based justice relies to a high degree on procedures and their legitimacy, the idea of need specifies what can count as a legitimate procedure for recognizing a demand as a need. A legitimate procedure must, in cases of recognition of needs, be aimed at assigning to particular demands the status of necessary, compelling demands called needs. This deviates from the idea of Rawls' "pure procedural justice" (Rawls 1971, 83–87). It is, therefore, not possible to interpret political recognition of needs as a mere application of the theory of procedural justice with pure procedural justice as the highest standard.

Which procedures can be considered legitimate is pre-structured by the concept of need as a necessary, i.e. compelling, imperative, indispensable, essentially required desire or demand. Procedures for the recognition of needs must, therefore, make it possible to determine what is necessary. A majority decision that recognizes something as a need without having dealt with the question of whether the need is necessary is highly problematic from the point of view of a theory of need-based justice, since the goal of political recognition, *recognition as a need*, has been missed. The concept of need is, therefore, in tension with decision-making procedures that are based exclusively on principles like consensus, unanimity or majority. In such proceedings arbitrary contents can be decided as legally binding without any reference to examinations of whether a demand can be seen as necessary. A theory of need-based justice *requires additional criteria for political procedures*, that can count as legitimate means of politically recognizing needs. In the modification of the well-known properties of fair political procedures, these must also guarantee that the recognition of needs is based on a discussion of what is really necessary.

Against a simple variant of legal positivism, processes of political recognition of needs are subject to an assessment by the social sciences that may be based on the assumption that not everything that is politically decided in a legitimate political procedure as being a need is a legitimate need. The recognition of needs should only be deemed legitimate if the political procedures include a debate about whether the demands are necessary, imperative, and compelling. Only procedures that include such debates can be regarded as legitimate. What is essential for a theory of need-based justice is a *combination of classical procedural justice and a specific substantive requirement*: the profound discussion of the nature of demands as necessary.

In processes of political recognition of needs, it is common to combine the usual procedures of democratic legislation with some form of expertise (Fischer 2009). Only procedures that include an element of expertise are usually considered appropriate for this purpose. However, the role of expertise is often emphasized to the extent that the democratic majority can only act in accordance with the results of the expertise and thus refrains from making its own decisions. This raises the question of whether the political recognition of needs should instead be realized through a scientific process. However, switching from majority decisions in parliaments to decision by experts transforms the political recognition of needs into a process of scientific investigation and expert consensus. These types of procedures are often criticized as expertocratic or technocratic and lack the inclusion of the public as the main element of democratic decision-making. Moreover, the delegation of decisions to expert bodies and the reframing of political decisions into an investigative process does not reflect the insight that the necessary must be constructed in an open and interactive process in which scientific expertise and research should have a voice but not the only voice (Landwehr (2013), see Chap. 5). A theory of procedural justice that takes seriously the political recognition of needs should include expertise in majority decisions without reifying the false objectivism of expertise.

7.6 Modes of Objectification

Hierarchies of needs or comprehensive lists of basic needs cover the spectrum of human activity that should be considered in theories of need-based justice, but they do not offer indications as to when needs can be regarded as satisfied.

Lists or hierarchically ordered levels of needs are frequently used in studies of need-based justice. Besides Maslow's pyramid of needs (Maslow 1970 [1954]), perhaps Martha Nussbaum's list of capabilities (Nussbaum 2000, 78–80; Nussbaum 2006, 76–78) is the best known example of such attempts (see also Braybrooke 1987, 33–38; Doyal and Gough 1991). The experience that bread and water alone are not sufficient to lead a prosperous life result in a wide range of human activities as potential sources of needs. In addition to the physical and biological necessities of pure survival, there are other necessities whose disregard does not immediately lead to death but nevertheless causes permanent damage and harm. It is obvious that needs cannot be based on biological principles alone. With the expansion of the list of needs to wider dimensions of human life, to societal, communicative, psychological and perhaps artistic and esthetic issues, the question arises of what may be considered necessary within this broad understanding of potential needs. All contributors to this debate agree on one statement: Securing survival cannot be the only criterion for deciding what is necessary. Nowadays, participation and inclusion in social life, being able to lead a worthy, valuable, and decent life is the most widely accepted reference point for the definition of what is necessary (Nussbaum 2006; Sen 2009; for Germany: Nullmeier 2018a).

With these categories, however, ethical questions—various notions of a good life over which justified dissent can exist—are used as the basis for a theory of justice. In the Rawlsian tradition, a theory of justice typically wants to free itself from questions of life plans and ways of living in order to develop a strong moral theory capable of universal consensus. In order to escape this tendency to ethics, attempts have been made to define a decent or valuable life negatively as the avoidance of serious harm. In these approaches, harm is understood as an objective event. With the argumentative combination or a type of mutual determination of harm and decent life, these approaches hope to develop a theory of need-based justice independent of deeper ethical questions (see Chap. 2, e.g. Thomson 1987).

While the question of objectification has been addressed in philosophy by clarifying the terms decent life and harm, a more empirical approach may regard the philosophical statements about harm and decent life as important inputs and argumentative sources for the public processes of social and political recognition. Objectification then takes place in the social and political processes, not by theory building and expertise. Additionally, terms like decent, valuable or worthy life leave a lot of room for interpretation and might call for theoretical approaches that further distinguish between the necessary, the appropriate, the affluent, and the luxurious. Alternatively, one can raise the social average or median in a society to the appropriate standard ("normal life") and consider the drop below a certain threshold as a case of need.

The experience that receiving bread and water is more urgent than making social contacts (McLeod 2014) makes the idea of a hierarchy of needs possible. *Urgency* gradations translate different demands into a hierarchy of needs, with the additional assumption that the less urgent needs only come into play when the most urgent needs are met (Maslow 1970 [1954]). This hierarchy introduces degrees of what is necessary. While all may be needs, some needs are more urgent than, and therefore, prior to others. Every form of hierarchization tends to start a process of inner decomposition of the concept of the necessary, with the danger that the entire attempt at objectification fails. Objectification can fail in a second respect. Maslow and his successors cannot show what resources are needed to satisfy the respective needs (see Chap. 3). Without any means to decide when a need is met, the dynamics of shifting needs from a lower to a higher level cannot be analyzed. If increasing demands for satisfaction over time cannot be ruled out, then the shift thesis itself is at risk.

In the case of lists that only provide clues for fields of human life in which needs can be searched, we have insufficient indications to identify certain levels of needs. A list of abstract fields of human life does not help to identify politically recognizable needs. For a normative theory of need-based justice that includes a comprehensive list of needs, it is meaningful to know the level of resources that is required for meeting the needs.

7.7 A Monistic Theory of Justice or the Role of Oversupply, Undersupply, and Scarcity

The attempt to base a theory of justice solely on needs as a criterion of justice leads to inconsistencies across different contexts. Oversupply and undersupply denote the relationship between available resources and socially and politically recognized needs, whereas scarcity is understood as the relationship between available resources and basically unlimited desires. Situations that in the context of a desire-based definition of scarcity has been regarded as states of scarcity are to a large extent states of oversupply in a need-based analysis.

As stated in Chap. 3, in psychology, no theory of justice has been developed that is solely based on the principle of need. This is also true for the disciplines of political science, economics, philosophy, and sociology. In all these disciplines, no theoretical approach emerges analogous to an egalitarian theory of justice, albeit with need as the only criterion from which the entire theory is developed.

Even if no purely need-based theory of justice has been developed so far, one can learn from a thought experiment of a monistic theory. Is it conceivable to develop a monistic theory of justice as a theory of need-based justice? The answer to this question is closely related to how the relationship between (recognized) needs and economically available resources (understood in a very broad sense) is framed. Let us suppose that the social or political recognition of needs has been completed. Two situations have to be distinguished. Either the resources exceed the sum of the needs or the totality of the needs exceeds the level of resources. The situation of complete congruence of resources and needs is the highly unlikely borderline between these two possibilities. Nevertheless, only such an unlikely case allows the principle of need-based justice to regulate the distribution. Even the smallest deviations from the congruence between needs and resources raise the question of which criteria can be applied in situations of over- or undersupply. If the principle of need-based justice is to solely determine the distribution, the quantitative congruence and the qualitative fit of resources and needs must be induced and constantly reproduced. Congruence and fit between needs and resources can be tackled from two sides: Needs can be adapted to resources or resources can be adapted to needs, both in the state of over- or undersupply.

One objection to the idea that needs should be adapted to resources is that this would destroy the idea of need as what is necessary. If the recognition of needs becomes resource-dependent, the element of necessity seems to be lost. On the other hand, the discussion on poverty in the social sciences has revealed that poverty must be determined relative to the level of prosperity in a certain society. A link between the level of available resources and the recognition of needs cannot be completely denied. Consequently, the notion of ensuring need-based justice as the sole guiding principle by adapting needs to resources cannot be generally rejected.

In the state of oversupply, the argument against a monistic theory of need-based justice is that it cannot be decided with reference to needs whether needs should be adapted to the available level of resources or the resources to the needs. The establishment of congruence by adjusting the needs to resources implies an increase in needs. The need level might be increased in proportion to the previously recognized needs. Or each person receives the same absolute increase in their needs until the total amount of available resources is reached. In both cases, however, the principle of need is combined with a second principle: either with proportionality or with equality. Such a theory of justice would have to fall back on a second principle and could, therefore, not exist in a strictly monistic form. It is also possible to identify another solution: Once there is a surplus of resources above the level of the recognized needs, a society can enter into a new process of recognizing needs and redefining what is to be considered a need. This process may be repeated until the matching of needs and resources is achieved through upward adjustment of needs. The weakness of this solution lies in the fact that the matching of requirements is predetermined. Why should the necessary correspond exactly with the available? Nothing in the idea of need stipulates that needs and resources must coincide. As long as one only reflects on what is necessary, the need level can be below the level of available resources as well as clearly above this level. The congruence of needs and resources is added as a further criterion. However, this additional criterion is *external* to the idea of need.

The congruence between needs and resources in the situation of oversupply can also be achieved by adjusting, i.e., reducing, the available resources. As far as resources are concerned, which have to be made available by human labor, this means a reduction of the (technically mediated) labor input. If, however, more is available than is needed, why should this not be used for a supply that goes beyond the level of what is necessary? To argue against this option would mean establishing the principle that a greater amount than what is necessary can no longer be tolerated as just. "Only what is necessary" instead of "what is necessary first" then becomes the pinnacle of need-based justice. The conclusion that a theory of justice is intolerant of the production of more than what is necessary cannot be derived from the concept of need.

If needs are socially and politically recognized and the society identifies a lack of resources in comparison to the total sum of recognized needs, we speak of undersupply. The ideal of congruence then requires either the adaptation of the needs to the available resources, i.e., a reduction of the recognized needs, or an expansion of the available resources to the point of meeting the needs. A discussion of these cases would lead to the same conclusions as in the situation of oversupply. A second criterion different from need is essential to justify the congruence between resources and needs. Any pure theory of need-based justice quickly gets entangled in contradictions. A monistic theory can, therefore, be excluded as logically impossible.

Beyond the discussion about either monistic or pluralistic theories of justice, the literature on needs deals intensely with the question of assessment and measurement of needs in situations of scarcity (see Chaps. 2 and 6). In economics, scarcity is understood as the relationship between available resources and basically unlimited desires. By contrast, the terms oversupply and undersupply refer to the relationship between available resources and socially and politically recognized needs. Because the level of needs is significantly lower than the level of desires, and needs is a concept limited to what is necessary, situations deemed as states of scarcity according to the desire-based definition of scarcity are largely considered states of oversupply in a need-based analysis.

The controversial question of the satisfaction of needs in the case of scarcity (Chap. 2, e.g. Miller 1999), which is so dominant in the literature, concerns a much smaller range of situations than previously assumed. Nevertheless, in these special situations, if it is not possible to satisfy all recognized needs, how can we evaluate the degree or fulfillment of the principle of need-based justice? If the lack of resources is seen as given and not changeable, is it possible to determine a just distribution solely by the criterion of need? Purely need-based solutions are conceivable by redefining the necessary as the most essential. However, this is an attempt to gradate the category of the necessary. Linear or proportional reductions of need might fall under the verdict of using a second criterion and offering a mixture of the principle of need and the principle of equality or proportionality as a solution. In their contribution to this volume, Siebel and Schramme (Chap. 2) offer a new solution to this problem by integrating elements from non-comparative (Platonic) and comparative (Aristotelian) versions of the principle of need.

7.8 Need Gaps and Corrective Justice

The origins of need gaps are decisive for the role need plays as a criterion of justice. Socially and politically recognized needs are often not met or only met to a limited extent if the origins of the need gap can be attributed to the person in need and his or her intentional behavior. A self-inflicted need gap leads in many cases to a denial of the distribution to this person according to need. If such a need gap, caused actively or by inactivity, is assigned to a group in a generalized manner, this can lead to the rejection of need fulfillment for this group. The normative question of the legitimacy of group-specific differentiation of need fulfillment raises questions of the interference between distributive and corrective justice and the existence of a kind of negative desert-based justice.

Certain perceptions of the origins and causes of need gaps can raise questions of responsibility and guilt (Miller 1999, 228–229). A recognized need may not be met because the need gap seems to be self-inflicted. This does not affect the social or political recognition of the need in general, but it does restrict the fulfillment of the need in a special case. Self-inflicted need gaps usually lead to punishment in the form of a (partial) denial of the meeting of these needs. The assumption is that the situation of need is entirely avoidable, i.e., that the need gap is the result of the individual's intentional behavior and not the effect of social institutions or economic situations or some type of misfortune. Guilt, responsibility, and punishment are *classical topics of corrective justice*, a type of justice that is concerned with the reversal of wrongs or the undoing of transactions. In the Aristotelian framework, it is an element of commutative justice, just like its counterpart distributive justice. The rejection of need fulfillment in these cases may be interpreted as an *overlapping of distributive and corrective justice*.

The second interpretation of these cases remains within the realm of distributive justice and does not raise the question of how distributive and corrective justice can be offset against each other or related to each other. This would be possible within the framework of Equity Theory developed in psychology. However, this would imply a return to a monistic theory in which the character of need-based justice would be completely lost. Within Equity Theory, the argument of guilt can be understood as the attribution of a lack of individual contributions. The rejection of need fulfillment is not a response to misconduct that has to be punished, but rather the consequence of a lack of contributions by the individual. Being at fault is interpreted as lacking achievement. Instead of the criterion of need, the criterion of desert dominates. The existence of a need might be accepted, but the self-inflicted need gap leads to the predominance of the criterion of desert in the fulfillment of needs. The inclusion of self-inflicted lacks in the provision of one's own contributions as an argument for the fulfillment of needs represents a specific variant of the *combination of need-based and desert-based justice*.

7.9 Empirical Findings and Future Tasks for Theory Formation

Deciding which criteria of justice to apply in a situation, and in which combination and with which weighting, depends not only on the specifics of the situation or on its perception, but also on the social relationships in which the persons concerned are involved and on the individual characteristics of the persons acting or judging. Situational, social and personal characteristics together determine the extent to which the principle of need is met.

Extensive empirical research in psychology, economics, and sociology has identified three groups of causes that determine the criteria used to evaluate distributions: situational, social, and personal determinants.

Situational: Decisions about just distribution may be made in a constructed state of nature, about social policy in a particular country or about constructed constellations of social problems in a laboratory experiment. Empirical evidence from different fields concludes that the characteristics of the respective situation do not remain without influence on the weighting between the different criteria of justice and the respective role of the principle of need. Today, the total available (but highly unequally distributed) resources are far greater than the sum of basic needs, defined as the socio-cultural subsistence minimum or the enabling of social participation. A situation of oversupply is given, and not only in OECD countries. For distributive decisions, however, it is not the situation as such but the *perceived situation* that plays the decisive role. Minor deviations in the situational constellation have a lasting effect on distributive decisions and can vary normative constructions of a just distribution. A plethora of detailed findings can be found in Chaps. 5 to 6 of this book. As mentioned above, a preliminary review of these findings seems to support a contextualist version of a theory of need-based-justice. To turn these findings into building blocks of a strong pluralistic theory of need-based justice, further research will be needed on how to classify the relevant aspects of distributive situations. Based on such classification, it might be possible to integrate the diverse empirical results by developing a multifaceted *typology of distributive situations*.

Social: The existence of particular relationships between the persons concerned plays a significant role in the weighting of the criteria of justice (Chap. 4). If this were the case in general, the scope of need-based justice would be severely limited, and the idea of meeting global needs to overcome hunger and extreme poverty as the cornerstone of global justice would be nearly impossible (Brock 2009). Need-based justice would be re-framed as a normative ground for human aid and bringing it closer to parental love, compassion, and mercy. For a normative theory of need-based justice, it would be highly problematic to accept that close social relationships are a prerequisite for a need-based distribution. However, empirical studies from psychology (Chap. 3) show that need-based decisions can be made even if there is no strong interdependence or relationship between the decision makers and the persons in need. These findings should initiate theoretical efforts to develop typologies of social relationships with several dimensions as a baseline for systematic testing in experimental settings.

Personal: Studies in psychology, economics, and sociology have shown that the extent to which needs are taken into account and how they are combined with other criteria of justice is determined by socio-demographic, cognitive, and attitudinal characteristics of the persons involved in the distributive decision. However, the individual characteristics do not seem to be so powerful that certain combinations between different criteria of justice are consistently preferred for all situations and all forms of social relationships. There is no such close connection that one could speak of a more need-oriented and a more performance-oriented group of persons. Personal factors do not determine the results of distributive decisions, but they modify the relationship between need, equality, and desert in a particular situations in a particular way. The drift to contribute to a contextualist theory of justice seems to be strong. Therefore, systematic variations in personal characteristics should be a mandatory consideration when testing the validity of previous findings in certain experimental settings.

7.10 The Principle of Basic Priority for Needs as Part of a Strong Pluralistic Theory of Need-Based Justice

Need is applied as a central criterion for distributive decisions in experimental settings. Need is also mentioned as one of the few criteria of justice in normative theories. Need is, therefore, an indispensable part of any theory of justice. An integrated theory of need-based justice can be developed as part of a strong pluralistic theory of justice.

The findings on the determinants of justice criteria allow for a merely contextualist theory as well as for a strong pluralistic theory of need-based justice. It is still unclear whether the determinants identified in the huge bulk of literature can be theoretically united in such a way that there are clearly defined types of distributive constellations for which a particular combination of criteria of justice is characteristic. Until now, research on need-based justice from empirical as well as normative perspectives has oscillated between a strong pluralistic theory and contextualism. It is still unclear to what extent theory formation in the field of need-based justice will be successful.

Nevertheless, it is evident that a monistic theory grounded on need cannot be defended. Everything speaks for a pluralistic theory of justice with need as a central criterion for fair distributions. Need is a central point of reference in distributive decisions both in experimental settings and in normative theories. Consequently, the most promising perspective of a theory of need-based justice consists in the development of an *integrated and strong pluralistic theory of justice with need as a central and indispensable component*.

Perhaps a theory of need-based justice might go further in the *normative direction*. A strong pluralistic theory allows for the justification of a demanding principle of need-based justice, the lexicographic principle that before any other criterion comes into play, the complete satisfaction of all needs must take place. This *"lexineed" principle* or some of its variants has been rejected so far because the search for efficient allocation of resources demands a distribution according to desert. The Rawlsian difference principle ("leximin") is based on an argument of this kind as a reason for the deviation from the principle of equality.

The key argument in support of the priority of the criterion of need is that there is such a wealth of resources worldwide that the needs of all people could be met easily—and there would still be a huge surplus of resources. Globally, and in all macro dimensions, there is a situation of considerable oversupply, which does not immediately collapse even by cutting back on distribution according to performance. A *principle of basic priority for needs* always applies when the condition of a considerable oversupply of resources exists. Naturally, the prioritization of needs in assessments and decisions on distribution does not apply in those cases of local distribution in which underproduction, measured against the level of what is necessary, still prevails for certain individual resources. Aside from these rare cases, a theory of need-based justice would strongly contribute to general political debates on economic and social distribution.

Acknowledgments This chapter has been written as part of DFG Research Group 2104 "Need-based Justice and Distributive Procedures", Project C1 "Limits of Proceduralism? Experimental Studies on the Stability of Procedures of Need Determination" (Nullmeier, reference NU 108/4 – 1). This funding is gratefully acknowledged.

References

Adams, J. S. (1965). Inequity in social exchange. In L. Berkowitz (Ed.), *Advances in experimental social psychology* (Vol. 2, pp. 267–299). New York: Academic.

Braybrooke, D. (1987). *Meeting needs*. Princeton: Princeton University Press.

Brock, G. (2009). *Global justice*. A Cosmopolitan Account, Oxford: Oxford University Press.

Deutsch, M. (1975). Equity, equality, and need: What determines which value will be used as the basis of distributive justice? *Journal of Social Issues*, *51*(3), 137–149.
Doyal, L., & Gough, I. (1991). *A theory of human need*. Houndmills: Palgrave Macmillan.
Fischer, F. (2009). *Democracy and expertise*. Reorienting Policy Inquiry, Oxford: Oxford University Press.
Fraser, N. (1989): Struggle over needs: outline of a socialist-feminist critical theory of late capitalist political culture. In N. Fraser (ed.), *Unruly practices. power, discourse, and gender in contemporary social theory* (pp. 161–187). University of Minnesota Press.
Hamilton, L. A. (2003). *The political philosophy of needs*. Cambridge: Cambridge University Press.
Konow, J. (2001). Fair and square: The four sides of distributive justice. *Journal of Economic Behavior and Organization*, *46*, 137–164.
Konow, J. (2003). Which is the fairest one of all? A positive analysis of justice theories. *Journal of Economic Literature*, *41*(4), 1186–1237.
Konow, J., & Schwettmann, L. (2016). The economics of justice. In C. Sabbagh & M. Schmitt (Eds.), *Handbook of social justice research* (pp. 83–106). Heidelberg: Springer.
Landwehr, C. (2013). Procedural justice and democratic institutional design in healthcare priority-setting. *Contemporary political theory*, *12*(4), 296–317.
Lerner, M. J. (1974). The justice motive: 'Equity' and 'parity' among children. *Journal of Personality and Social Sciences*, *29*(4), 539–550.
Liebig, S., & Sauer, C. (2016). Sociology of Justice. In C. Sabbagh & M. Schmitt (Eds.), *Handbook of Social Justice Theory and Research* (pp. 37–59). Heidelberg: Springer.
Maslow, A. H. (1970 [1954]). *Motivation and personality* (2nd ed.). New York: Harper and Row.
McLeod, S. (2014). Absolute Biological Needs. *Bioethics*, *28*(6), 293–301.
Miller, D. (1999). *Principles of social justice*. Cambridge: Harvard University Press.
Nozick, R. (1974). *Anarchy, State, and Utopia*. New York: Basic Books.
Nullmeier, F. (2018a). Germany: Justice as a dominant political value. In G. Craig (Ed.), *Handbook on global social justice* (pp. 129–140). Cheltenham: Edward Elgar.
Nullmeier, F. (2018b). Verfahren und Mechanismen. Theoriebildung und Kausalitätsverständnis in der politikwissenschaftlichen Verwaltungsforschung. In M. W. Bauer & E. Grande (Eds.), *Perspektiven der Verwaltungswissenschaft* (pp. 279–302). Baden-Baden: Nomos.
Nussbaum, M.C. (2000). *Women and human development. The capabilities approach*. Cambridge: Cambridge University Press.
Nussbaum, M.C. (2006). *Frontiers of justice. Disability, nationality, species membership*. Cambridge: Belknap Press of Harvard University Press.
Pritzlaff-Scheele, T., & P. Zauchner (2017). *Meeting needs. An experimental study on need-based justice and inequality*. FOR 2104 Discussion Paper No. 2017–7, Hamburg.
Rawls, J. (1971). *A theory of justice*. Cambridge: Belknap Press of Harvard University Press.
Rawls, J. (1993). *Political liberalism*. New York: Columbia University Press.
Rawls, J. (1999). *A theory of justice* (Revised ed.). Cambridge: Belknap Press of Harvard University Press.
Rawls, J. (2001). *Justice as fairness. A restatement* E. Kelly (Ed.). Cambridge: Belknap Press of Harvard University Press.
Sabbagh, C., & Schmitt, M. (Eds.). (2016). *Handbook of social justice theory and research*. Heidelberg: Springer.
Sen, A. K. (1987). *The standard of living*. Cambridge: Cambridge University Press.
Sen, A. K. (2009). *The Idea of Justice*. New York: Penguin.
Thomson, G. (1987). *Needs*. London/New York: Routledge and Kegan Paul.
Walzer, M. (1983). *Spheres of justice. A defense of pluralism and democracy*. New York: Basic Books.

The manufacturer's authorised representative in the EU is Springer
Nature Customer Service Centre GmbH, Europaplatz 3, 69115 Heidelberg,
Germany. If you have any concerns regarding our products, please
contact ProductSafety@springernature.com

Printed and bound by CPI Group (UK) Ltd, Croydon, CR0 4YY
05/10/2026
02228121-0013